THE MERCHANT *of*
POWER

THE MERCHANT *of* POWER

SAM INSULL,
THOMAS EDISON, *and*
THE CREATION
of the
MODERN
METROPOLIS

JOHN F. WASIK

palgrave
macmillan

First published in hardcover in 2006 by PALGRAVE MACMILLAN® in the US–a
division of St. Martin's Press LLC, 175 Fifth Avenue, New York, NY 10010.

Where this book is distributed in the UK, Europe and the rest of the world, this is by
Palgrave Macmillan, a division of Macmillan Publishers Limited, registered in England,
company number 785998, of Houndmills, Basingstoke, Hampshire RG21 6XS.

Palgrave Macmillan is the global academic imprint of the above companies and has
companies and representatives throughout the world.

Palgrave® and Macmillan® are registered trademarks in the United States, the United
Kingdom, Europe and other countries.

ISBN-13: 978-0-230-60952-5
ISBN-10: 0-230-60952-X

Library of Congress Cataloging-in-Publication Data
The merchant of power : Sam Insull, Thomas Edison, and the creation of the modern
Metropolis / John F. Wasik.
    p. cm.
    Includes bibliographical references and index.
    ISBN 1-4039-6884-5 (cloth)
    ISBN 0-230-60952-X (paperback)
    1. Insull, Samuel, 1859–1938.   2. Businesspeople—United States—Biography.
3. Electric utilites—United States—History.   4. Commonwealth Edison Company—
History.   5. Holding companies—United States—History.   6. Public utilities—United
States—History.   I. Title.
HD9685.U61578   2006
333.793'2'092—dc22

                                                                                    2005051711

A catalogue record of the book is available from the British Library.

Design by Letra Libre, Inc.

First PALGRAVE MACMILLAN paperback edition: January 2009
10 9 8 7 6 5 4 3 2 1
Printed in the United States of America.

To my parents,
Virginia Frances Wasik
and Arthur Stanley Wasik

Sto lat

CONTENTS

PREFACE

A bike ride on my favorite trail always ends in the same place. Once I emerge from the path of the Liberty Prairie, a reserve about 40 miles north of Chicago, I end up under a forest of high-tension towers, which carry 345,000 volts of power across the country. The lines hum and pulse intensely above me like rhythmic rain falling on a metal roof, creating pockets of ozone and delivering electrons to points unknown. Like watching freight trains as a kid, I wonder where the power came from and where it is going. Charting this journey led me to one man.

The widespread availability of electricity occurred because men like Samuel Insull made it happen. While the names of Edison and Westinghouse are better known, it was Insull—the Bill Gates, Warren Buffett, and P.T. Barnum of his time—who brought electricity into nearly every home, office, commercial building, and factory. Unfortunately, Insull is not a person treated kindly by history since most of his empire collapsed in 1932 and his legacy was largely blackened by the largest business failure of that time.

Out of the ashes of Insull's debacle, though, rose a great many social benefits, foremost among them were efficiently distributed electricity throughout the world and a stronger government hand in policing Wall Street chicanery.

Insull wrangled with and frequently outwitted the most corrupt politicians of Illinois. A rare combination of brilliant financier, CEO, visionary, huckster, arts patron, philanthropist, tyrant, and scoundrel, Insull lived a remarkable life that started in the steam age of the robber barons and lasted into Roosevelt's radio-obsessed, progressive New Deal era. Even more notable was what happened in tandem with Insull's rise and fall. Emerging during his lifetime were modern corporations, skyscrapers, and our electron-crazy way of life. These foundations of modern civilization were being invented in the dynamo of the Chicago metropolis, an epic story of unbridled energy and folly that shaped human history far beyond its borders. Insull lived in a Chicago in which few public figures rivaled him for supreme notoriety, power, and infamy. Along the way, Insull's role as the merchant of power also influenced other geniuses ranging from Franklin Delano Roosevelt and Frank Lloyd Wright to John Dos Passos and Orson Welles.

Ironically, Insull's "superpower" creation anchors one of the greatest electrical and information networks ever created—an infrastructure that makes everything from cellphones to the Internet possible. While few truly understand the accomplishments of some of Insull's contemporaries such as Freud, Tesla, Einstein, and Fermi, anyone with electrical outlets and appliances can grasp the infinite importance of easily accessed power. Yet the acquisition of this Promethean energy was not without a cost. With it came unsustainable appetites for electrical and political power, a polluted environment, and perhaps the largest downside of all, global warming.

Insull's career also begs some compelling questions about the troubled soul of capitalism that resound with us today: How much wealth and control should executives have? Should employees be buying their employers' stock? How much of the corporate governance process should be made transparent so as to prevent malfeasance and bankruptcy? As we contemplate the meaning of corporate power in the context of even bigger contemporary failures (Enron, WorldCom and many dot.com blowups come to mind), consider what Insull helped foster. This is nothing less than the modern global metropolis—an expanding network of energy, and information that is not limited by geography and certainly not by imagination.

—John F. Wasik, 2006

left 1. Samuel Insull in his 20s, when he was a secretary to Thomas Edison. Photo Credit: Loyola University of Chicago Archives: Samuel Insull Papers.

right 2. Gladys (Margaret Bird) Wallis in a publicity photo during her acting days in the 1890s. Photo Credit: Loyola University of Chicago Archives: Samuel Insull Papers.

3. Three generations of Samuel Insulls, taken in the early 1900s. Photo Credit: Loyola University of Chicago Archives: Samuel Insull Papers.

4. A photograph of Samuel Insull at the height of his powers in the mid-1920s. Photo Credit: Loyola University of Chicago: Samuel Insull papers.

INTRODUCTION

Paris, July 16, 1938

The stout, 78-year-old businessman with the creamy white moustache turned around to gaze upon the city of light one last time. In front of him, a huge metal fence with gold filials offered mock protection to one of Paris' loveliest parks, the Jardin de Tuileries, from the angry, vengeful mobs of the past. He reflected upon the violent history of the place. Louis XVI and Marie-Antoinette were arrested and confined to a palace that once graced the grounds after they had been caught in Varennes fleeing the revolution. The day the bells rang in Paris on August 10, 1792, the rabble stormed the last refuge of the Bourbons, leaving 1,000 corpses in Les Tuileries. The exquisite garden, designed by Notre, once strolled in by Catherine de Medici in the late sixteenth century, now, as then, featured generous flowerbeds and lined paths where sculptures longed to dance into the ponds. Lovers, children, and lonely pensioners sat on the green metal chairs.

The old man reflected on what the palace must have looked like as he returned from his shopping trip along the Champs Elysée. The mansion had burned down in 1871 after a confrontation with the Communard government. He empathized with the horror of facing the unwashed masses and a government ardently desiring to see *his* head in a guillotine. His enemies had compared him to a Bourbon monarch and worse. He chuckled with a sense of stinging irony when it occurred to him that he had once owned a corporate empire spanning the size of France, and a 4,000-acre estate that far eclipsed this mere city park. He knew what it was like to lose nearly everything and to have the angry government and people of a powerful country transform one into a beast that deserved to be hunted and slain.

His sigh was cut short as he felt his breath constricted. Turning around, he had hoped to get one last glimpse down the Place de La Concorde and the

3,300-year-old obelisk that had marked the entrance to the Luxor palace of Ramses III. He tried to imagine the scaffolds where the nearly 3,000 condemned in the Reign of Terror were guillotined in the Place de la Revolution. He felt a dreadful heaviness on his chest, perhaps associated with his imagined horror of the counterrevolution. More likely it was a descent into his own abyss only six years earlier.

Turning toward his left again, he wondered if he should walk the length of the gardens to the Place du Carrousel, where Napoleon's version of the Arch of Constantine was crowned by the equestrian statue that the little corporal had stolen from San Marco in Venice: *I had once been a Napoleon of industry, known and feared throughout the world. Now here I am, in exile, after my Waterloo had sent me here where few knew or despised me.*

He stared at the florid metallic entrance to Le Metro, which painfully reminded him of the subway he could have built in Chicago, a subway that would have been the envy of the world. The Art Nouveau grillwork reminded him of the first time he came to Chicago and noticed how the new buildings of Louis Sullivan were alive with organic ornament. It was 1900 when the first Paris Metro line was opened, a year in which he was well on his way to buying and running a great urban transit system and creating one of the largest power systems on the planet.

He started down the stairs, thinking of his luncheon appointment. As always, he was impeccably dressed, wearing a gray suit with red stripes and a brown felt hat that covered his white hair. He despised tardiness, yet felt a growing pain spreading through his neck, shoulders, and arms. In the middle of the descent into the subway, he felt nausea and dizziness and started to sweat. He wanted to make it to the ticket booth and struggled to catch his breath. The doctors had warned him not to exert himself since he was quite portly and diabetic. His wife Gladys had warned him never to take the subway because it was bad for his heart, but he was never one to take other people's advice. If only he could get to the ticket booth, he could rest and catch his breath. Then his heart could regain its normal rhythm. He reached into his pocket for the fare.

The world was about to suffer something far worse than the undiscovered country where the old man was headed. A few months earlier, Hitler had annexed Austria and opened his first death camp. Franco had declared victory in the Spanish civil war. Japan had declared war on China. Two days earlier, Benito Mussolini had published an anti-Jewish, anti-African manifesto. A few months hence, British prime minister Neville Chamberlain would sign the infamous appeasement policy with Hitler in Munich. Nazi leaders, proclaiming that a Jew had shot a German diplomat in Paris, would incite the riots that would later be called the *Kristallnacht,* starting the Holocaust.

While depression-wracked Western countries distracted themselves by dancing to Benny Goodman and the other big bands, watching Joe Louis knock out Max Schmeling in the first round, and following an odd businessman named Howard Hughes fly the first passenger flight around the world, the battle lines were forming. And a young Orson Welles would scare the heck out of his CBS radio audience with a mock invasion from Mars. Ironically, Welles would later use the old man in Paris as a partial model for his older Citizen Kane, even instructing his makeup artist to copy the white moustache.

At the ticket booth, the elderly gent felt the crushing dark drapery descend around him. Much like the curtain of the opera house he built, it was both beautiful and terrifying, recalling a scene from *Aida* and the tragic conclusion of the first opera staged in the auditorium he built for the people. As he extended his hand to the booth, the black pachyderm smashed his heart; he threw up his hands before he could get his ticket punched. He fell on his face, smashing his pince-nez glasses into a thousand pieces as the blockage in his coronary arteries silenced his heart.

Samuel Insull was dead on arrival at the hospital. He had to be identified from a hotel laundry bill and a handkerchief bearing his initials. His wallet had apparently been stolen, possibly containing up to $20,000. The man who had, in 1932, been worth more than $100 million, had 84 cents in his pocket when he died, according to Paris police agent #2023. His actress wife Gladys Wallis, the former Margaret Anna Bird, sobbed when she told the press her husband would be buried in his native London.

The man Thomas Edison called "one of the greatest businessmen in the USA" had survived the financial destruction of his investment companies, a public excoriation by Franklin Delano Roosevelt, three trials for fraud, and public vilification. Some 600,000 shareholders in his companies, as well as 500,000 bondholders, who had been devastated in 1932 when his utility holding companies folded, reviled him as if he were a deposed tyrant. His name became as infamous as his contemporary Al Capone. Insull was so powerful in the 1920s that Scarface had once offered the services of his bodyguards to protect the industrial titan. Ironically, most solid citizens in the mobster's dominions would fondly recall Capone's charitable gestures before they would remember Insull in the same light, a man who had donated millions, controlled utility and railroad companies in 38 states, generated 10 percent of the nation's electricity, yet had not physically harmed a soul. There are 20 times as many biographies on the mobster.

Insull was the premier financier-entrepreneur of his time, making Edison's basic idea of electricity generated by central stations work in thousands of cities, thus making the modern metropolis possible. As a brilliant financier, builder, manager, civic leader, philanthropist, and promoter, Insull was a man of his time and ahead of his time. His remarkable journey touched nearly everyone who ever turned on a light, used an electrical appliance, stepped foot in a modern factory, home, or office, or tapped into the vast informational riches of computers and the Internet.

How did this one-time assistant to Edison become one of the most celebrated, hated, and mostly forgotten figures of the twentieth century? His was certainly a Horatio Alger story; he was a self-made mogul who gave electricity to the masses by financing, charming, cajoling, finagling, and outfoxing the most graft-loving politicians in a city where corruption was an ancient established art form.

Harold Ickes, FDR's interior secretary, who had several run-ins with Insull in the 1920s, remarked upon hearing of Insull's death: "after I came to know him, I had a sneaking liking for him, as I have found myself having for so many people of whom I have not been able to approve as citizens. He was a strong man even if he was dangerous to our economic well being and a threat to our American institutions."[1]

Insull was the classic American enigma. Coming from poverty and eventually building an empire, he had few true friends and was cast as a corporate demon even though his enterprises had a large role in seeding the fruits of modern civilization. Perhaps Insull's poetic answer to the question he constantly heard on the streets of Chicago, around the time of his fraud trials in the early 1930s—"Sam, where did the money go?"—provides some insight. "Where the woodbine twines," he supposedly replied, perplexing his once-adoring public at the end of one of the most spectacular business careers in America. Insull is more than a forgotten titan, though. His accomplishments took root in nearly every corner of the industrialized world. Through great imagination and force of will, Insull attained what Alexander Hamilton called "a dangerous greatness"[2] that forever linked commerce and technology with social progress.

To understand Insull and his place in creating the modern metropolis at the dawn of the twentieth century, you have to imagine the end of the steam age, when Mark Twain was guiding his readers on a paddlewheeler down the Mississippi and "ran some exceedingly narrow and intricate island-chutes by aid of electric light."[3] It was a time when electric illumination was a genuine novelty, and a wizard in Menlo Park, New Jersey, was about to change everything.

TIRELESS AS THE TIDES

Edison Summons Insull

So doth the woodbine the sweet honeysuckle gently entwist.

—William Shakespeare, *A Midsummer Night's Dream*, iv.

The power which electricity of tension possesses of causing an opposite electrical state in its vicinity has been expressed by the general term Induction.

—Michael Faraday, *Experimental Researches in Electricity*[1]

The great inventor was awaiting the arrival of his new, young English secretary. While possessing a mind that had given the world an incandescent lightbulb only two years earlier, Edison, as usual, was trying to figure out how to finance his growing empire. The first lightbulb would beget billions more—higher in efficiency, brighter in illumination, longer lasting, and, most important, available to anyone. Edison's vision of the future was clearly a democratic one, a world in which every street, factory, office, and home would be blazing with his creations. But how to get that electricity transported and delivered? It took money and some ingenuity to pry capital from the tightfisted New York bankers who initially looked upon Edison's ventures as amusing novelties compared to sure bets like telegraph lines, steel mills, and railroads.

At 6 p.m. on February 28, 1881, a wisp of a man made his way into Edison's business office at 65 Fifth Avenue, an unassuming building with a second-floor entrance and striped awnings: Edison's new secretary, Samuel Insull, whippet-thin, about five-foot-three with a pallid complexion, spectacles, high cheekbones, sideburns down to his jaw line, and thin, neatly cropped brown hair. The 21-year-old looked more like a refugee from the Franco-Prussian war than a future empire builder. The Englishman had the blush of youth on his face and little meat on his bones. He weighed only 117 pounds, having spent most of his rough, two-month voyage on the *City of Chester* unsuccessfully trying to keep his food down. Soon after he left the ship, Insull was ushered into Edison's office, where the two men stared at each other and were initially paralyzed in an awkward silence. The unshaven 34-year-old Edison, in his trademark Prince Albert coat, a white kerchief tied sloppily around his neck, his tumbleweed hair under his floppy sombrerolike hat prematurely gray, leaned back slowly in his wooden chair to take in the neatly dressed Insull. The inventor who had given the world superior forms of the telegraph, telephone, mimeograph, stock ticker, phonograph, and lightbulb was measuring up the lad with the burning dark eyes. Edison then broke into a smile, introduced himself, warmly shook Insull's hand, and launched into describing Insull's first project.

"Sammy, this is what I need," Edison began in his casual, Midwestern drone. "I've poured thousands into my experiments and I need money. The banks won't give me any more and I've got a lot to do. I may have to sell my securities and borrow against my patent rights to raise more cash."

Edison pulled out a checkbook and showed Insull how much money he had in the bank: "I want to launch a machine works, an underground conductor works, and an establishment for the manufacture of small appliances. I have only $80,000. Now Johnson [Edison's London agent] is going to Europe tomorrow to see what I can turn into cash over there, and we have been waiting for *you* to get here to tell us what there is over there that we can convert into money."

Insull gaped at Edison, partially in awe, partially in fear, horrified that Edison was looking for someone with an entirely different skill set and that he would not fit the bill. Insull had little experience in finance beyond bookkeeping and spending hours perusing records in Edison's London office. The Englishman also was having trouble parsing the prairie-flat vowels of the upper Midwest, where Edison had spent his formative years as a quicksilver telegraph operator.

As straight as a coat rack, Insull mustered up a reply in a formal manner that he had reviewed all of Edison's European interests and contracts and was confident that he could be of assistance. Now it was Edison who had a problem with the spoken word, and not because of his growing deafness. In this case, Insull's thick cockney accent, with its taffy-pulled diphthongs, tripped up Edison.

"Okay then," Edison winced. "How much should I pay you? How about $100 a month? And here's a check for $200 to cover your travel expenses. You had better go get your supper. Then we have a lot of work to do before Johnson heads back to London on the steamer *Arizona* for London at 5 a.m."

"That's fine, sir," Insull replied, not expecting to be reimbursed for his voyage. While agreeing to only half what he was making in London, he maintained a stoic face to contain his exaltation. He was now employed by his idol, the most famous inventor in the world.

Despite being physically depleted from the voyage, Insull went to work immediately around 8 p.m., scouring the untidy mass of Edison's financial documents. Insull had a hunch that Edison could leverage his European interests to procure more financing. Where Edison simply saw assets and an ability to write checks to the Morgan bank against them, Insull saw a cornucopia of collateral, mortgages, bonds, and debentures, all waiting to be harvested and cut up like fruit in an orchard of ledger books. Insull had arrived at this knowledge through hard study, luck, intense curiosity, and a serendipitous meeting.

Born November 11, 1859, in the London district of Lambeth, Samuel Insull was one of three surviving children, the fifth child of eight. Born in near poverty at the corner of Union Street and Westminster Bridge Road in South London, his home was only five minutes from the Houses of Parliament. As Congregationalist nonconformists, his family was among a group of dissenters that had separated from the Anglican Church. Consequently, they were not afforded the social privileges of state-supported Church of England members and their chapels were modest and often ramshackle. His often underemployed father, also named Samuel, worked as a merchant, dairyman, and eventually as a temperance minister. The elder Samuel, "whose ideals were more in his mind than his pocketbook," wanted his son to become a minister as well. The elder Insull joined the United Kingdom Alliance, a group that was agitating for permissive or partial prohibition throughout England. He became a lay preacher for the movement and became the alliance's paid representative in Oxfordshire. One of young Samuel's uncles had been a pastor in John Bunyan's meeting house for 20 years. Other uncles were involved in manufacturing.

Emma Short Insull, his adored mother, also took the temperance pledge. The "fine English matron" would implore young Sam always to be the best, follow his ambition, and keep the pledge. She was to remain a powerful force in his life long after he had achieved success in the business world. Both grandparents were of solid yeoman stock; his maternal grandparents, the Shorts, were also temperance minded. The most illustrious of the Shorts was his uncle George, who was a master mason involved in the restoration of St. George Castle at Windsor Castle. Prince Albert admired his work so much that he obtained a position for him in the army, where he became known for his fortifications in the Crimean War. Like most English dissenters, the Insulls and the Shorts were at the social margins of English society. Their coreligionists largely emigrated before and after the English Civil War and became influential forces in American society as Quakers (Philadelphia), Congregationalists (New England abolitionists), and Baptists (John D. Rockefeller). Samuel the elder became a preacher four years after young Samuel was born. The family then moved to Reading and later to Oxford, where young Samuel received a fairly good education for a boy of his class before moving back to London as a teenager.

Since his father had no money to educate him as a proper clergyman, young Sam was sent to work in London at the age of 14. He quickly picked up the myriad skills of an office clerk in 1870s London. Following his mother's edict constantly to improve himself, Insull embarked on a business education campaign, learned shorthand and bookkeeping on the side, read everything he could get his hands on, improved his awful handwriting, and took various jobs as an office boy and shorthand clerk. At the time, everything was written out in longhand since typewriters were not yet widely accepted. Working his way up to the rank of correspondence clerk in a real estate auction firm—basically a stenographer who accepted and wrote down dictation—Insull was ready to advance. On a chilly day in January 1879, one of the partners of the firm called for Insull to come into his office.

"Is all of your work up to date?" the partner asked in his high-collared business tone.

"Yes sir, everything is in shape," the boy responded.

"Samuel, you have served us well and we want you to know that."

Insull knew something was afoot, but did not flinch.

"Unfortunately, we have an articled clerk coming in the following Monday morning. As he will work for *nothing*, we will have no further need for your services. You can stay on until you have found another position."

The up-and-coming clerk was being replaced by the son of a wealthy client, but Insull restrained his anger, easing out a curt yet controlled reply.

"Well, it's half past eleven. I will stay until 12 noon, then I will be going and I shall *not* be back. If my services are not worth anything to you, and it pays you better to have a man not only do my work for nothing, but pay *you* to do my work, I think it is time I got out and went somewhere else. So instead of taking a few weeks, as you have offered to allow me to do, I will take my pay to date, and I will quit at noon."

Insull quietly walked over to his desk and started cleaning it out, feeling liberated from the insulting pay of five dollars a week. It was quadruple what he was making when he first started out as an office boy, but he knew he could do better and was already working lucrative part-time jobs as secretaries for a newspaper publisher, the editor of *Vanity Fair,* and a member of Parliament. Insull wanted what the upper-class merchants of London probably would never give him, a chance to take charge of an office, a business, an enterprise.

Paging through the *Times,* the right opportunity soon caught his eye. "Wanted: private secretary for an American office in London, Hours from 11 until 3." The hours conveniently dovetailed with his other jobs, so he applied. The position was for the Mercantile Trust Company of New York and Edison's European agent, Colonel George Gouraud. Insull was more than familiar with Edison. As the secretary of a South London literary society, he was well read on Edison's life and inventions and even presented a paper to the society on the inventor. Insull was smitten with the ideas of self-reliance, self-improvement, and personal character. He was aspiring to be a Victorian gentleman who was well read, kept his word, and would be known for his industry and undisputed determination. He enthusiastically consumed the writings of the Scottish writer Samuel Smiles, who was the British counterpart of Horatio Alger, telling stories of poor boys who made good in inspirational vignettes. Smiles's *Self-Help* and *Lives of the Great Engineers* were well-worn books.

The other boys in the new office snickered when Insull arrived, immediately telling him that the only reason he got the job is because he offered to do it for less than anyone else. Insull ignored them and knew he was there primarily to do simple correspondence, enjoy the work, and "improve my mental faculties." He also liked being among the technical men wandering in and out of the office, engineers who, in a time when there was no formal university electrical engineering training, were trying to improve upon Edison's installations of phones, batteries, and wiring.

Since very few specialties existed in the burgeoning telephone and electrical industries at the time, young Edison men were expected to be jacks-of-all-trades. In addition to being a stenographer and file clerk, Insull was the first switchboard operator for Edison's small London telephone system. He also maintained batteries for the phones along with a headstrong Irishman named George Bernard Shaw. At the time, Edison was marketing a telephone that employed a transmitter with chalk within a diaphragm. While vastly inferior to the telephones of today, it was said to produce significantly more volume than the competing Bell product, a distinct advantage considering how little volume phones of that day produced. When the "loud-speaking" telephone was being introduced to the powerbrokers of London, Edison's company had strung a line so that the prime minister William E. Gladstone and his wife could be among the first to use the new instrument at Burlington House. The first conversation, with Mrs. Gladstone at the receiver and Insull at the switchboard went something like this:

"Is this a woman or a man at the other end?"

"It's a man!" came the indignant shout.

Shaw was unimpressed and quickly convinced himself that he was not cut out for the telephone business of 1879, calling the loud-speaking phone "a much too ingenious invention as it proved, being nothing less than a telephone of such stentorian efficiency that it bellowed your most private communications all over the house instead of whispering them with some sort of discretion. This was not what the British stockbroker wanted; so the company was soon merged into the National Telephone Company after making a place for itself in the history of literature, quite unintentionally, by providing me with a job." Shaw would later use the experience in his novel *The Irrational Knot* and recall of the telephone pioneers:

> These deluded and romantic men gave me a glimpse of the skilled proletariat of the United States. They sang obsolete sentimental songs with genuine emotion; and their language was frightful even to an Irishman. They worked with ferocious energy which was all out of proportion to the actual result achieved.[2]

It is unlikely that Shaw and Insull had much of a relationship, given the respective size of their egos and aspirations. As a lover of grand opera, Insull the Puritan industrialist was heading in a different direction than the libertine, socialist Shaw. Insull also wanted to build something tangible and did not live in a world of abstraction. Ironically, Shaw and Insull would connect indirectly 30 years later when Insull's wife would star in Shaw's *Heartbreak House,* a production Insull would finance.

Shortly around the time of the telephone demonstration, as Insull was sitting in the office, Edward Johnson, Edison's chief engineer in London, walked in, cussing up a storm. He was angry because he could not find a stenographer to prepare a legal brief in Edison's litigation against the Bell interests, one of many suits Edison would file over his long career to establish that his technology was the first, the foremost, and the most deserving of future millions in licensing and royalty fees. Insull saw his opening.

"Well, Johnson," Insull said, his eyes blazing intently. "I will do it for you. I *was* going to a cricket match, but I will do it for you," he said with icy calmness, as if he was putting off a memo for the Queen herself to accommodate the engineer.

"Why are *you* offering to do it?" Johnson shot back, reacting to Insull's cockiness.

"First of all," his tone that of a country squire, "I would like to oblige you, and second, I think I will get some information from it."

It was more than information that Insull derived from the dictation. It plunged him into the technical mysteries of the Edison telephone. There were also the contracts, licenses, and financing of Edison's other varied interests across the continents. While he had no technical background, Insull immersed himself in Edison's business, knowing where the income came from and how it was spent. Entranced by the prospect of Edison's mushrooming technologies, Insull talked Johnson into letting him become his private secretary, squeezing Johnson's work in between his other responsibilities at night. Since Insull only seemed to need four hours of sleep or less a night, he was now writing Johnson's weekly letters to Edison on the changing "electrical situation in Europe."

Shortly after beginning to work directly for Johnson, Insull was offered a stenographer's position in the New York office of Drexel, Morgan & Company, the colossal House of Morgan at the corner of Broad and Wall Street that dominated U.S. investment banking at the time. Insull casually mentioned the job offer to Johnson with an ulterior motive lurking in his haughty tone.

"The only way I would ever go to America, though, is as Mr. Edison's private secretary," Insull said with firmness.

"Are you really serious?" Johnson barked in surprise. "Mr. Edison badly needs a private secretary. His correspondence is abominably handled. Do you want the job?"

"I can tell that from running the London end of it," Insull said wryly. "Yes."

Johnson finished up dictating some letters to Edison's assistant in Menlo Park, New Jersey.

"Let's start a new letter, Sam. 'I am dictating this letter to a young English friend of mine who does my work when he is not engaged in the office of private secretary to Mr. Edison's London agent. He is the kind of fellow Mr. Edison ought to have for his private secretary.'"

Insull blushed at the subtle praise and the recommendation letter that would spring from his own hand. He was on his way, as soon as he devoured all of the files on all of Edison's operations.

Although it may have surprised Edison that Insull had memorized and was fluent in every detail of Edison's business affairs in Europe and America, what most impressed the 24/7 Edison was that Insull was keeping up with him, a man who had disdained sleep and often took catnaps on a cot right in his lab. The two men worked through the night to come up with a novel financing plan. By dawn of the next day, Johnson would have his marching orders, which originated from his former assistant, whom Edison would say was as "tireless as the tides."

Insull's work ethic embodied a potent mixture of Calvinism and temperance. As nonconformists, the Insulls were not on the fast track for wealth and prestige in the England of the late nineteenth century. Up until 1828, this dissenting group of "dry" Protestants was even banned from attending Oxford or Cambridge. Temperance crusaders from the Quakers and the Salvation Army had worked with the British Liberal Party to restrict the sale of alcohol, equating the drink trade with immorality. In fact, most of the nonconformist ministers in the 1870s had "signed the pledge" to abstain from alcohol. Some 2,500 out of 3,000 Congregationalist ministers were teetotalers. Insull would be a lifelong supporter of the temperance cause, even during the "wet" days of the 1920s in Chicago, where Prohibition was a laughable failure.

Having been largely excluded from the power structure of class-entrenched Britain, nonconformists like Insull did well in the New World where the class system was not fused to Church of England membership. While temperance had its origins in a religious and moral movement, it also gave outsiders like Insull a chance to direct their energies toward self-development, application to the business world, and achievement.

Insull kept his emotions under check as he concentrated on the tasks at hand. The young Edison men rooming with him at 65 Fifth Avenue often teased him for his serious demeanor and accent. Insull did not make much of an attempt to blend in, either. He was not the congenial type. The only open emotion Insull was known to have displayed in his early days in New York is when he stood by a window, homesick for London, listening to the other boys talk about their homes in the city. "Home! Home! You chaps all have homes to go to—mine is far away." Francis Jehl, one of Edison's lab assistants at the time, felt sorry for Insull, often inviting him to stay in his home in New Brunswick, New Jersey. Jehl also got his jibes in at Insull, who took everything in stride. When Insull made his way down to the Menlo Park lab in New Jersey, shortly after he arrived in New York, he encountered Jehl alone in the lab.

"What's on your mind?" Jehl asked.

"Oh, don't ye know?' Insull said perkily. "I am Mr. Edison's new English secretary and my name is Mr. Samuel Insull."

Mocking Insull, Jehl, the tough New York east sider, quickly retorted in a cockney drawl. "'Pon my word, Mr. Insull, it's mighty jolly to meet you and I shall be glad to show you around in Mr. Thomas Edison's laboratory."

Activity at Menlo Park was slowing to a crawl in 1881. Its heyday had passed since Edison produced the lightbulb. His burgeoning operations had outgrown its handful of buildings, along with its copper mine, and small electric rail line. Edison's tinfoil cylinder phonograph lay dormant on the lab's tables as Edison, weary of patent suits, conceded to Insull: "Well, Sammy, they never will try to steal the phonograph; it is of no commercial value and therefore nobody will ever have the incentive to try to get it away from me."

A new machine works and conductor plant was springing up on Goerck Street in lower Manhattan, while the bulk of Edison's basic research was moving to West Orange. Henry Ford would later re-create the Menlo Park lab in his Greenfield Village park near Detroit in homage to his friend and mentor.

After a brief tour of the Menlo Park machine shop and glassworks, Insull spied a small electric locomotive and asked Jehl if it could haul several trailers of people. Jehl, still ribbing Insull, replied "certainly my *dear* sir. Would *ye* like a ride?"

Jehl started up the locomotive and unhooked the cars. They tootled around the track at about 30 miles an hour. Insull seemed pleased with the third of a mile excursion, which ended at the small copper mine on the property.

"Have you ever heard of the Flying Scotsman?" Insull smiled, referring to one of England's fastest trains, which ran from Edinburgh, Scotland, to London. "The speed of your locomotive is nothing compared to this train."

"Oh, it's speed that you're hankering after!" Jehl laughed. With that, Jehl started the motor again and the little train went hurtling down the track. The burst of speed startled Insull, who grabbed the brake handle and begged Jehl to slow down. Some small objects appeared on the tracks ahead and in an instant an explosion of feathers puffed up. Jehl pulled the brake so hard that the handle came off in his hand. Insull managed to engage his brake successfully, stopping the train. They both looked back to see two turkey carcasses lying on the track. A fellow Menlo Park worker was keeping them for a future feast.

"Well, Jehl, an electric locomotive *can* attain a surprising speed and will no doubt compete with steam locomotives," Insull said, wiping the sweat from his brow. As a future financier of electric interurban lines, Insull never forgot the experience, writing Jehl thirty years later that the ride "nearly scared the life out of me."

⋘⋙

Other than his perennial financial shortfall, Edison had two distinct dilemmas in the early 1880s. He wanted to establish the first urban central power station and factories that would make the necessary equipment to make his electrical transmission system work on a large scale. As Edison's secretary, Insull had his hand in all of these activities, gaining Edison's power of attorney, paying bills, ordering supplies, and watching the money flow in—and mostly out of—Edison's coffers. Insull also had to keep Edison's personal matters on track by buying him clothes and paying some of his personal debts.

It was not a lack of will, ideas, or applications that held Edison back in the mid-1880s. It was a chronic shortage of capital that slowed the Edison combine's unstoppable culture of innovation. Up until Edison's time, there were relatively long periods when little or nothing happened in the thrilling world of electromagnetism. Ever since Franklin had first described electricity in the middle of the eighteenth century as a discrete force of nature that could be captured, the world had longed to harness this Promethean energy. There was a lull in research between the American Revolution and the Napoleonic wars. Sir Humphrey Davy discovered in 1801 that an arc of electricity between two carbon electrodes would produce a continuous light source. Faraday's brilliant electromagnetic experiments of the 1830s provided a catalyst for the explosion in Victorian-era science. In 1839, the first fuel cell to liberate electrons from hydrogen and oxygen was invented by another Englishman named Grove. The first lead-cell battery was invented in 1860 by a Frenchman named Plante. The first effective dynamo, or a device with moving parts that generated electricity using electromagnetism, was invented by a Belgian named Gramme. Arc lighting, the bright illumination that came from crossing a high-voltage current between two carbon electrodes, was part of the innovation in the early to mid-1800s. In the closing years of the steam age, large-scale electric arc lighting was a breakthrough, although it was a poor solution. Arc lights required tremendous voltage to operate, burned out frequently, and had to be replaced. They were unsuitable for most indoor applications because of the blinding harshness of the light. Interior modes of lighting were mostly done either by the dangerous use of kerosene, candles, or gas manufactured from coal. Gaslights, besides posing the threat of explosion, had the additional danger of asphyxiation if the flame went out, so they required large rooms with big windows. Though the best available technology for indoor lighting, gaslight also flickered, had a strong odor, and could only be increased nominally in brightness. They often gave people headaches. In a word, they were noxious.

Edison, along with Joseph Swan—who invented an incandescent light at about the same time with considerably less fanfare—realized early on that if his new approach to lighting was to succeed, it would have to be self-contained, be long burning, use relatively little power, and be safe from explosion. And these newfangled lightbulbs would need ready power to keep them lit at any hour of the day. Batteries were not up to the task (neither then nor now over long periods of time). That meant either steam-driven dynamos on every property, or the more efficient approach of central station power.

Power stations, though, required dynamos, pulleys, cables, fuses, junction boxes, switches, and untold lengths of wire and conduit. Edison had purchased a site on Pearl Street in lower Manhattan for $65,000 for his first large central station and had most of the equipment he needed to make that station run. Then there was the small matter of getting the power to his customers, which required huge conduits—copper wire in iron pipes surrounded by cardboard, asphalt, and linseed oil.

Edison's enterprises were now spread out over several companies, which needed to be managed and coordinated to make Pearl Street a working operation. Edison's Electric Lamp Company made lightbulbs. His Electric Light Company owned the patents for lighting and power equipment. The Electric Tube Company made conductors for supplying the current. The Edison Machine Works made heavy equipment such as dynamos and motors. Edison also had an interest in the Bergmann Company, which made electrical fixtures, telephones, and telegraphic equipment. For establishing power plants outside of New York, the Edison Company for Isolated Lighting was created. The flagship for the power plant on Pearl Street was the Edison Electric Illuminating Company of New York. Edison's associates were either officers or directors of the various companies, which were all nominally headed by Edison, though they lacked a central management structure.

Insull did his best to keep up with the overlapping interests and financing needs of the various companies, although they were continually plagued by lack of capital, space, and direction. Within two years of arriving in America, Insull was secretary of most of Edison's companies. Edison, for example, made Insull secretary of his Electric Tube Company, which was located in a 20-foot-long building at 65 Washington Street. Like most of Edison's ambitious projects at the time, it was underfinanced. Since the conductor tubes were more than 20 feet long, they had to be pushed out the window so that they could be turned around. On Washington Street, Insull worked closely with the clever bearded Swiss engineer John Kruesi, who spoke only broken English.

Seeing firsthand Edison's relentless money woes, in his first year in New York, Insull often asked Edison to pay him exclusively with stocks and interests in the myriad Edison concerns. By the end of 1881, Edison had given Insull securities worth close to $15,000, a princely sum at the time. The most Insull had earned with all of his jobs in London was $2,000 a year. Insull felt he was worth it. He was available to Edison at any hour and worked directly with the bankers, engineers, and workers in all of his enterprises. There was almost nothing that Insull did not do for Edison, a fact that often earned him the derision of the top "muckers" at Menlo Park, many of whom specialized in certain aspects of experimentation and development. Edison noted in his journal that Insull was peeved that one of his workers called the English assistant the "valet to my intellect." While Insull must have absorbed constant put-downs in his role as factotum, he continued to examine every detail of Edison's scattered business plan and finances.

Although constantly anxious about money, Edison moved on with his projects. Driven by his internal compass that always guided him to create a better product for the public, Edison still needed another triumph to regain his momentum. The Pearl Street station would be that prize, one that not only would get Edison into the power generating business, it would provide Insull with the knowledge to transform Edison's vision into a national system. It also would be the fulcrum to pry some needed capital loose from the House of Morgan.

THE PEARL IN THE OYSTER

Edison's Power Plant

Edison was still only 35 [in 1882]. Enticed by his opportunity to transform night into day for millions of Americans, he declared that he had definitely become a businessman, and would take a "long vacation in the matter of inventions."

—Daniel Boorstin, *The Americans: The Democratic Experience*[1]

Edison savored a juicy practical joke in between experiments and grappling with bankers. Shortly before he planned to take the Pearl Street station on line, one night he summoned Insull to his lab. From the twinkle in Edison's eye, Insull knew his boss was up to something devilish. Edison had called in two of his best mathematicians and asked them to determine the exact volume of one of his lightbulbs, stressing that he wanted the result as quickly as possible. Turning to Insull, he said, "Sammy, you had better go down to the house and go to bed. Tell the watchman to call you at 6 a.m. tomorrow morning, and when you get up, come over and wake me up. I am going to lie down and take a sleep, as these fellows have got quite a long job ahead of them."

The next morning Insull woke up Edison and they headed to the lab, where the mathematicians were still working, exhausted, tormented, and swimming in scraps of paper covered with various formulae. Edison turned to Insull and quietly asked him to get a lightbulb and a graduated cylinder for measuring liquid volume. Edison then filled the bulb with water and poured the contents into the cylinder, which gave the volume of the bulb. Edison then walked over to his workers and elaborated on his method.

"A little practical experience is sometimes of more value than all of the theoretical knowledge in the world," Edison said in a serious tone. "You might have been figuring until doomsday and not get the accurate results that this cylinder gave me in a minute." With that, Edison, Insull, and the workers guffawed and went off to breakfast.

For all of his legendary doggedness in solving serious problems, Edison had a powerful sense of humor and loved to entertain (he had a pipe organ in the Menlo Park lab). When Insull asked him if he believed in genius, Edison replied that "I believe more in a real good memory and knowledge of the thousands of things that don't work." Insull would remember this remark for several decades as he built upon his knowledge every day, knowing in his heart that he knew he could apply the pragmatic spirit of Edison on a grand scale.

For most of 1882, Edison was working on the Pearl Street station. Thousands of details needed to be attended to, and Insull was enlisted as a part-time troubleshooter. The streets had to be torn up for installation of electrical conduits. That meant negotiating with the Tammany Hall hacks controlling the street cleaners, who already had their hands full picking up three million pounds a day of manure from the nearly 150,000 horses that provided most of New York's transportation. The city bosses also wanted inspectors to supervise the work on the streets—and were to be paid $25 a week directly by Edison's company. In keeping up an unsavory tradition of patronage employees in the Tammany days, the inspectors showed up only on Saturdays to accept what amounted to little more than bribes. There were other setbacks. Other street workers would destroy some of the conduit laid by Edison, causing further delays and prompting horses to bolt when they hit live current from the severed wires.

The summer heat bore down and intensified the already Augean stench of garbage, stale beer, horse manure, and urine while Edison kept postponing the opening date for the Pearl Street station. The powerhouse would essentially serve a half-mile radius of businesses in the nearby financial district, so he wanted to get it right. If he failed, it would set him back for years. If he succeeded, the most important city in the country would be at his beck and call and other cities would be clamoring for central power. The other benefit was that illuminating the financial district would show his bankers and stockholders that it could be done and was worthy of more investment. After all, up until this point he had been creating all of the equipment for the modern electrical industry on the fly out of small labs and storefronts. His principal competitors Westinghouse and Thomson-Houston were also small operations, nothing like the giant equipment manufacturers of today.

Edison needed to win the public relations battle by getting Pearl Street on line so that the bankers would see he had a viable concern. Capital would then flow into his companies and enable him to build power plants in every city. He staked nearly everything on Pearl Street, wiring all of the major businesses in the financial district. Even the *New York Times* was wired to illuminate 52 bulbs.

The few power plants of the early 1880s were tremendously inefficient. Dynamos attached to steam engines would be housed either in basements or on adjacent properties. They were noisy, constantly broke down, were used only for lighting, and typically did not run 24 hours a day. John Pierpont Morgan was one of the few residential electric customers. His clattering little power plant rankled his Murray Hill neighbors because of its constant noise and smoke. His Madison Street mansion had electric lights, but the great banker was one of the few people in the world who could afford them. One of Edison's other first isolated plants was not even on land. He installed a lighting system in 1880 on the yacht S.S. *Columbia,* owned by the financier Henry Villard. Like Morgan, Villard had extensive interests in railroads and was an early supporter of Edison. It was Villard who encouraged Edison to build an electric train, hoping that such an idea would eventually catch on in every city and stem the huge amount of pollution that horse- and steam-driven trolleys were creating. Edison built the train, yet left the project idle while he concentrated on Pearl Street. Villard and Morgan, however, likely did not trust each other, even though they traveled in the same circles and owned two of the most celebrated mansions in New York. Villard took more of a hands-off approach to Edison, which the inventor preferred. Morgan was more conservative and had a supreme interest in control and consolidation. While Villard knew his investment would take time to show profits, Morgan wanted to see results in a short time through large, consolidated operations (that he could control) before he opened his checkbook to Edison, who depended heavily on Morgan for the bulk of his early financing.

Edison spent his evenings in and around Pearl Street testing various elements of the power station. Insull usually accompanied his boss and assisted him in running tests. Although Insull was exhausted from doing Edison's business virtually around the clock, he agreed to help.

A typical week meant working through the night Monday and Tuesday, sleeping Wednesday night, working through Saturday, and taking a break on Sunday. Insull usually handled correspondence and paperwork in the morning and early afternoon and followed Edison into the lab for the evening. Since Insull did not have much time to take and transcribe dictation, he usually wrote and signed Edison's letters and business directives himself. He had power of attorney for the inventor, who trusted him implicitly.

Insull marveled at Edison's energy; the inventor claimed he could work for ten days straight with little sleep. The young assistant also blushed with pride at the idea that he was part of something historic and wrote to a friend in England before the inauguration of Pearl Street and the illumination of more than 15,000 lights.

> I suppose that this district will be all lighted up in from three to four months and then you will see what you will see. You will witness the amazing sight of those English scientists eating that unpalatable crow of which Johnson used to speak in his letters to me when I was in the old country.[2]

There were countless technical details to work out before Edison could bask in his glory. Rather than the tangled skein of high-voltage lines strung overhead for arc lighting, Edison wanted his lines underground, which created a raft of problems since they were expensive, less accessible, and needed heavy insulation. Edison wanted no part of the jungle of wires strung carelessly above the streets. The lines carried as much as 3,500 volts, which caused frequent electrocutions.

One night Insull had fallen asleep while watching a galvanometer (electric voltage indicator). A friendly cop who was supposed to wake him up failed to rouse him as Edison ambled down the street. Edison, slightly perturbed, woke Insull and remarked, "I suppose galvanometers are adapted to absent treatment."

Toward the end of that summer, the newspapers became natteringly skeptical as delay after delay caused several more postponements. After a capital investment of $600,000, Edison was finally ready to throw the switch by early September. If it worked, every newspaper adjacent to the financial district would know it immediately. If he failed, it would be back to Menlo Park in humiliation.

Donning a brown frock coat and white high-crowned a derby hat, Edison appeared more like the dandy Diamond Jim Brady than a rumpled inventor on September 4, 1882. He made a bet with one of his assistants for $100 that the lights would go on. Pulling out his pocket watch, he waited for the moment when electrician John Lieb would pull down a circuit breaker at Pearl Street to send current into his new system. Edison was stationed in Morgan's Wall Street office, huddled with a group of investment bankers. At 3 p.m., Lieb sent the electricity flowing into Wall Street and Edison pulled a switch at the Morgan headquarters.

"They're on!" shouted the directors. Some 100 Edison bulbs slowly started a fluttering glow, then reached full luminosity. All told, 400 bulbs lit up the cavernous financial district. As night fell around 7 p.m., the staff of the *New York Times* witnessed in its own newsroom one of the world's most significant moments of progress.

"The electric light made itself known and showed how bright and steady it was," the *New York Times* reported. "It seemed almost like writing by daylight . . . the light was soft and mellow and grateful to the eye." The *Times* account waxed poetic about the relatively low heat the bulbs produced and the mellowness of the light. A happy medium was now in use that straddled the blinding harshness of the arc lamps and the dangerous dimness of the gas lights. No longer a novelty for wealthy financiers, power and illumination could be widely distributed, as the Pearl Street victory showed. It was clearly a conquest for Edison as Insull took detailed notes.

Edison called the event "the most responsible thing I had ever undertaken, there was no parallel in the world." As the capital started to seep into Edison's manufacturing operations, the price of gas stocks in that $400 million industry plummeted. While the use of gas for lighting continued well into the first two decades of the twentieth century, gas was technically obsolete. The great barrier now was producing enough—and the right kind—of power equipment to meet the demand, which accelerated exponentially after the Pearl Street experience.

Insull became a frenzied whirligig in his new role to sell and manage power station equipment production. As secretary of most of the companies, he had to review their financial statements, ensure that Edison was up to date on their operations, and try to keep them solvent. Edison's interests were now more than four times larger than his operation at Menlo Park, and there was no centralized method of keeping track or managing the whole enterprise. In addition to making thousands of lightbulbs, Edison's companies now needed to build the machinery and parts that would go into his power plants, conduits, and installation. That entailed an endless list of devices that needed to be invented, tested, perfected, and manufactured. Connectors, fuse boxes, circuit boards, switches, and insulators all needed to be born and reared in the then tiny Edison manufacturing operation if he was to compete with Westinghouse and Thomson-Houston. And the most stringent reality of it all was that it needed to be produced at a profit.

The lightbulbs and the overall system needed to become more efficient as well. If lightbulbs used less power and lasted longer, that meant it would eventually be less expensive for the customer. Knowing how much power the customer consumed was a moot point since Edison charged by the bulb. This was before the time of the electric meter.

The key to making electricity work on a large scale was to make the cost of lighting fall relative to the rate of efficiency in producing the energy. As detailed by economist John Kay, for example, the physical efficiency ratio of light to energy (or lumens to watt in electrical terms) is 0.002 for a wood fire. That means you have to burn a lot of wood to create light, relative to say a candle, which has an efficiency of 0.01. With a gas lamp, the efficiency expanded by a factor of 25. By 1890, the efficiency rose by another factor of 10. A century later, and lighting was seven times more efficient. Today, the most efficient form of non-electronic lighting is more than five times as efficient as in 1990. At each step of the technological ladder, efficiency translated into less electricity doing more work (or illumination) for less cost. Such a progression means that electricity was becoming increasingly more cost-effective for multiple uses in factories, municipalities, offices, and homes. Edison knew this formula intimately, and Insull was learning how to apply it.

Ever less-costly electricity not only would provide the financial incentive for customers to use it, it also would change the way commercial and residential buildings were constructed. The Ansel Cook home in Libertyville, Illinois (where Insull's portrait now hangs, although he never lived there), is a case in point. Built in 1878 by a wealthy teacher, legislator, and stonemason who constructed the famous Chicago Water Tower, the Cook home features a neoclassic exterior and a typical Victorian interior. The rooms have high ceilings and were largely designed to prevent gas explosions since the larger rooms could hold a considerable volume of gas. Heated by seven fireplaces, the house had two parlors, a front room for guests, and an adjacent space used largely for funerals. Before gas lighting was installed, the chandeliers were kerosene fueled. As Cook was one of the most prosperous men in the county, he could afford to install a private generator for lighting in 1887, which was extremely rare at the time. The dynamo was in the backyard. The town of Libertyville did not have streetlights until ten years later, and its main street was not paved until the mid-1920s. As seen in the Cook home, electricity in the late nineteenth century was the exclusive province of the upper class until it became widely and efficiently distributed by central power stations, as Insull saw firsthand.

Three weeks after Pearl Street started up, Insull had a commanding view of Edison's finances. He had pored over every ledger, invoice, bill, and meager bit of income. As usual, Edison was overextended, and Insull had to marshall Edison's dwindling resources to keep the operation going. Although Insull had been in

Edison's employment less than three years, the inventor trusted the young Englishman for his bookkeeping and secretarial skills. Now the future of Edison's amorphous enterprises was being overseen by Insull, who had no background for guiding the finances of what would become one of the world's greatest industrial concerns.

Financial details, though, seemed to inform and educate Insull the way experiments gave Edison critical insights. There was no item too insignificant for Insull to ponder as he canvassed company records for ways of cutting costs and raising capital. Acting as the chief financial officer Edison never really had, Insull made Edison's top managers account for everything they were spending money on, something that they had not been accustomed to doing during the freewheeling experimenting days at Menlo Park. Whether he knew it or not at the time, Insull, attempting to fulfill Edison's many goals, was trying to establish the kind of fiscal discipline that would befit a modern corporation and not an entrepreneurial venture.

Insull began his crusade to police Edison's troubled books with Charles Batchelor, one of Edison's many capable vice presidents. Batchelor was instrumental in running Edison's research and growing manufacturing operations, and was one of the pioneers from the Menlo Park days. It is not clear exactly how he regarded Insull, who had neither served in Menlo Park nor was with Edison in the 1870s, yet it was now Insull, in a martinetlike tone, who was issuing marching orders. In a letter to Batchelor on September 28, 1882, Insull outlined his fiscal strategy, combing through each of Edison's main units: "I think it well to deal with the most expensive subject first. The Lamp Factory continues to absorb money right along. They are turning out at the present time from about 800 to 1,000 [lightbulbs] a day and still lose on everything that they sell."

Insull not only criticized the profit-and-loss statement of Edison's most vaunted division (a separate company at the time), but also went into specific detail about the stock that capitalized it and how company finances could be bolstered, including raising the price of the lamps: "If we met this increased price on lamps, it would appear that everything would be solid at the lamp factory. In addition to this, we are going to claim from the Light Co. an amount equal to about $50,000 for purely experimental work. We propose to debit this sum to the Light Co.'s account and wipe it out by means of crediting them with any future profits on manufacture that they may be entitled to after the Lamp Co. has received 5 cents per lamp as its regular profit."

In addition to his accounting finesse, Insull, who had even less experience in engineering than he did in big-company accounting, delved into the technical details of the Machine Works, which was producing equipment for the power plants. He made an effort to understand Edison's many dilemmas in getting all of his equipment to work, even making a surprising technical suggestion to Batchelor:

> My electrical knowledge is too slight to describe the causes of this difficulty to you . . . all I can do is state the facts and leave it to Edison to give you the theory. Up to 2 or three days ago, it was quite impossible to run more than one dynamo in the [Pearl Street] central station. The night before last Edison had this coupling arrangement for locking engines together tried and it worked with perfect success. . . . There is no reason why as soon as this coupling device has been fixed up permanently we should not connect up to 4,000 or 5,000 more lights. At present, we have consumers using our light constantly from Drexel, Morgan & Co., to the Times Building and from there down to the East River.[3]

Despite his precocious grasp of accounting realities, ultimately Insull trusted Edison's projections that his lighting business would continue to grow apace: "So Edison is very confident that everything will be all right so far as this economy goes. Johnson [one of Edison's top engineers] is assisting Edison in cutting in consumers and immediately Edison gives him the word to connect 4 or 5,000 more he will put a large force of men at work and then we shall have probably the Edison boom that we have been so long hoping for."[4]

Power company workers in 1882 were ombudsmen. Edison's companies not only produced and sold power, they made lightbulbs, all of the fixtures, wired the buildings, and installed the infrastructure to generate and transport electricity. Imagine Microsoft, the software company, in addition to writing computer operating systems, making every component of the computer *and* supplying the electricity to run them, wiring houses *and* owning and running power plants. Such was the nascent electrical industry before the turn of the century.

In addition to operational concerns, Insull was intimately involved in how Edison's companies were capitalized. He monitored the stock prices of each concern, advising on which shares could be sold at a profit and which should be held. Edison routinely gave Insull and his top managers shares in his companies, and they were free to buy and sell whenever they liked. Since salaries at the time were meager and often unpaid when Edison ran short of cash, the free shares were often the only compensation, so Insull paid close attention to each security.

Edison's men hoped to profit handsomely since they were exchanging their sweat equity for thinly traded stock. Insull was no exception, yet none of the wealth that would flow from Edison's operations would be created immediately after the Pearl Street bonanza. Insull was also in the position of offering advice and taking orders from Edison's lieutenants when they wanted to buy or sell their stocks. He pointedly discusses the stock performance to Batchelor:

> The parent stock has not sold at very high prices as yet in consequence of our lighting up. There were at least 150 shares thrown on the market. I consider this price extremely good and shows public confidence in this enterprise. . . . I think as soon as 4 or 5,000 lights are running, we shall see a very considerable rise in Edison's stock, although as I have just stated, it is passing hands [trading] at about $600, there is practically none offering [being sold], everybody is holding for higher prices.[5]

Insull goes on to note to Batchelor in the letter that "nothing whatever is doing" in the Illuminating Company stock while the Isolated Company (power plants) "is doing extremely good business from $235 to $240 a share," mainly because, unlike many of Edison's other operations, the power stations are generating a "gross profit of 50 percent."

The power company was one of the strongest Edison concerns. It had more orders than it could fill and had a three-month backlog. Insull even mentioned to Edison that "he bought some [stock] himself at the $110 premium."

The overseer of the books of the Edison companies, Insull gained invaluable experience on how growing companies used capital to expand and the importance of keeping the business moving in the right direction. As charismatic as he was, Edison was no manager. The wizard preferred being in the workshops or on the front lines of his most promising ventures. One of the reasons he hired Insull was to gain control over the mundane necessities of ordering parts, paying bills, and keeping the money flowing. Without Insull's prodding, Edison would fall behind on any number of business matters, much to the routine frustration of Insull, who wrote in July of 1883:

> My Dear Edison: I telegraphed you the other day asking you what I should do about regulators and switches for the Louisville Exposition. You have not yet answered my telegram. There are piles of matter requiring your attention, and I am very anxiously looking forward to your return, else I am afraid the plaster will grow so horribly thick it will be set hard in our stomachs.[6]

Edison's lighting system was being shown all over the world in expositions and demonstrations. Gone was the single goal of efficiently producing lightbulbs and his other inventions. Now Edison was rapidly trying to dominate the central station business, which meant setting up the Edison electric franchises in large cities, many of which have retained the "Edison" name in the local power companies to this day. Since Edison's focus was on global expansion, Insull could not fully handle the affairs of the Edison power companies, which had expanded from Pearl Street to the main street of every town wanting illumination. Economically, widely-distributed electricity was a breakthrough commodity that not only was priced cheaper than gas, but also offered power for other uses. It was becoming essential in the formation of the modern metropolis.

Although the workload must have been unbearable, Insull also took it upon himself to evaluate the status of Edison's customers, a hands-on approach that he would retain through most of his career. One of Edison's first power station clients, the *New York Herald,* was watching carefully how much it was spending on electric bills. The Herald building was one of the first structures to be wired when Pearl Street opened. Insull knew that the Herald was paying about $20,000 for gas lighting, which not only was unsuitable for the high-intensity lighting needed for newspaper work, it also carried all of the other safety problems of gas, especially around all that paper: "The Herald people are keeping an exact amount of the cost of running them [the lights], and I expect at the end of the year they will come out in their columns [accounting] with a very strong endorsement of our isolated plants."[7]

If the Herald could save a significant amount of money by running Edison's lights, which he estimated would cost the publisher about $8,000 a year, not only would it cut the paper's operating expense, it also would create a possible future endorsement. Insull, now almost 23, was thinking about marketing research and advertising, another area in which he had absolutely no training.

Edison's companies were riding a new wave of technology and industry that many historians say began with the invention and distribution of the telegraph by William F.B. Morse before the Civil War. Edison had a role in that early technological push, having invented a multiplex telegraph that improved upon Morse's invention and transmitted messages rapidly. There had been a huge gap between the end of the Civil War and Edison's phonograph development, and finally, the incandescent lightbulb. It was still the Gilded Age, when robber barons like Rockefeller dominated their industries and most of the country's wealth was concentrated in a few families and firms. While steam was the dominant source of new power during this time, the great cities still reeked of horse excrement and modern urban sanitation was in its infancy. Typhus, tuberculosis, and cholera epidemics devastated nearly every urban community. Unpasteurized milk and drinking water that was fouled by raw sewage were prime sources of bacterial contamination.

Social critic Lewis Mumford called this period the "Brown Decades," referring to the haze, grime, and soot that blanketed streets, buildings, and urban skies. Coal-stoked fires belched out poisonous smoke everywhere from the multiple urban train stations to the family hearth. Public transportation consisted of a horse-drawn taxi, a horse-drawn streetcar, or steam-driven trains belching smoke and spewing cinders throughout the heart of cities. To many observers of the late nineteenth-century city, this urbanscape made Dante's vision of hell somewhat pleasant by comparison.

Before the great engineering visionaries of the steam age could better harness the toxic brawn of coal, they took some steps along the way to build the modern city. In Chicago, the first skyscrapers were being erected with steel skeletons, enabling architects using a new kind of structural steel to make a building taller than ten stories without having to build thick masonry walls to support it. Electric elevators also made taller buildings more practical. With cities becoming ever more crowded and property costing more, creating more vertical space made efficient use of land. Yet the building boom was reaching out in all directions as urban areas mushroomed. New engineering techniques meant taller buildings and longer tunnels and bridges.

On the evening before the Brooklyn Bridge opened, on May 23, 1883, Edison and his associates (Insull was probably working that evening) took a stroll on the new structure, a magnificent engineering achievement designed and managed by John and Washington Roebling and the nearly 30 workers who died building it, including the designer John Roebling. Local superstition had it that nature itself conspired against the designers and builders. The crowds that walked on the bridge on the day of the opening were panicked when someone tripped and fell near the center of the bridge, causing a dominolike line of people to fall. A dozen people were crushed to death as the mob tried to escape what they thought was the bridge's imminent collapse. Despite the tragic accident, the dual-towered colossus more than held.

Along for the bridge walk with the Edison associates, Alfred O. Tate, Edison's energetic new Canadian office boy (and Insull's protégé), later remarked about the bridge melee that "the evil spirit which appeared to hover over it and resent its construction was appeased." While Edison rarely referred to superstition or religion, he knew that he, too, was another modern Prometheus, attempting to defy the gods of nature. Around the time of the bridge's opening, while Insull and Edison were working in the Fifth Avenue office one evening, a brilliant flash of lightning flooded the room with light.

"That's the Opposition, Sammy," Edison quipped with his wry smile. "There's an engineer—Somewhere."

❦

In 1884, the Edison Machine Works became the crucible for new power plant machinery. The company was incorporated in January of that year with a capital stock of $100,000, hardly enough to produce more than a few large dynamos and related equipment. As was Edison's design, Insull became the secretary. Charles Batchelor was appointed the general manager, having recently returned from France, where he successfully established the French Edison company at Ivry-sur-Seine in 1882. Batchelor would soon be promoting the Edison company's new three-wire system, which allowed power system builders to reduce their copper costs by 62 percent. Copper was essential to the Edison system, since it was a relatively easy-to-work-with electrical conductor and readily obtainable. The biggest drawback of copper, though, was that it was expensive, and Edison's direct-current (DC) operations used enormous amounts of it. The wires carrying electricity from the power stations to customers were as big as tree trunks. The conduits had to be elephantine since low-voltage DC power demanded it, and the power could be transported only about a mile before it lost its original intensity. Even with the three-wire system, there was no getting around the fact that DC made sense only within a few blocks and in traction systems. A rival system using alternating current (AC), where the electrons phase back and forth within the wires—versus moving in a virtual straight line with DC—made much more engineering sense for efficient large-scale power generation over distances of several miles.

Batchelor followed the Edison model in hiring his staff in France: find young, inexhaustible, hardworking, and hopefully brilliant young men who would follow orders and work untold hours for very little money. Before he embarked upon his management of the Edison Machine Works in New York, he would have an interesting encounter with one of his European workers.

Nikola Tesla was a rail-thin Croatian who had an aversion to shaking hands and a voracious intellectual and physical appetite. Educated in Gratz, Austria, he had worked for a phone company in Budapest before joining Batchelor in France. Tesla came from a part of Serbo-Croatia and Montenegro that was part of the Austro-Hungarian Empire at the time of his birth in 1856. His father was a Serbian Orthodox priest. Tesla did not fit the Edison worker mold, however. He was arrogant, incredibly self-absorbed, and despised working with a team. He also had odd habits. When swimming, he would swim precisely 27 laps, then quit. He insisted that all of his meals be served with 17 napkins so that he could wipe the germs off his cutlery. Microbes were his sworn enemy and he hated being touched in any way. A modern diagnosis would probably conclude that he was suffering from an obsessive-compulsive disorder. More at home in Parisian cafés than he was in the Edison workshop, in between spouting visions of a more efficient alternating-current motor, he would be silenced by an enticing chateaubriand. He would enjoy the meat so much he would place a second order. He would frequently leave for lunch and never come back to work, stopping to take a long cup of coffee, play cards, or shoot billiards. He would often sleep in and not show up until noon. Batchelor was not enamored of Tesla's work habits, although he knew Tesla was brilliant.

Tesla was the anti-Edison. He saw specific engineering ideas in mind pictures and formulas while sitting in cafés, while Edison and his lab "muckers" would take the trial-and-error approach through thousands of experiments. Tesla could work through abstract, complex math to arrive at a solution. Though Edison was no slouch at math, it was not his preferred route and he typically took a more concrete approach. Tesla, about six foot six, 140 pounds, and darkly handsome, was usually impeccably groomed and attired. Edison was dumpy and indifferent to dress. Tesla not only had a visionary solution for an efficient means of using and delivering electricity, he also was brashly confident. Edison stubbornly (and wrongly) stuck with his DC system, even to the point of starting an industrial war to defend it and to associate AC with pure evil. Tesla regularly talked with pigeons and sincerely believed he had a rapport with them. Edison had captured the imagination and modest support of Morgan, Villard, and all the great minds of the time. Both Tesla and Edison, however, loved the idea of running their own labs without interference and showing the world their inventions on a grand stage.

Tesla grew tired of his less-than-strenuous Parisian routine and asked Batchelor if he could follow him back to New York. Batchelor bluntly discouraged him, but Tesla came to the Goerck Street works anyway. Upon seeing Pearl Street, Tesla said he could make the power plant run more efficiently, even though such a project would involve a herculean reworking. Edison reportedly bet Tesla $50,000 that he could not do it. Several months later, after virtual nonstop work, Tesla completed his task, only to be insulted by Edison, who claimed the $50,000 offer was a *joke*. Pouring salt on Tesla's wounded ego, Edison only offered to raise Tesla's salary $10—to $28 a week. Tesla left in a huff to start his own laboratory at 89 Liberty Street in Manhattan. After finding some financiers for his own lighting company, he immediately started work on his AC motor and polyphase system. He would patent his ideas without a challenge three years later (highly unusual in those days considering all of the patent challenges Edison endured) and sell them to Westinghouse for $60,000, 150 shares of Westinghouse stock, and a royalty rate of $2.50 per horsepower of electrical capacity sold. The windfall would make Tesla wealthy, but, like Edison, he would spend most of his money on building a lab and pursuing electrical experiments.

"The woods are full of men like him," Batchelor reportedly said of Tesla after Edison humiliated the Croatian genius. "I can get any number of them I want for $18 a week."

Insull and Tesla apparently had some regard for each other in their brief acquaintance, although they were as different as a donkey and a thoroughbred. Tesla would fondly recall 50 years later Insull's role in shaping his industry. Whatever Tesla's influence may have been on Insull at the time, Insull sensed that Tesla was on to something profound and took note of it.

Batchelor, however, was as wrong about Tesla as Edison was about the prospects of DC power succeeding on a large scale. Edison could have easily kept Tesla and cornered the technology that would dominate the central station business. Edison was so entrenched in his DC power system, though, that Tesla became this buzzing fly of truth that he thought he had swatted when he denigrated him and effectively sent him packing.

For the time being, Edison was facing more serious setbacks as his companies lurched ahead without adequate support from the New York banks and cried out for capital. While Pearl Street was the face that would launch more than a thousand power plants, it was difficult for his small shops to keep up with the orders. By the end of 1882, Pearl Street was supplying 231 customers with more than 3,400 lightbulbs. Edison Electric Light Company had 431 houses wired with more than 10,000 lights. Six months later, 300 plants were in service all over the country, including the first hydroelectric plant in Appleton, Wisconsin, which powered up to 300 lights.

Profits were not streaming in as fast as the plant orders. Edison was losing money on his lightbulbs, priced at 40 cents, although they cost $1.40 to make. To bolster his power equipment shops, he created a unit called the "Thomas A. Edison Construction Department" in 1885, and assigned Insull to manage it. Like his other operations, it, too, was underfinanced and ran up losses. Insull would later call it the "destruction" department since it was little more than a poorly capitalized contracting firm whose main purpose was to build power plants.

"It achieved the objective for which it was started," Insull would later recall of the construction department, "but it was not a financial success. Its work resulted in the necessary impetus being given to the development of the central station business in the United States. The companies were slow in getting into earning [profitability], and some of them, as a result, were slow in their payments, consequently the financial difficulties were very great. It was eventually necessary to liquidate the department. Mr. Edison's personal resources had to carry the burden of the liquidation, although it was accomplished without substantial loss."

With cash flow down to a trickle, despite all of Edison's leaps forward into the power business, he could not run his company without a steady source of capital. All of Edison's personal resources were tied up in his companies, and the banks were not receptive to his constant pleas for money. The inventor got so frustrated with the banks that he put 90 percent of the capital into the machine works, with Batchelor investing the other 10 percent. Since the banks were not seeing immediate profits, they also withheld funding from the power plant business. Edison once again took the initiative and promoted the contracting of the power stations through the ill-fated construction department.

It got to the point where Insull was unable to draw a salary from any of his positions or pay his weekly expenses. Sigmund Bergmann, Edison's partner in manufacturing electrical fixtures, generously stepped in to lend Insull $50 a week. Insull was embarrassed when he approached Charley Delmonico, the proprietor of the great New York restaurant, to tell him sheepishly that he could not afford to take his meals there. At the time, Insull was living in a miniscule two-room apartment on the tenth floor of 247 Fifth Avenue. Now he was seriously challenged to pay his rent. Delmonico generously agreed to let Insull go on credit until he could pay. Insull hated owing anything to anyone, but paid Delmonico in full once Edison's operations became flush again.

While generous in the company of his colleagues, Insull had a banker's policy on personal debts. One day while running errands with his young charge Alfred Tate, he admonished the Canadian for paying in cash, saying that offering a 30-day note was more prudent. That way, he could conserve cash until he could repay the debt. Insull would later apply this principle to many of his later business dealings.

Edison himself would have been broke except for some modest royalties from some of his telegraph inventions. The wizard had yet to see the bottom of the abyss, though.

CRISIS AND CONSOLIDATION

The Morgan Takeover

Electricity effected an improvement in our mechanical civilization: the neotechnic period dawned.

—Lewis Mumford, *The Brown Decades*[1]

While Edison was lighting up the world with his central stations, the flame of life was fading in his wife Mary. In July 1884, she contracted typhoid fever. She had never been in good health, but Edison was optimistic she would recover in their New Jersey home while he tried to rescue his companies. After battling the disease for a month, she died on August 9. The cause of death was initially called "congestion of the brain." Edison was bereft. As an entrepreneur who lived his business, he was rarely at home, seldom saw his children, and felt her loss deeply. Mary Stillwell was devoted to Edison and his neglect clearly took its toll. She had been isolated for so long while Edison worked his 18-hour days in the lab—often sleeping there—she had a fear of being raped and robbed and often slept with a revolver under her pillow. One night when Edison was returning from the lab and found himself locked out, he climbed up the outside of his house to his bedroom window, where Mary nearly shot him. Her mental health was clearly in decline in her final years. Nevertheless, she was Edison's loved and cherished companion. The pain and shock of having lost his 29-year-old wife immediately threw him into emotional turmoil as he could not immediately summon the words to tell his children. Insull, too, deeply felt the loss of a dear friend, as the kindly Mary, fully aware of his homesickness and empathizing with his loneliness, frequently had him over for dinner and some indirect mothering.

At 37, with two sons and his doting, beloved daughter Marion, whom he called "Dot," Edison was now the center of attention in nearly every social circle in the greater New York area as the campaign began to find the world's most eligible widower a wife. After meeting a string of eligible and well-bred young ladies, Edison was struck by 19-year-old Mina Miller at his friend Ezra Gilliand's house. The self-assured beauty had lustrous brown hair and a lovely figure. Her father Lewis also had the proper pedigree, having made a fortune in farm implements in Akron, Ohio, and cofounded the Chautauqua Association for adult education. Edison was smitten and even more enamored of her lively intelligence. This was a young lady who had traveled abroad and could hold her own in the parlors of the Morgans and Vanderbilts. During a few dates he had taught her the Morse code, which suited his purposes when he proposed to her in the telegraphic language of his youth. Shortly before his marriage in February 1885, he bought Glenmont, a 13-acre estate and mansion near West Orange, New Jersey. That would be his principal residence for the rest of his life and the home for three more children. His research complex would be built nearby. Edison declared to Mina that he would make the valley "beautiful" by building factories, something he made good on in subsequent years.

Back at 65 Fifth Avenue, the cash evaporated in Edison's companies and his business situation grew even dimmer. He finally sat down with Insull and laid it out. Insull had rarely seen Edison so discouraged. Through perseverance, pluck, and that ineffable trait called "stick-to-itiveness," Edison achieved before he was 40 the equivalent of several lifetimes of accomplishments of other men. While the plow, railroads, cheap land, and the U.S. Army may have bludgeoned their way into the shrinking American frontier, Edison and his men took his ideas and made them working realities on another frontier. His lightbulbs and power plants banished the darkness, increased productivity in the workplace, made streets safer, and made unnecessary the horrific dangers of gas lighting. Under Edison's incandescence, civilization and culture were moving into a brave, new world. The "Great White Way" was born, as the exterior and interior of Broadway theaters were illuminated. Signs could be lit up for advertising. Department store windows and floors could properly showcase the goods of an ever-expanding consumer culture. Everything from toothpaste to the latest frock could be shown in pure, white light. None of it mattered, though, if his companies ended up in receivership and he was humiliated.

"This looks pretty bad," the gray-haired wizard said in a drooping tone to his secretary. "Do you think I could go back and earn my living as a telegraph operator? Do you think, Sammy, you could go back to earn your living as a stenographer?"

Insull curled his upper lip, which many thought expressed impatience or even anger. It was, however, a physical expression that showed he was sorting out a situation. Seizing upon his fundamental but increasingly sophisticated knowledge of accounting and Edison's ledger books, Insull suggested that he could aggressively get Edison's bills paid to bring in some money. Now every dime in Edison's accounts receivable loomed large, and Insull was going to grab every one of them. First he applied himself to collecting debts for the construction department, then shut it down. Then, with the assistance of Edison Isolated president Edward Johnson, Insull hit the road. Their mission was to visit every town that wanted a new power plant and help the local people raise the money. That would lift the burden of having to finance the stations out of Edison resources. It would also promote Edison's money-saving three-wire system.

"The scheme is to raise from fifty thousand to a quarter million dollars, according to the size of the town or city, and form a local Edison electric illuminating company," Insull told Edison, his eyes like embers. "Then we form a local Edison illuminating company, paying the Edison Electric Light Company for the use of their patents by giving them a percentage of the stock of the local company, and by this means, to give an impetus to the growth of the central station business."

Insull's idea was to find towns willing to accept this financial arrangement, cut them in on the business, then build the plant once the cash was in hand. It was similar to a turnkey franchise today, where local business interests buy all of the equipment and supplies from the franchiser and share in the profits when the business is up and running. This technique gave Edison some fiscal breathing room and eventually convinced the bankers that he was on a sound footing.

Shortly after Mary died, Edison did something he had never done before. He shook up the board of directors of the light company to give himself more control. Key Edison men such as Batchelor, Francis Upton, and Edward Johnson were installed. He waged a proxy battle to dump the directors he thought were hostile to his rapid expansion. Insull helped orchestrate the *coup*, which ultimately packed the company board with Edison men and allies who represented more than half of the votes he needed to get what he wanted. One of the directors that Edison was successful in ousting was Sherbourne Eaton, a corporate lawyer who was relentlessly critical of Edison's experimental expenses. Insull developed an enmity toward Eaton largely because of Eaton's criticism of Insull's handling of the construction department. When the proxy battle of the electric company was decided in Edison's favor, Insull bragged to Tate, "There is no one more anxious after wealth than Samuel Insull, but there are times when revenge is sweeter than money, and I have got mine."

The tone of Insull's letter reveals one of Insull's demons. The Englishman hated to be bested, and he competed with his peers to show them that he could get business done. Insull also had a control complex that often alienated others. Consequently, this made him unpopular, particularly when he was trimming expenses or leaning on managers to stick to their budgets. In his role of financial enforcer, Insull certainly did not endear himself to any of the Menlo Park pioneers. Yet he felt he was doing something that Edison himself was never able to do: watch the bottom line.

Insull's loyalty to Edison also contained an implicit promise that his boss would support him in his climb within the organization. Coming from a family of eight, Insull wanted to do more than distinguish himself in commerce. He wanted power and control, things that were conferred upon him if he maintained certain alliances. As a shrewd businessman, Insull sized up his adversaries quickly and chose his enemies carefully. Eaton came between him and Edison, so he was more than happy to rally the proxy vote against the lawyer. Insull had his reservations about Edison as well, particularly when it came to his management skills, although he never voiced them openly nor did anything to undermine the inventor.

Insull did all he could to bring Edison's companies back from the brink. Whether he was hedging his bets or simply exercising an entrepreneurial urge, he started a business on the side in late 1885. He had acquired control of patents over an invention called a "cash carrier" that enabled large stores to transport cash without the use of "cash boys," thus saving labor costs. In November, Insull wrote to his father in England, with the hopes of setting him up in the business in London: "My business promises extremely well here as I have control of the finest territory in America in this class of business. I already have 4 or 5 agents actively at work and my partner is on the road all the time starting fresh business agencies and drumming up business. . . . Your knowledge and experience in insurance business of this character stand you in extremely good stead."[2]

While his father considered the opportunity, Insull said in a letter that he could not help out his brother Joseph, a farmer to whom he had sent some money. Sam advised him to get a mortgage on his farm and was optimistic that he would be of more help when Edison's financial woes were resolved: "Matters with me are improving somewhat and by the time 1886 comes round, I shall be fully on my feet again. . . . I hope your children are all right and that there is no immediate prospect of another one coming along! Big families are expensive."[3]

By the end of 1886, both Insull and Edison were in better financial condition, although Edison was now facing some meaningful competition. Westinghouse was now fully committed to the electrical industry through the formation of his Westinghouse Electric Corporation. The Pittsburgh industrialist, though, had something Edison did not have: he had Tesla's AC technology behind him. Tesla was building a complete AC transmission system. Around the same time, a transformer was invented that could "step up" or "step down" the high voltage that an AC system produced. The growing flexibility of AC was becoming the foundation for a large-scale power network. One could generate thousands of volts of power at one location and efficiently send it dozens or even hundreds of miles using central power plants, transformers, substations, and local feeder lines. In contrast, the Pearl Street station and its many DC cousins could transmit power efficiently for only a few blocks. While the actual AC or "polyphase" system did not exist on a large scale in 1886, the means for creating it did. The Thomson-Houston Company of Lynn, Massachusetts, run by the estimable Charles Coffin, a former shoe manufacturer, also vied for the lead in creating AC equipment. Within the next five years, Tesla, Westinghouse, and Coffin would be running rings around Edison's staid DC orthodoxy and it infuriated the wizard.

Henry Villard was not a man who would be left behind as the electrical industry aspired to be as civilizing an influence on America as the railroads had been. Having known Edison since 1879, the barrel-chested, broom-mustached financier was an enthusiastic backer of the inventor and had hopes for establishing an international conglomerate that would dominate the industry. Like Edison, Villard was confident that electrical distribution had limitless commercial potential and had promoted Edison's patents across Europe, particularly in Germany, where the Siemens brothers were building an empire of their own.

Born Ferdinand Heinrich Gustav Hilgard in Bavaria in 1835, Villard was trained to become a lawyer. His prominent, imperious father was a supreme court justice and had mapped out Henry's life for him. Rejecting his father's wishes for his future, while in a German law school in 1853, Henry left Europe and ended up in Illinois, where he had family. He soon took the name of a French classmate to avoid detection from his father. Working various jobs in Chicago, he settled into journalism and worked for the city's leading German newspaper. The wild, adolescent city had a large, thriving German-speaking community, and Villard wanted to be at the center of it. A robust, gregarious fellow who loved ideas and adventure, he was willing to go anywhere that promised to give him a new experience.

In 1860, Villard got his chance as the horrors of the Civil War unfolded. He became a principal correspondent for the *New York Herald,* posting detailed and balanced dispatches of every battle he witnessed. Working for one paper was not enough for Villard as he invented what later became newspaper syndication. With a keen eye on the business of his trade, he sold his eyewitness accounts of the war to several papers across the country, working deftly with messengers and telegraphers to ensure that his stories were published as soon as possible after the battles. Nearly a full volume of his scintillating two-volume memoirs was devoted to the epic slaughter of the war between the states. Along the way, he was befriended by Abraham Lincoln and the family of abolitionist William Lloyd Garrison. In 1863, he married Garrison's bright, compassionate daughter, Fanny.

Once the war ended, Villard headed west. He was already a world-famous journalist who had written brilliantly in two different languages, but there was something that beckoned him as the great frontier opened up. Seeing the enormous potential of providing transportation in the sparsely populated but resource-rich Pacific Northwest, he enlisted the backing of German bankers to build railroads. As a partner in rail ventures, he secured financing for the Kansas and Pacific; Wisconsin Central; Oregon and California; Oregon Railway and Navigation; Northern Pacific; and Oregon and Transcontinental. His talent for brassy promotion and financial partnerships made him one of the most powerful men in the country as he completed transcontinental routes and threw huge celebrations to mark his triumph.

By 1879, Villard was ready to move onto something even more enervating as his railroad investments began to mature or, in some cases, become mired in financial chaos. A noveau riche financier rivaling the Morgans and Vanderbilts, he had arrived in the upper strata of society and built his renaissance palace in Manhattan. As one of the most adventurous dealmakers of the nineteenth century, Villard had a personal stake in seeing Edison do well on a large scale. Visiting Edison at Menlo Park, Villard marveled at the electric light displays, yet was more captivated by the moneymaking potential of electric traction. The idea of running faster, less coal-intensive trains had great appeal to him and he advanced Edison $40,000 to start work on an electric engine. After Edison had started up Pearl Street three years later, Villard would come back into the picture again with financing for Edison electrical systems in Wisconsin.

As an exhausted Villard was completing a transcontinental link in Gold Creek, Montana, in September 1883, his rail empire started to fall apart. The man who had been feted as a hero from Oregon to Montana was now witnessing a dramatic decline in the value of his stocks. As Insull had done with Edison's holdings, Villard was shuffling his finances to avert receivership, pouring in more of his own money, remortgaging, and dodging creditors. His German bankers had staked him $20 million, although it would not be enough for him to retain control of his railroad boards. Villard's enemies on Wall Street were stoking the destructive rumor mill and running down his stocks. Blamed for mismanagement, he was forced to resign from two Oregon railroads and the Northern Pacific board. Fanny called Edison for advice; the best the inventor could do was return his $40,000 from the electric train project. Edison tried to console his friend, whom he held in gratitude because he was a true believer in the Menlo Park dream.

"When Villard was all broken down and in a stupor caused by his disasters in connection with the Northern Pacific," Edison recalled, "Mrs. Villard called for me to come and cheer him up. It was very difficult to rouse him from despair and apathy, but I talked about the electric light to him, and its development, and told him that I would help him win it all back and put him in his former position."[4]

On the brink of bankruptcy and physical collapse from the stress, Villard and Fanny decamped for Europe. When Villard was staying in Berlin, he regularly talked with the Siemens brothers and monitored the German Edison company, Deutsche Edison Gesellschaft, which was having financial setbacks of its own. At the request of Edison, Villard reorganized the company. Villard was once again in the right place at a turning point in history. Northern Pacific investor Georg von Siemens, who was also founder and president of Deutsche Bank, introduced Villard to his brother Werner, an inventor-engineer who was the Edison of Germany. Werner wanted to build electric railroads in the U.S. When Villard told Werner about Edison's Menlo Park electric train, the proverbial light went on in both men's minds and the seeds of a partnership were sown.

After a three-year tour of the Continent and a needed respite, Villard returned to New York revived and determined to resolve his unfinished business. He also wanted to propose to Edison that he join forces with the Siemens. He sold his mansion at 457 Madison Avenue, which cleared most of his debts, and took up residence in a Tiffany-decorated home at 72nd and Madison. Then the Villards threw a lavish welcome-back party for themselves in which Edison slipped on his showman's cape and entertained everyone with his new phonograph. Soprano Lilli Lehmann sang into a giant funnel to record her voice on a cylinder. Edison flipped a switch and her scratchy solo was replayed for the astounded crowd.

Like a Teutonic phoenix, Villard had reemerged as a key player in his railroads, which he worked to reorganize. He was also excited about the conversations he had with the Siemens brothers and Deutsche Bank. Once again he was sanguine about the possibilities of Edison's companies, envisioning an international concern that would eventually be joined with his German partners to dominate North America and Europe, and possibly thwart the ambitions of his rival, Morgan.

Insull was absorbing Villard's business practices the way an Oxford student learns from a great don, taking mental notes on how the German financier created investment deals across borders. While he was not quite ready for the heady world of international venture capital, he certainly absorbed the modus operandi of Villard's negotiations. As Edison's operations moved into the black, however, he had other more mundane concerns. Edison's Machine Works was bursting at the seams in lower Manhattan. His boss needed more men, more machine tools, more output, and more capacity. Labor troubles in the Goerck Street shop—the workers wanted to start a union—provided another impetus to convince Edison that he needed a full-fledged industrial complex instead of slapdash workshops. The lamp works was moved to a larger facility in Harrison, New Jersey. The Electric Tube operation relocated to Brooklyn.

Edison and Insull were shopping for a large parcel of real estate for heavy manufacturing. With Insull at his side, Edison then purchased ten acres in upstate Schenectady, New York, to build a larger facility for producing dynamos and other electrical components. Two large buildings were already on the property, having once been part of the McQueen Locomotive Works, which had been merged into the American Locomotive Works. Edward Johnson was complaining about the sluggish production of equipment because a small crew was working in the ridiculously cramped Goerck Street shop. After dining with Johnson at his home on West 36th Street, Edison formed a plan and called Insull into his office the following day. It was decided that the Goerck street operation was to be moved in its entirety to Schenectady as soon as possible. Edison put Insull in charge of the move.

Since Insull was a subordinate to both Batchelor and Kruesi, he was reluctant to usurp the two executives, both of whom knew infinitely more about the heavy machinery that needed to be moved, reinstalled, and brought into production mode again. Edison insisted that Insull move ahead with the transfer. As Insull predicted shortly after he completed the move in a month's time, "I had a great deal of trouble, resulting in a great deal of confusion." The Menlo Park pioneers may have resented that the English secretary, whom they may have regarded as a glorified bookkeeper, was now thrust into the role of manager, even though he had Edison's blessing.

Undaunted at having ruffled the feathers of the Edison elders, Insull returned to Fifth Avenue to report on his progress. Edison was so impressed with Insull's diligence, he told him to move to Schenectady to oversee the operation. Insull said no, saying that he still did not have "the proper authority." Edison gave him a verbal slap on the back and sent him back into the fray.

"Now you go back up there and run the institution, and whatever you do Sammy, make it either a brilliant success of it or a brilliant failure," Edison barked. "Just do something. Make it go."

These were the words that the former London office boy had longed to hear ever since he dipped his feet into the waters of commerce. He was to succeed Batchelor as the general manager of the Machine Works. The secretary was now fully empowered by the world's most illustrious inventor to *make it go!* Were there three words in the English language that were more attuned to Insull's mind, body, and soul?

Having steadily groomed Tate to take over as Edison's secretary in New York City, Insull was ready to manage the satellite world that was to form the basis of Edison's manufacturing dominion. Although now a viceroy over the making of generators, fuses, and junction boxes, Insull was still only making $4,000 a year. Yet he felt every bit the country squire that his father aspired to become. He was starting what would become one of the largest industrial enterprises practically from the ground up. As such, he needed to keep a country house to entertain Edison employees and clients, so he summoned his sister Emma to run the home. Unlike the cosmopolitan climate of lower Manhattan, there was little in the way of entertainment in Schenectady. Despite his meager salary, he felt obliged to keep a stable of horses for the pleasure of his customers. He did this at his own expense and did not consider asking Edison for an expense allowance.

Two hundred men came up from New York City with Insull. In the summer of 1886, Edison shuttered the Brooklyn-based tube works and relocated the operation to Schenectady. Kruesi, who was running the tube shop, came upstate as well. To Insull's surprise, Kruesi did not mind working for Insull at all, proving to be both an excellent mechanic and loyal submanager. Kruesi and Insull worked together to "develop manufacturing methods of the most economical character." While Insull did not have a clear idea of how to achieve economies of scale as a mechanical engineer, he did know what to do on the accounting side.

Running the Machine Works and getting Tate up to speed in New York City drove Insull to his limits. He would often show up in the shop at 7 a.m., work until the end of the day, then hop onto a train for the city, arriving at 1 am. He was still troubleshooting Edison's financial difficulties throughout most of 1887 while trying to manage the Machine Works. Tate was not up to the task quite yet and was slow to appreciate Insull's often obnoxious obsession with detail. Every source of income was treated as if it was the only Christmas present under the tree, and Insull may have regarded Tate's attitude as too cavalier, so the Englishman micromanaged the situation.

In September 1887, Insull lost his patience with Tate. He upbraided the secretary for misusing one of Edison's accounts. His typically formal "My Dear Tate" was reduced to an icy "Dear Sir" in this seething letter from September 2: "You seem to forget that Mr. Edison has got to meet a note of some $1,600 tomorrow morning. I must ask you to leave Mr. Edison's account alone, so far as drawing out money, unless you are prepared to take hold of providing him with funds to meet his liabilities. . . . Don't you realize that the first thing in business should be to meet a man's notes and let everything else stand?"[5]

Insull had been irritated by Tate's inattention to details for some time. When Insull had instructed Tate to order a British flag in June, Tate sent him the wrong flags, resulting in this petulant missive: "I received today an express package containing two flags. What I wanted when I asked you to get me a 'Union Jack' was not an American flag, but a British flag. What you have sent me is a regular American flag and also the flag of the Revenue Department of the United States . . . if you don't now understand exactly what I want, please write for further instructions."[6]

The strain of being Edison's financial overseer and Machine Works chief was bearing down hard on Insull, who took every misstep by Tate as a personal affront. Earlier in the year, Insull practically accused Tate of stealing: "I wired you Friday to bring me 100 cigars. I received 75 by mail. Who kept the other 25?"[7]

Insull would ride Tate constantly in his correspondence, being piqued about everything from misplaced photographs to the handling of Edison's minor accounts. While Edison was more and more retreating to his castlelike home Glenmont, Insull lived for his work in the absence of a domestic life. Insull did not take a real vacation during the Schenectady years. Mina Edison had managed to reel in her husband somewhat from the unrelenting pressure of his business, even venturing to explore some interesting property in Fort Myers, Florida, where Edison would later build a winter retreat alongside an identical white house owned by Henry Ford. Edison needed the rest, having been sick on and off with respiratory infections and taking increasingly longer periods to recover.

There was no respite for Insull, who was still on a mission to make the Machine Works profitable and revive Edison's general finances. In order to keep up appearances of an influential electrical industry executive, Insull was spending about $16,000 just to commute to New York, keep his home, and entertain clients. By the end of the first year of managing Schenectady, he was ready to have a heart-to-heart with Edison and requested a meeting at Glenmont.

It is not clear whether Insull expected a confrontation with Edison in his home, where he was cordially received by Mina. He stuck to business, hoping that his employer would have some sympathy for his deteriorating personal finances. Insull presented a report on the Machine Works and Edison was pleased.

"Where do I come in?" Insull implored after giving the report, diplomatically probing Edison for some kind of raise.

Edison smiled and pulled out of his waistcoat an option for Insull to buy stock of the Edison Machine Works, stock that only he and Batchelor owned. Insull would later value the option at $75,000.

"And Sammy, who paid for all of your entertainment expenses up there?"

"I have."

"From now on, I'm going to give you a substantial raise and a considerable amount to cover your entertainment bill."

Villard believed he could do an end run around the Morgan interests by marrying the Edison companies with the Siemens electrical concerns to create an international combine that would dominate North America and Europe. In conversations with the German industrialists, Villard became interested in technology that would provide better cabling of underground lines for street lighting. Fully exposed overhead lines were messy and dangerous. It was Villard's belief that the Germans could offer a superior method of cabling in the U.S. in concert with the Edison interests. Edison's cabling method, in contrast, was awkward, expensive, and unreliable. Cables were dropped into wooden troughs, then covered with gutta-percha, an asphaltlike substance. Siemens made a cable that was covered by an armament and lead cover, so it was much less prone to damage and leakage of current.

Edison signed on with the Siemens and proposed a separate company that would manufacture the cables in the U.S. Newly emboldened, Villard then addressed the heart of Edison's financial morass. Villard wanted to combine all of Edison's interests into a single entity. The new corporation would have one board of directors, have one set of stockholders and inject much-needed capital into all of Edison's financially bulimic companies. It must have become clear to Villard that Edison's tightfisted control over all the separate companies and lack of central management were holding them back from raising money, especially in the New York investment banking community, which always wanted a large stake and a large voice on the board of each company.

Villard formed a syndicate of investors to purchase control of the Edison companies. By the end of 1888, the Siemens were part of the investment group, subscribing to 2,700 shares at $92.50 per share, which they later sold at a healthy profit. Edison and his executives also received shares, as did the Morgan interests as minority shareholders. Villard became the president of the new company, Edison General Electric, thus denying the Morgan men full control of the Edison consolidation, at least for now.

While Insull was not Villard's confidant on the capitalization of the new company, he was certainly vetting the financing structure. On September 27, 1888, he corresponded with Edison to confirm what little he knew about the transaction: "I came back from Schenectady this morning and called on Mr. Villard. He told me that he had seen the Drexel, Morgan & Company people twice and got their absolute agreement to that deal. The entire $500,000 by Drexel Morgan is to be paid in deferred stock. Mr. Villard said that no papers had been signed, but there was no chance of Morgan backing down."[8]

Villard had boosted the syndicate's capitalization of Edison GE to $2 million. Considering that Edison had started the Machine Works with $200,000, this was a major league deal for Edison that would relieve him of all of his debts. It also would make him more than financially independent. Now essentially bought out, Edison was free to pursue any interest he wanted at West Orange and enjoy his much-deserved wealth. In snipping off the many frayed ends of Edison's finances, Insull did the paperwork by liquidating all of Edison's debts and transferring the new Edison GE securities into Edison's account. After 40 years of begging for cash from everyone from Jay Gould to J.P. Morgan, Edison now had $3.5 million in the bank from those stocks. All told, he was now worth about $5 million.

With a combination of relief from the stress of constantly fretting about money and the sense that he was losing something in the bargain, Edison said of the deal, "we concluded that it was better to be safe than sorry; so we sold out for a large sum."

Villard quickly moved to appoint Kruesi general manager of Schenectady, which was now able to expand aggressively. Insull, who was not in the least slighted by Kruesi's promotion, was relocated back to Manhattan to become second vice president of Edison GE. With Edison subtly pushed into the virtual role of founder emeritus and chief experimenter, Villard would now become Insull's primary superior and full-time financial mentor. Insull was now poised to focus on marketing the new, large company so that it could compete with Westinghouse and Thomson-Houston. He began to travel extensively to visit the company's offices from San Francisco to Montreal. Since the successful installation of an electric trolley system in Richmond, Virginia, in 1888 by the Sprague Motor Car Company (later absorbed by the Edison company), a new front was opening up in the electrical industry. In addition to making power and lighting devices, the triumvirate of electrical titans—Edison, Westinghouse and Thomson-Houston—were engaged in making electric traction systems. The era of the horse and cable car (except in San Francisco, of course) was coming to a grinding halt. Cities that were clogged with equine waste and choking on coal smoke yearned for a clean, reliable source of transportation as the new electric trolley systems expanded to swallow thousands of acres of real estate. Before Insull could pursue the traction business, he was still needed to deal with Edison on a much more contentious issue.

Thriving in the lucrative embrace of Westinghouse, Tesla had created a working AC system, which was now being fully marketed by Westinghouse and Thomson-Houston to every city in which there was an Edison power system either being proposed or installed. The industrial free-for-all that became to be known as the "battle of the currents" was now about to get ugly. Although relegated to a lesser role in Villard's new corporation, Edison was still the one calling the shots on the technical side. He had ordered some work to be done on AC equipment in his labs, but it was not coming to market fast enough to meet the demand created by the Tesla-Westinghouse lead.

Tesla's polyphase system made the widespread use of electricity possible. It was to power generation and transportation what the incandescent bulb had been to illumination. Instead of being limited to about a mile with DC power, the entire continent, and world, as Tesla later theorized, could be served by remote generators at any point. Hydropower was now practical, making Niagara Falls a potent source of energy. In turn, any location that had significant river current or where a dam could be sited was a candidate for hydropower. Despite the versatility of the concept, Tesla's AC motor at first did not fit in with Westinghouse's system. Westinghouse's 120 power plants ran at 133 cycles and Tesla's motor ran on today's standard 60 cycles. Tesla agreed to work out the problem for free, as he had formed an emotional attachment to the Pittsburgh magnate, who was now his padrone.

Unlike Edison, Westinghouse was flexible when it came to new ideas on electrical transmission systems. An energetic and solidly built man with a sense of fairness, Westinghouse paid his workers well and expected them to work in teams to come up with marketable solutions. He was the antithesis of the lone inventor in the lab. He was one of the first industrialists to offer a half day on Saturday when the six-day work week was standard. A Christmas turkey was given to his employees as a year-end bonus. His workers were so enamored of Westinghouse's compensation and working environment that they refused to start a union. Tesla never fit into the Westinghouse culture and preferred to work alone, rarely sharing his ideas. Few of his assistants knew what he was working on at any given moment. For all of his antisocial tendencies, though, Tesla was an excellent speaker who not only could present his ideas, but could present them with a dramatic flair. Many of his early demonstrations involved him sitting on stage while thousands of volts ran through his body, creating an aura of sparks. While he did not want to be bothered by showing up in a standard workplace, Tesla savored being the center of attention.

Edison was eager to grab center stage again. Perhaps embittered that Tesla had worked with Westinghouse, Edison was ready to go to war with Westinghouse. It was not that he hated Westinghouse—Edison rarely showed strong disdain for anyone—it was that he abhorred the idea of alternating current. Many theories abound as to why Edison despised AC. Possibly he was incensed at the idea of someone else having a technical advantage in the marketplace, or perhaps he did not have a complete vision of what AC could accomplish. Or maybe he just dug in his heels because most of his factories were producing DC power equipment and he was trying to protect his franchises across the country. In any case, Edison was determined to tar Westinghouse and make AC look like the devil's work.

A shadowy engineer named Harold Brown was enlisted in the anti-AC campaign along with Insull. Brown had worked in Chicago for Edison's electric pen company and had an obscure past in sales. Edison did not care where he came from so long as he could be an unflinching public crusader against AC. It just so happened that Brown had a virulent hatred of AC. The first line of attack was calculating the number of people who had been electrocuted by AC power. Brown drew up a list and discovered, much to his disappointment, that Westinghouse did not have a power plant running in any of the cities where the deaths occurred. Edison took to the press: "Westinghouse will kill a customer within six months after he puts in a system of any size. . . . There is no plea which will justify the use of high-tension and alternating current, either in a scientific or a commercial sense."[9]

At the time, New York State was looking for a "humane" way of executing felons. A commission was appointed and reached the macabre conclusion that "the guillotine was the most merciful but also the most terrible to witness." Electricity, it was decided, was the least objectionable of the execution methods. It became the death inducer in New York State as of June 4, 1888. Edison and Brown seized the moment to put AC in the headlines.

The sparkling new West Orange lab became an AC electrocution center for hapless stray cats and dogs. Edison reportedly paid street kids of West Orange a quarter each for every animal they brought in to be fried. After a few experiments, Brown was ready to take his show on the road to show the general public how a creature could be "westinghoused." At the Columbia School of Mines, Brown demonstrated a mild shock on a dog using DC. When he brought another dog up to be toasted with AC, the crowd refused to let him pull the switch. Then Brown offered to duel Westinghouse using the two voltages. Brown would be hooked up to DC and Westinghouse to the evil AC. Brown concluded his gory demonstration by electrocuting a calf and a horse.

Horrified by the bizarre publicity, Westinghouse refused to sell an AC generator to the state of New York for the execution of axe-murderer William Kemmler. The convict was strapped into the country's first electric chair anyway on August 6, 1890. The first wave of electricity did not kill him; the second wave started to roast his flesh. It was a horrible way to die and indirectly proved Brown and Edison's contention that AC was lethal and repugnant. Westinghouse remarked "they could have done better with an ax."[10]

While he had lost this salvo of Edison's ill-fated battle, Westinghouse would bounce back triumphantly to reclaim market share since AC was the only true universal power. Elihu Thomson, the founding, savvy engineer at Thomson-Houston, saw what Westinghouse had seen, and started his men to work on AC technology years earlier. No matter how well Edison did on the public relations front, he was behind in developing AC. No amount of newspaper headlines would help him regain the lead in a short time.

While it is not known how much Insull contributed to the battle of the currents, his business sense told him that Westinghouse was right and that Edison was chauvinistically embracing the wrong technology. A universal system that did not have to be in close physical proximity to its customers made much more sense than the highly inefficient DC power. As early as 1886, Edward Johnson also knew AC was going to be the dominant force in the business and was frustrated with Edison's commitment to DC.

Insull was fully aware of the Westinghouse threat, having been on the road and having talked to Edison customers across the country. All the time he was attacking Westinghouse, Edison was conducting experiments with AC. He did not have anywhere near the headstart that Westinghouse had on AC and was corresponding with Insull on the subject. At a meeting of Edison utilities in the summer of 1889, local power company executives said they were losing the battle to the new Westinghouse systems. Seeking to quell the uproar, Insull promised the managers that they would have AC systems within six months and personally instructed Edison GE engineers to forge ahead.

The last year of that decade would be a trying one for Insull. Still working out of two offices (Schenectady and 19 Dey Street in Manhattan), Insull spent a great deal of time in the field troubleshooting seemingly minor technical problems in a customer service capacity. At the beginning of the year, the company had a number of incidents with junction boxes exploding, which was a perennial bugaboo for the unreliable Edison cabling.

"We have had two more explosions of junction boxes," Insull wrote Edison. "Within the last two months two boxes have exploded in Chicago and one in Boston. . . . This is a matter that requires immediate attention as, if these explosions continue, our reputation will be very seriously affected."[11]

Three months later, Edison thought he had a solution. Insull suggested Edison confer with Frederick Sargent, an engineer with the Chicago Edison Company and someone who would play a prominent role in Insull's future: "The experiment suggested by you of placing a bottle of chloroform [a chemical used as a general anesthetic] in junction boxes, has been and is now being tried in the New York uptown districts, but sufficient time has not elapsed for us to make any kind of report as to the result."[12]

For some unexplained reason, all of the lights went out in Manhattan on October 14, 1889, extinguishing more than 1,000 bulbs. Well-to-do Gothamites and major businesses had become used to the constant illumination and the evening was referred to as "A Night of Darkness." New Yorkers characteristically carried on in the face of this unique adversity as extra police were sent to patrol the darkened streets. Dozens of power plants now dotted the city, which were becoming major sources of annoyance for residents. A stream of coal trucks clogged the streets, as they needed to supply the smoke-belching plants around the clock. If the populace had known about the virtues of AC and learned that the sooty, noisy power plants did not need to be in the central city, perhaps there would have been more public outcry to bring in Westinghouse's regime. As it was, New Yorkers were generally happy with the new, ubiquitous lighting and were grateful that the wonderful Edison had bestowed it upon them.

In the battle of the currents, though, Insull was becoming a discontented general fretting over the lack of matériel. More than a year had passed since Edison had promised to deliver AC equipment to his customers. Not only did Insull think that Edison was stonewalling, Insull could not keep his promise to his customers. That was a black mark on a man who valued integrity and keeping one's word. By July of 1890, Insull wrote to Edison of his pique: "It is of utmost importance that we should be able to go ahead on [the] alternating apparatus, so as to be ready for our next season's business. I would like to know definitely from you what I can promise to our district managers throughout the country." Like his fuming letters to Tate, this was a stony "Dear Sir" letter, which was unusual for Insull since he typically began his letters "My Dear Edison."[13]

Edison likely delegated the matter to Kruesi, who responded to Insull within 30 days that the Schenectady works had completed *one* AC dynamo for testing, although it was apparently not up to standards.

By the fall of that year, Insull advised Edison to quit the war of the currents and wrote to Edison on October 17, "Do you think it advisable for us to take part in a fight of this character, in view of the fact that we will probably be putting out [an] alternating apparatus within the six months?" It was now a year and a half since Insull had first asked Edison for AC equipment, and all the while Westinghouse was winning the day in every one of their markets. Thomson-Houston was also making huge inroads with its own line of AC products.

"I find that the Thomson-Houston people are offering to sell entirely new [AC] equipment for next year's delivery," Insull writes Edison on December 22. "They have taken a large number of contracts for next season, and if we were in a position to offer your new [AC] motor for delivery, I am sure we could head them off on a good many of the contracts they are now endeavoring to obtain, and which it is hopeless for us to expect to get with our present apparatus."[14]

With the diligent Charles Coffin at the helm, Thomson-Houston was moving quickly into the traction business, which it had exhibited at the Paris Exhibition of 1889. Organized in New Britain, Connecticut, in 1880 by Thomson and Edwin Houston, Thomson-Houston had been a major manufacturer of arc lighting systems. By 1883, the company had installed 22 arc-lighting plants and more than 1,500 lights. The company had also partially solved of the technical problems associated with DC generators, which sparked excessively (AC generators did not). In the traction business, Thomson-Houston also pioneered a 250-kilowatt railway generator, which gave the company a decided advantage in producing power for the energy-intensive electric trolley lines that were being installed in every major city. Westinghouse, which had several years earlier cross-licensed some of its AC patents with Thomson-Houston, countered with even more powerful generators.

Long-distance power transmission was coming on strong and it would not be dominated by Edison's DC system. At the International Electrical Exhibition at Frankfurt, Germany, in 1891, an AC line carried power from Lauffen, which was 100 miles away. Engineers found that the line was 77 percent efficient: for every 100 watts sent down the line, only 23 were lost. The following year, the Cataract Construction Company, which was researching the systems for a power plant at Niagara Falls, concluded that AC technology was the best route. The company reached this conclusion even after it had personally asked Edison to consult on the progress. Naturally, the wizard recommended a DC system, which never would have worked. Angered at the company's choice of AC, he refused to accept a $10,000 consultancy fee.

The battle among Westinghouse, Edison GE, and Thomson-Houston also entailed a vicious price war as each company did whatever it could to gain market share. Edison, who had a virtual monopoly in his lighting business for several years, rued over the "ruinous competition." The intense business climate took its toll on Edison GE finances. In the midst of the war, Insull was undertaking a $250,000 expansion in Schenectady. Villard, who had been battling Edison ever since he took over the chief executive role of Edison GE and was beset with railroad cash-flow problems, was now asking Edison for money.

Edison refused to part with his cash and told Villard, "when I sold out, one of the greatest inducements was the sum of cash received, so as to free my mind from financial stress, and thus enable me to go ahead in the technical field. To put it back into the business is something I never contemplated."[15]

Happily tinkering away in West Orange on his phonograph and an iron-ore separation process, Edison had no intention of reentering the hyperstressful sphere of financing his businesses. When he was bought out it was with the understanding that he would be supported in his experiments. Now Villard wanted to renege on the deal in an effort to free up cash. Faced with other debts from the Northern Pacific coming due, he returned to Germany. He needed $6 million in a time of tight money. The large British banking firm Baring Brothers was near insolvency, making investment capital difficult to obtain in Europe. Villard compounded his financial distress by organizing a holding company that controlled Edison GE (called North American) to float more stock. When Villard failed to secure the financing he needed, North American stock slid from $50 to $7 a share. The squeeze forced Villard to sell 10,000 shares of the holding company and Edison GE. They were immediately bought by Morgan and the Vanderbilts.

Insull was nearly in his own sphere at Schenectady. The complex was being run efficiently, was expanding to meet market demand (except for the immediate need for AC components), and was the most highly valued of all of the Edison GE properties. Insull's relationship with Edison had also changed. Since the Villard takeover, Insull was given much more independence to manage the more centralized offices of the new company. He was no longer paying Edison's bills, nor did he need Edison to sign off on any major decision. Insull was practically running Edison's heavy manufacturing operation and making a profit. While Insull did not approve of how Villard was handling the Edison General Electric finances, there was little he could do about it since the financier and his German friends controlled the company. As the nominal president of Edison's phonograph works, Insull still had a stake in the "old" Edison company. Yet he was not happy with the carefree way Edison was soaking up money at West Orange without having to account for it.

Insull was at loggerheads with Edison in 1892. The men had reached an impasse over the money spent at the phonograph works. In dramatic fashion, Edison abruptly shut down the phonograph factory and fired all the workers. This would be the harbinger of a year in which both men would reach a fork in the road.

The great consolidator J.P. Morgan saw his opportunity the way Insull had seen his 11 years ago, when Edison took him on as secretary. Never trusting his rival Villard and always dubious of Edison's business practices, Morgan saw a unique vision of a megacompany that would dominate the electrical business. Thomson-Houston, Morgan surmised, had a profitable portfolio of railway and AC products. Edison produced nearly everything else from lightbulbs to switches. Both companies had gross sales of about $10 million, although Thomson-Houston was twice as profitable and quicker to get products to the market. Both companies were slashing prices so aggressively that they were selling at a loss. Consolidation, the hallmark of Morgan's legacy, made obvious sense. Since Villard was unable to raise the capital to keep the company afloat, Morgan stepped in, calling together a committee of six financiers, which included all of his Wall Street allies and the Vanderbilts. At the time, Thomson-Houston was worth about $17 million and Edison GE $15 million.

By February 1892, the General Electric Company was born as Morgan consolidated all of the companies. Villard was shut out of the $50 million deal— the second-largest corporate consolidation of its time (after U.S. Steel)—and was forced to resign as president. Coffin was chosen to run the new corporation with four out of five of his managers in charge. The only Edison man in the executive suite was Insull, who was unceremoniously named second vice president.

Morgan knew that Insull, despite his dislike for him, was more than a capable manager, and he foresaw a role in which Insull would stay in Schenectady.

"Send for Insull," barked Edison, who turned white as a collar when Tate informed him of the deal. Insull came into the office and the men talked in private.

While there is still considerable debate as to whether Edison was aware of the complete nature of the consolidation, from Insull's point of view neither Villard nor Edison were in complete agreement with the terms. Insull, however, thought the merger made eminent sense for all concerned, although he knew it meant his own "eventual elimination from the organization."

Perhaps supremely trumped that he had lost control to Morgan, Villard found a scapegoat. When the consolidation was announced in the papers, Villard was quoted as saying "that the impaired financial condition of the Edison company, due to the extravagant management of Mr. Insull, made the fusion imperative."

Edison's name disappeared from the new company, although he was given a 14 percent stake and was chuffed with the value of his holdings. Was it a humiliation for the wizard, after building up those companies over more than two decades, only to have Morgan wrest control and take his name off the door? Many of Edison's associates were appalled by the consolidation when the greatest name in electrical manufacturing was forced out of his own company. Morgan kept the negotiations secret until the deal was finalized. Rumors circulated that Insull knew about the deal and "sold out" Edison. There is no evidence that Insull had sway over Villard. It is unlikely that the financier would have fully confided in Insull anyway. At the time, Insull was swamped in Schenectady, building GE. Having started with 200 workers and an informal machine shop constantly running in the red, Insull finished 1892 with 6,000 men and led Edison's most profitable operation. The resulting company became an industrial colossus that is one of the most successful and highly valued industrial corporations on the planet. Had Insull failed in organizing it into a competitive concern, Morgan never would have bothered consolidating it with Thomson-Houston.

Tate later rebuffed the allegations that Insull "had been paid heavily for maintaining silence. To anyone who knew Insull's character as I did, that story is incredible. No expression of this nature ever to my knowledge came from the lips of Edison."

Despite his many tiffs with the churlish Insull over the years, Tate defended Insull in print. "Villard was fully aware of Insull's intimate association with and loyalty to Edison, and working secretly, as he did, Insull was the last man that he [Villard] would take into his confidence. The risk was wholly unnecessary and Villard was a man too shrewd to assume unessential risks."

Insull would write in his memoirs nearly 40 years later that Edison's companies were unable to raise any more money and that a "consolidation or reorganization was therefore inevitable. I believed then, and I believe now, that it was best for the best interests of Mr. Edison and his associates that the consolidation take place. . . . Some of the men around him knew that he was not very sympathetic to the consolidation of the two big electrical companies."

Insull seemed to hold no ill will toward the Edison men who believed that Insull had betrayed the wizard. Neither did he mention any animus toward Villard or Morgan. He was tainted, though, and could not stay in New York. Working for GE under the Morgan interests was not what he had in mind for his career. He did not want to be second or third banana anymore: "I was quite young, having but recently completed my thirty-second year, and was doubtless indiscreet in arousing the hostility of a good many enemies, and due to Mr. Edison's attitude towards the consolidation, which I had very strongly urged him to acquiesce in, these enemies took advantage of the situation and prejudiced Mr. Edison against me. The misunderstanding lasted but a very few weeks and our friendship was shortly resumed, never to be broken until the day of his death. However, the spell was broken."

THE WIDE-OPEN CITY

Insull Comes to Chicago

There was, at this time, several elements in Chicago—those who, having grown suddenly rich from dull poverty, could not so easily forget the village church and the village social standards; those who, having inherited wealth, or migrated from the East where wealth was old, understood more or the savoir faire of the game; and those who, being newly born into wealth and seeing the drift toward a smarter American life, were beginning to wish they might shine in it—these last the very young people.

—Theodore Dreiser, *The Titan*[1]

A strange testimonial dinner was held for Insull at Delmonicos as he was preparing to leave New York to lead Chicago Edison. A considerable number of those present did not mind that Insull was exiting the Edison fold and probably even cheered his departure. It was, as one host said, a gathering of Insull's "most intimate friends and intimate enemies." Insull did not endear himself to those staying with the combined Thomson-Houston-GE interests when he practically toasted himself: "Eventually Chicago Edison will probably equal or exceed the investment of the General Electric Company."

Henry Villard, who watched his power shrivel as Morgan swooped in to consolidate General Electric, likely had a sly smile on his face. He knew that Insull was more than capable of backing up his boast. Although Villard offered Insull the vice presidency of his electric holding company—he had owned streetcar lines and utilities in Milwaukee and Cincinnati—he knew Insull was more interested in running his own company.

C.H. Coster—the Drexel Morgan partner in attendance—probably blanched and stared at Insull the way two predators would fix their eyes on each other in a standoff. Perhaps at this moment, Insull signaled that he would be an open rival to the Morgan interests, carefully establishing his territory in Chicago before the New York bankers could get a foothold in the nation's fastest-growing city. Why Insull would want to alienate a future source of capital was puzzling. Here was a former assistant to Edison, yet not known to be a proven financier like Villard or Morgan, practically spitting in the eyes of the most powerful investment bankers in the world.

Edison, who was seated next to Insull, likely flashed his knowing smile, cognizant that Insull was ready to start his new venture with everything he had learned from him, Villard, and Morgan. For the record, Insull had always maintained that the Morgan consolidation was best for Edison. The wizard was now able to fully remove himself from balance sheets and stifling executive suite matters and return to West Orange to work on anything he wanted from iron-ore processing to motion pictures. Edison gave his blessing to Insull and would remain his supporter up until his death.

Was Insull more aggrieved at having Edison's name removed from the General Electric combination, insulted that he was not tapped to run the new concern or more at the way Morgan handled the consolidation, so that it seeded a lifelong grudge? Certainly Insull held no animus toward Charles Coffin, who was the first president of GE. He respected Coffin immensely and would work with him on countless projects in Chicago.

If Insull wanted to make a stellar career move, he probably could have landed a top position with Westinghouse or stayed in New York to work for Coffin. Insull held the new company (GE) in such high regard that "it was not a possibility for me to contemplate joining in the management of any concern competing with or in any way in opposition to the consolidated company which owned Mr. Edison's rights and patents."

Chicago Edison was one among several power suppliers in the Windy City and hardly dominated that fractured market. While Edison himself had noted upon several visits with Insull that Chicago would be a prime location for a growing central station business, getting established in the colossally corrupt city would require a baronial war chest for bribes and the deftness of a master operator. Insull's decision, however, was not influenced by Edison, Coffin, or Villard. It was his mother who urged him to conquer the Midwestern mecca.

Shortly after the Morgan takeover, Insull had an intimate talk with Edison about his future. It is not known what Edison told him—it is unlikely Edison discouraged him—although his mother's message was clear. She had been visiting New York and staying with his sister in his apartment at 120 Madison. When Insull returned, he told them that he had explained his situation to Edison and his limited chance for advancement in working under the Morgan-controlled regime at GE. Insull, still stung by the Edison men's portrayal of him as a Benedict Arnold for his veiled role in the consolidation, wanted to be "free from any criticism of joining an opposition concern." To wit, joining Westinghouse would confirm to his enemies that he had betrayed Edison. Insull was a geyser of ambition, but he was no turncoat.

In a dynamic city that sweat new business opportunities, the presidency of Chicago Edison was a step down for Insull. Like Edison's pre-Villard companies, Chicago Edison was acutely undercapitalized and profits were scant. Insull's salary would be a pittance of what it was under Villard, and he would virtually have to build the company from scratch. Unlike his positions with Edison or GE, Insull would be running a puny also-ran in a competitive market. Chicago Edison's headquarters at 120 West Adams served as an office building, a power plant, and a coal bin. Its meager capacity was 8,000 horsepower—the equivalent of a large portable generator today. Its territory covered the 56 square blocks of the downtown Loop district, which was encircled by train tracks. The capitalization of the company was $833,000, and the company struggled in an environment in which bankers were reluctant to lend money to power producers since most of them would fail, and margins were thin or nonexistent. Few believed they would stay in business. Moreover, there were more than 45 electric companies in Chicago at the time, not counting the single power plants that businesses ran on their premises. Finally, after hearing her son lay out his arguments, his mother chimed in, her eyes tearing up with pride that her son had so many options and the best opportunity was within his reach.

"Son, you will write your friends in Chicago and submit your name to be president of Chicago Edison, luv," Emma Short Insull said with the confidence of a stage mother. As usual, his mother knew what her son needed to do. He needed a place where he could *make it go*. A place where his mind, soul, and energy would be unfettered. Although she had never been there, Chicago precisely fit the bill.

That evening, Insull wrote Byron Smith, a securities broker and director of Chicago Edison, and Edward Brewster, another director and investment banker. He offered his services, stating that "I desired to close my connections with the electric manufacturing business and to engage myself in the operation of a central station business."

On March 17, 1892, Insull met with Smith, Brewster, and with Frank Gorton, secretary of Chicago Edison, and John Doane, president of Merchants Loan and Trust of Chicago and chairman of the Edison executive committee. They were all impressed with Insull's verve and knowledge of the power business. In his capacity as vice president under Villard, Insull familiarized himself with the economics of central stations and had visited Chicago several times. There was little question that some major financial bolstering was needed at the company, and Insull did not hesitate to mention that at his interviews. The position was offered to him at a salary of $12,000 a year, half of what he was making at Edison General Electric. While the compensation and business prospects of the company looked dismal, Insull glowed over the most priceless aspect of the new position: the prospect of something much larger that needed *him* to make it grow.

Chicago was an audacious, brawny, scrappy, opportunistic bastion of opportunity that had no idea how influential a player it would become in the development of the twentieth-century metropolis. Insull was now as much its child as Carl Sandburg, the poet-singer-journalist from sedate Galesburg, Illinois, who dubbed Chicago "the city of big shoulders and hog butcher to the world." If Sandburg was its poet laureate, barding in a city of writers, architects, philosophers, graft artists, and thugs, then Insull was its Prometheus. Chicago was awaiting Insull the way the stage awaited Sarah Bernhardt. Literally built on a foundation of mud and swampland, the nation's second-largest metropolis was ready to be formed and molded into a world-class city.

Some 60 years prior to Insull's arrival, Chicago was little more than smelly, insect-infested wetland, which was the diplomatic description. Long used as a trading post because of its access to Lake Michigan, the town was a Potawatomi (People of the Fire) settlement largely because in the spring, an unceremoniously large puddle named Mud Lake filled with enough water to allow a portage-free route from Lake Michigan to the Mississippi River system through the turgid Chicago River. Translated from the Native American tongue, *Checagou* literally meant "smelly onion" owing to the wild onions growing in the swamps abutting Lake Michigan. The French voyageurs used the area as a trading post for their fur trade, and through the explorations of Father Marquette, Louis Jolliet, and Robert Sieur de la Salle, the Bourbon dynasty was in the seventeenth century able to establish dominion from the eastern St. Lawrence River down the Illinois to the Mississippi, eventually reaching New Orleans. Little thought was given to agriculture during the French era. At the time, furs were among the most valuable commodities in Europe.

To the west of Chicago lay the Great Plains, the boundless sea of grass and bison that stretched nearly one thousand miles to the foot of the Rockies. Two waves of glaciers that retreated 13,000 years ago flattened the area, leaving some of the most fertile soil on the planet, perennially enriched by the biomass of the tallgrass prairie, which efficiently took nitrogen from the air and restored it to the soil. The undulating, bountiful ocean of flowers, forbs, and grasses reached the height of ten feet, enough to dwarf a man on horseback. Most major transportation prior to the arrival of railroads and European settlers in the late 1830s was conducted on the waterways in the warmer months as the smaller rivers and streams froze and the biting prairie wind in winter was unbearable. At the center of the eventual metropolis, Fort Dearborn had been built in the early 1800s and burned down during the War of 1812, accompanied by a massacre of the white settlers. Not much had happened between 1816 and 1840, when the area around the fort was reoccupied by settlers and traders. By 1832, the town had a cabin, store, and two taverns. The Potawatomi signed a treaty and agreed to leave the smelly swamp town in 1835. They moved north and west, triggering an influx of settlement, bringing hopeful farmers, merchants, bankers, and railroad entrepreneurs from the East and Europe. While offering a pitiful harbor that was constantly being blocked by a sandbar—before the federal government appropriated the money to open up the mouth of the Chicago River on the lake—Chicago was destined to become the gateway to the rest of the continent, quickly surpassing St. Louis, the debarkation point for Lewis and Clark, as the most important city in the Midwest.

Fire would again ravage the city in 1871, when most of the central section of the city was destroyed, leaving 100,000 homeless. Not only did Chicago recover, it quickly became the manufacturing, meatpacking, and rail center of the nation. During the Civil War, the city's grisly slaughterhouses provided tons of (often rancid) meat to Union troops. Cyrus McCormick, the inventor of the reaper, the device that helped make farming profitable in the natural grasslands, also decided to locate in the city and build the largest agricultural implement plant in the world. He expanded his plant after the fire, as did hundreds of other businesses. The phoenix on the prairie was on its way to becoming the world's fourth largest city by the end of the nineteenth century.

Chicago was a cauldron of every imaginable industry, transportation mode, ethnic group, religion, and vice. Immigrants came to Chicago to build canals, slaughter cows, make steel, peddle booze and sell bodies. Advertisements for Chicago's bustling factories circulated across Europe. There was very little that was not made or sold in and around Chicago. And what Chicago did not sell, it could distribute through catalogs such as those of Montgomery Ward and

Sears and Roebuck (founded in 1893 and merged with K-Mart in late 2004), both of which grew tremendously in the 1890s. As a rail and water hub with access to the Great Lakes, Mississippi River, and the Atlantic, Chicago was the nation's transportation center.

While Chicago was unrivaled in the rate of population growth and the cornucopia of employment it offered, it was an ecological and public-health disaster. Prior to major public works improvements that began in the latter half of the nineteenth century, millions of gallons of raw sewage spilled into Lake Michigan from the Chicago River. Every factory and abattoir along the river dumped its sewage into the river with abandon. One hapless stream near the meatpacking district on the South Side was known as "bubbly creek" for its brown, oozing, gurgling quality. The river was nothing less than a witch's brew of industrial filth and disease that relentlessly sickened and killed Chicagoans.

Though fouled every minute of the day, the lake was the city's primary source for drinking water, having been tapped with tunnels and water-inflow "cribs" beginning in the late 1860s. Cholera and typhus ravaged entire neighborhoods regularly since the poisoned river water ran directly into the lake. Unpasteurized (and largely unrefrigerated) milk was also unsafe and carried diseases such as tuberculosis. Through one of the largest civil engineering feats of modern times, engineers working for the Metropolitan Water Reclamation District of Greater Chicago, locally known as the "Sanitary District," managed to reverse the flow of the Chicago River. From 1892 to 1900, the district redirected the flow away from the lake, channeling the city's effluent down the Chicago River and eventually into the Mississippi. The result was the expenditure of $35 million and a polluted system of canals and rivers below Chicago, which resulted in much litigation and little relief for those living downstream from Chicago's offal. The district later built some of the largest wastewater and stormwater systems in the world, reclaiming water that had previously been fouled. The waves of waterborne diseases stopped and Chicago was a much healthier place, at least when you turned on the water tap.

In the days of tainted water (and well beyond that period), Chicago fostered a much more insidious public health crisis: public drunkenness. From its earliest pioneer days, the plethora of saloons frequently dominated local commerce. Chicago was a city in which alcohol was as much as fact a life as working and recreating. By the end of the nineteenth century, the number of saloons equaled the number of meat markets, groceries, and dry goods stores combined. Also regarding alcohol as a medical anesthetic, quack medicine, and winter bloodwarming agent, Americans spent $1 billion on booze, compared to $900 million on meat, $200 million on public education, and $150 million on churches. Alcohol was cheaper and safer than milk, more plentiful, and easier to deliver. Chicago became an unrivaled mecca for demon rum.

It was the social curse of alcoholism that Insull's family devoted itself to in trying to cleanse the drunken streets of major cities. Like all temperance advocates, they believed that by replacing the dependency of drink with moral virtue and hard work, their alcohol-free lifestyle model could uplift society from its squalor. Alcoholism was a prime women's issue as well. Drunks were typically men who came home and abused their wives, often leading to broken homes. Since women in Victorian times were seen as domestic goddesses and protectors of morality, they campaigned for temperance while ensuring that they would gain the right to vote and further enforce their moral crusade. It was in Chicago that the great suffragette Susan B. Anthony, after the 1871 fire, proclaimed that "women were the greatest sufferers from drunkenness." About two years after Insull arrived in Chicago, the growing Women's Christian Temperance Union, a leading crusade, equated drying out the country with a battle for women's civil rights. Alcoholism, which was seen more as a disease in the 1890s, frequently led to feminine poverty when their men took to drink. The mostly Protestant temperance leaders also saw a need to convert those who could take the pledge, in a vain hope of emptying the brothels as well. This progressive spirit, born of the dissenters' crusades, branched out to include every urban malady and attracted some of the most successful social reformers in history from labor leader Mary "Mother" Jones to Jane Addams, who established her Hull House as a way to help immigrants.

No matter how much the temperance preachers inveighed against liquor, the unstoppable nature of a lusty city overwhelmed their cause at every turn. There were thousands of jobs to be had in the city that worked. And workers needed their saloons. The potent mixture was a cocktail for corruption. Theodore Dreiser, who had come to the city from Indiana via St. Louis in setting his immortal *Sister Carrie* in Chicago, wrote:

> In 1889, Chicago had the peculiar qualifications of growth which made such adventurous pilgrimages even on the part of young girls plausible. Its many and growing commercial opportunities gave it widespread fame, which made of it a giant magnet, drawing to itself, from all quarters, the hopeful and the hopeless—those who had their fortunes yet to make and those whose fortunes and affairs had reached a disastrous climax elsewhere.[2]

To the moral purification army, the immorality of Chicago was as pervasive as the dirty drinking water prior to the sanitation improvements. The reformers had sought to reverse the crime and indecency the way the Chicago River had been made to flow in the opposite direction of its natural course. William T. Stead, the English investigative journalist, was not afraid to name the owners of each Chicago bordello he documented. He listed the madams and the men who paid the taxes on the whorehouses, along with indictments against abusive industrialists like George Pullman, who created a city for his workers adjacent to his railroad-car plant on the city's South Side. As part of a manacled dystopia, workers had to pay exorbitant rents to Pullman, who set up the employer-owned experiment as a for-profit enterprise. Pullman made 600 percent profit on the gas he sold his employees, who, when they could not pay outright, were garnished on their substandard wages. The sleeping-car baron even rented the church he built in "Pullman." Labor unrest had been growing in the city for years. The railway union leader Eugene Debs organized the Pullman workers and they struck the plant in 1894. Though the strike was defeated when President Grover Cleveland called in federal troops and Debs was thrown in jail, it rallied the city, which generally supported the strikers. It also introduced a brilliant young defense lawyer named Clarence Darrow to the progressive scene, who was dared by Debs to quit his law firm to defend him.

During that period, Stead's classic *If Christ Came to Chicago* revolted the established, civic-minded families of Chicago. The British scribe was unafraid to lump together labor woes with prostitution and grossly unfair property taxes with public safety issues. In addition to the moral shortcomings, the city was being overrun by trains of every kind. At the time, the city had 2,500 miles of streets and 1,375 miles of railroad track with more than 2,000 grade crossings. This horrendous confluence of horse-drawn carriages, steam-driven trains, cable cars, and new electric trains made for an ongoing public-safety debacle. From 1889 through 1893, more than 1,700 people died in train accidents.

"In the last five years, there have been fewer soldiers killed in our wars all round the world than have been slaughtered in the streets of Chicago at the grade crossings," Stead wrote in 1894. "The railroads ride roughshod over the convenience, the rights and lives of the citizens."

Along with railroad hazards that threatened citizens daily, Chicago teemed with criminals of every stripe, who extended their domain far beyond liquor, prostitution, and gambling. Herbert Asbury, who documented Chicago's underworld in *Gangs of Chicago,* noted:

> The good and the bad of Europe poured into Chicago by the thousands, bringing with them their historic methods of revenge and reprisal, settling in national groups and in the main resisting the slight efforts which were made to Americanize them.[3]

Asbury documents extensively how the Irish, Sicilian, and other gangs formed alliances, fought turf wars, and conducted their operations, usually unchecked by an inadequate police force and graft-hungry politicians. Chicago was a tribal place that reinforced affiliations within the diverse communities that formed within the neighborhoods. By 1890, Chicago had the largest U.S. concentration of Poles, Swedes, Norwegians, Danes, Bohemians, Dutch, Croatians, Slovakians, Lithuanians, and Greeks. It boasted more Bohemians than any city outside of Prague. The Germans and the Irish, who had come earlier in the century, had already lodged themselves in cultural, civic, political, and criminal affairs. And the immigration was just beginning. From 1890 to 1910, the city added more than a million residents and expanded to an area of 200 square miles. Those immigrants fed the expansion of the brothels and the fortunes of madams like Carrie Watson, who "ran the finest bordello in Chicago"; Frankie Wright, who was in charge of the "'Library,' because it had a bookcase of a dozen never-read books"; and the Park Theater, which Stead said was "an exhibition which would be more in place in Sodom and Gomorrah than in Chicago."

Chicago attracted writers, reformers, and social activists the way the saloons attracted the thirsty. Naturalistic writers like Dreiser chronicled the horrors of Chicago's frontier. L. Frank Baum based his Oz series on the wonders of the city, particularly during the World's Columbian Exposition. Edna Ferber, the author of *Showboat,* and Willa Cather, who profiled pioneers, also got their literary feet wet in the city. Upton Sinclair's *The Jungle* showed readers the horrific life of a Lithuanian immigrant working in the slaughterhouses, a book that revolted the nation so much that it led to clean-food laws. Mark Twain, Sinclair Lewis, and Ernest Hemingway passed through the city on their way to greater adventures, infusing their uniquely American novels with the unstinting voice of the Midwest. By the 1920s, the critic H.L. Mencken anointed Chicago as America's literary capital. The social melee was front and center in Chicago. It was always within walking distance of the city's proudest facades.

In reaction to Stead's book and the crime that took root in the Levee District and other zones of licentiousness, at the urging of the leading newspapers, the old guard formed a social committee to address many of the miseries Stead highlighted. But Chicago was not quite ready for reform, to paraphrase the corrupt city alderman and saloonkeeper Paddy Bauler.

Rudyard Kipling echoed the sentiments of many non-Chicagoans who had been repulsed by the city's naked ambition, tribal fervor, squalor, immorality, and unabashed growth. "This place is the first American city I have encountered. Having seen it, I urgently desire to never see it again. It is inhabited by savages."

In 1892, Insull must have wondered how he fit into the Chicago milieu. The city itself needed many things, but he knew he was not there to be a temperance crusader. With a checkered history of utilities service, the first order of business for the city was to separate the chaotic business climate from what he needed to do. Fortunately for Insull, utilities in the city cried out for someone with organizational skills, since Chicago was late to the game and was playing by rules that changed with each packet of money handed to an alderman. The handsome ex-convict Charles Tyson Yerkes had bribed his way into controlling most of the city's trolley lines. While universally hated for his poor service and casual attitude toward "boodling," Yerkes, fictionally profiled in Dreiser's *The Titan* and *The Financier,* had one achilles heel: all of the city franchises granted for the traction lines were good for only a few years, which meant he was always reaching into his pockets to bribe the city council. When his attempt to finance legislation that would have granted him long-term franchises failed, he left the city forever, ending up in London, where he established the Underground system. Insull was aware of the Yerkes spectre and must have made a commitment to avoid his mistakes as surveyed the city's utilities businesses.

The city was already served by gas utilities, which started service in the 1860s and operated more than 50 miles of underground pipeline. Gas lighting, though, remained unaffordable for most homes as rates tended to stay high. Arc lighting came along in the late 1870s, but, as mentioned, was totally unsuitable for most indoor illumination because of its intensity. Chicago Edison's first station opened in 1888 and was followed by many others throughout the city, which seemed to boast a power station for every neighborhood that could afford it.

Edgewater was one of those rare upscale Chicago areas that championed the everyday use of electricity in homes in the late nineteenth Century. It took off when real estate developer J.L. Cochran talked the Chicago, Milwaukee, and St. Paul railroad into adding a stop in his suburb (now a part of Chicago). In his advertising, he promoted "Edison incandescent light" where you could "read your evening paper by the clear, steady light of an incandescent burner [bulb] in any room." By 1892, Cochran organized an electric trolley company that would allow his residents to take a faster train downtown. Wired for electricity and lighting, the Cochran homes were veritable palaces for the time, having been designed by Joseph L. Silsbee. Offering variations on Tudor and English cottage-style masonry homes, the houses were set in a semirural setting. A horse stable and large park was part of the package in a place where an urban worker could relax in a nearly bucolic setting.

As one of the first electrified commuter suburbs, the modern convenience of electric lighting allowed Cochran to charge more for his homes at a time when most city-bound Americans lived in cramped apartments or tenements. Cochran also made his community livable and kept his advertised promises by paving streets and opening gun and boat clubs and a bathing house for his residents.

A young draftsman in Silsbee's office named Frank Lloyd Wright studied Silsbee's plans with great interest. Working in his first job since coming to Chicago in 1887, the young Wright had dropped out of the University of Wisconsin to make his way in the booming city. A slight, handsome, Welsh Unitarian whose family had farmed a valley west of Madison, Wisconsin, Wright also had a strong mother who had great ambitions for her son. His mother encouraged Wright to build things. One of his first commissions was a boarding school run by his maiden aunts in Spring Green, Wisconsin, when he was 19. He was not headed down the moral path of his uncle, who was a noted preacher. While admitting Silsbee was "a kind of genius," Wright wanted to go beyond mere aesthetics and mate a structure with its setting in an organic harmony. His work would follow architect Louis Sullivan's dictum "form follows function." Although influenced by the writings of William Morris and John Ruskin, two pillars of the Arts and Crafts movement that stressed an anti-industrial love of craftsmanship, Wright was not at odds with the introduction of electricity in his homes. His most famous houses, including his own home and studio in Oak Park, Illinois, seamlessly integrated the electric light into homes decorated with stained glass, natural wood, and clerestory windows.

Wright also appreciated the subtle power of incandescent lighting within a space. When he first arrived in Chicago in 1887, he had never seen electric lights before but noted the "sputtering white arc-light in the stations and streets, dazzling and ugly. . . . This must be Chicago now. So cold, black, blue-white and wet." After working with his mentor Louis Sullivan, one of the world's leading architects, and a man he called his *lieber meister,* Wright established his own architectural practice in 1893 in Oak Park at the age of 26. Like Insull, he had studied with some of the finest minds in his business, learned quickly, and needed to be out on his own. He entered into his practice as a philosopher, writer, and revolutionary, tearing apart the conventional wisdom of architecture that rooms and buildings should be basic, inflexible boxes. He lectured on his new view of architecture throughout the Chicago area, including at Jane Addam's Hull House, which, in addition to providing social services for the immigrant poor from its inception in 1889, was a home for progressive intellectuals like Wright and the educator-philosopher John Dewey.

As Insull was assessing how to produce and sell electricity to a city busy creating the world's most inventive and dynamic architecture, Wright was aiming his intellectual shotgun at the conventional way of designing buildings:

> The pernicious papier-mâché elegance of our theaters is, in architectural spirit, level with the morals of the *Folies-Bergere.* The city's public buildings are foolish lies. The Art Institute itself is a stupid building with no countenance and elaborate flanks; the Public Library two buildings one on top of the other in disgraceful quarrel; the Post Office a boyish *atelier* project regardless of its purpose; the City Hall, a big bluff in vain "classic" costing the city many thousands a month for huge columns, themselves a troublesome and expensive load as columns used to do.[4]

Although Wright would design only a handful of buildings that would be built within city limits, he was moved by Chicago's energy and aspirations: "nevertheless, set against this fashionable folly with its fatuous inelegance there is something vital, indigenous to Chicago, the seeds of a genuine culture, the great hope of America quietly working here eventually to come up through this imposition, to show it for what it is and refute it."[5]

Wright, Sullivan, and their peers chose to reinvent architecture at a time when the expansion of cities, creation of new wealth, and the looming twentieth century demanded it. A quarter acre of land in downtown Chicago cost $130,000 in 1880. A decade later, the same parcel cost $900,000. Population also had doubled in that period. Widely available electricity changed the way homes and commercial spaces could be built. Electric illumination allowed architects to build smaller rooms with lower ceilings, as there was no threat of a gas leak causing a catastrophic explosion and fire. In the heart of the second industrial revolution, when buildings in effect became networks of machines, Wright saw the electric bulb as "an engine of light." More applications of electricity made buildings able to do more work with less human energy than ever before. Elevators and electric lighting allowed structures to grow into the sky, and Chicago was the world's foremost nursery for this vertical revolution. The Bessemer process of making steel was being adapted from making steel rails to structural girders. Concrete manufacturing and its use in buildings also took a quantum leap. William LeBaron Jenney invented the first iron skeleton building framework in 1883 and applied it to his Home Insurance Building in the city, which became the first true skyscraper in 1885.

Louis Sullivan declared that 1880 was "the zero hour of an amazing expansion." Blessed with easy access to iron, copper, wood, limestone, and every attendant building material, Chicago soaked up capital for new businesses at an astounding rate. Land values soared and the skyscraper was begat out of necessity and innovation, Sullivan recalled:

> The tendency in commercial buildings was toward increasing stability, durability, and height, with ever better equipment. The telephone appears and electric-lighting systems. Iron columns and girders were now encased in fireproofing materials, hydraulic elevators came into established use, superseding those operated by steam or gas. Sanitary appliances keep pace with the rest.[6]

The evolution of modern commercial architecture took shape within a few blocks of Insull's first office in Chicago. The old technique of masonry-supported walls was seen in the nine-story Montauk building, with its castlelike brown walls. Then came Daniel Burnham and John Root's 16-story Monadnock building, "an amazing cliff of line and surface, a direct singleness of purpose, that last word of its kind," Sullivan described it.

Sullivan and his partner Dankmar Adler then took their turn in designing the Auditorium building, which housed a hotel and one of the most acoustically perfect theaters in the world in 1889. The 63,000-square-foot structure was the largest and most complex building of the time. With its graceful arches, life-affirming organic ornament, and soaring, Tuscan tower, the building proclaimed to the world what American buildings should aspire to, and established Chicago as the birthplace of truly modern buildings.

In tandem with the development of the skyscraper came numerous changes in the city's transportation system, a chaotic jumble in 1892. Insull immediately saw that all of the urban streetcars could be driven by electric motors, which would create demand for electricity. Edison General Electric had absorbed the Sprague Company, a pioneer in electric traction, while Insull was in New York. Westinghouse and Coffin also knew the future of urban transit was going to be driven by the electric motor. The near-term problem for this type of transportation, which was far more reliable than what it was replacing, was that it required a lot of electricity. The small stations of the time were not up to the task. Fortunately, Chicago Edison was already planning to build the Harrison Street station before Insull arrived on the scene. As such, it would be one of the largest power plants in the country.

Seeking to ensure that he would have some working capital when he took the helm of Chicago Edison, Insull asked the board to increase the company's capitalization by $250,000. Accustomed to paltry salaries from his New York tenure, Insull also received an advance of company stock in the same amount, which he bought with a loan from the department store mogul Marshall Field. Asking for a contract of three years, Insull knew that if he stayed in Chicago that long, "I would be compelled to be here long enough to get used to living in a city smaller than New York. I very rapidly got over this feeling. The businessmen of Chicago, were, at the time, still imbued with the cooperative spirit of the early settlers, and I soon found myself enjoying very pleasant relations with a great many of them." Insull felt so much at home that he became an American citizen in 1896.

The mélange of different transportation modes, in Insull's view, came down to one solution: electrify everything. Horse-drawn omnibus carts, which had been on the streets since 1859, competed with steam-driven trains, which coexisted with the cable cars. By March 1894, there were 86 miles of cable-car lines and 450 cars powered by 11 power plants. While this system made the streets cleaner and somewhat safer, building the system cost $100,000 a mile because the streets had to be torn up and fitted for conduits that contained the ever-fickle cables. The cars were operated by devices called "grips" that literally clamped onto the endless, moving cable that was pulled by a steam engine. When the operator wanted to stop his car, he released the grip and applied the brakes. When Insull arrived in 1892, the city had decided to commit all new lines to electric trolleys. The horse carts and cable cars were relegated to routes not served by electricity or were sent to the junkyard and museums.

Charming, conniving, and boodling his way into control of the new electric system, Insull's predecessor Charles Tyson Yerkes built a relatively efficient electric system that spanned the city's South, West, and North sides. As a token civic gesture, he donated money to construct a large refracting telescope, one of the world's largest. Oddly enough, the telescope ended up in Williams Bay, Wisconsin, where it was used by the fledgling University of Chicago. The university, funded by a large gift by John D. Rockefeller, was built in Hyde Park about eight miles south of downtown in 1892. When an ordinance failed to pass that would have granted him long-term traction franchise rights, Yerkes made his way to New York, taking his millions and leaving behind a trail of mistresses, many of whom were wives of leading Chicago citizens.

Now that Chicago was a leader in everything from mail-order merchandising to meatpacking, it wanted to show the world what it could do and what the future could look like. The architect and civic leader Daniel Burnham was appointed to head a committee that would build a World's Fair for 1893. Serving with him were the landscape architect Frederick Law Olmsted, the designer of New York's Central Park; sculptors Augustus St. Gaudens and Lorado Taft; and to a very limited extent, Louis Sullivan, who designed the fair's Transportation building, its most original structure. Built on the swamps of Jackson Park near the University of Chicago, the fair would be an 11-block showpiece for agriculture, manufacturing, mines, fine arts, transportation, machinery and electricity.

The luminous "White City" used electricity in a way that the world had never seen before. Around Olmsted's pond, lagoon, and wooded island were built some of the most lavish—and gaudy—electrified buildings of the day. With the exception of Sullivan's Transportation building, gracefully highlighted by his signature Romanesque arched entrance, the White City looked like 1850s Paris taken to a Barnumesque extreme. Part spectacle, part carnival, and part educational, the fair was an exhibition that would display all of the world's latest technologies alongside romanticized sideshows of what had been lost as America lurched into a new industrial age. Buffalo Bill Cody's Wild West show performed to an audience of up to 12,000 people a day. The latest General Electric equipment was on display around the corner from knock-offs of Roman statutes. It was a shamelessly eclectic hodgepodge, but it was a lot of fun.

The Midway Plaisance featured the world's largest ferris wheel. Every ride imaginable was available and every known form of entertainment exhibited, including hoochie-coochie dancers. The $35 million extravaganza succeeded because it drew people from all over the country through the country's rail system. All told, 28 million passed through the gates of the White City, with 21 million paying. The attendance equaled nearly half of the population of the U.S., which had 66 million residents in 1893. The Illinois Central purchased 300 coaches and 41 locomotives just to transport people from downtown to the fair. On its busiest day, the railroad moved more than half a million people.

Every dignitary, local official, and writer visited the fair to marvel at the domed buildings, the crowds, and the international displays of "Little Egypt" and German villages. The world had not actually come to Chicago; the city was presenting a utopian postcard, an idealized international community through the eyes of mostly hack architects (Burnham and Sullivan excepted) and geniuses like Tesla and Olmstead. Yet it was the city—and all of its unrepressed urges to be great—that was the centerpiece, distracting its visitors from the unsustainable filth of the South Side stockyards, the ramshackle tenements, and the vice districts.

Louis Sullivan, appalled by the overwrought European facades that reflected the most grandiose pretensions of the Old World, said in his *Autobiography of an Idea,* "the damage wrought by the World's Fair will last for half a century from its date, if not longer. It had penetrated deep into the constitution of the American mind, effecting there lesions significant of dementia." While Sullivan's prediction that the fair's bellicose architectural style would rein supreme in future years in the building of other cities was partially correct, the White City's influence would certainly not last 50 years.

Burnham's utopian vision was one of splendid buildings, grand boulevards, and parks with commodious lagoons and progress manifested in every piece of machinery and artwork. From the designing of New York's Flatiron building (originally called the Fuller building), to a design for central Washington, Burnham was a visionary of big spaces and bold exteriors. In 1909, at the urging of the city's leading lights, Burnham would expand upon his ideas to create the Chicago Plan and spacious urban layouts for other cities. Chicago would later bravely try to build upon what the fair espoused, an industrial-era advance on every level that led to improved working and living conditions.

Insull, who would befriend and support Burnham, savored the connection between better living through electricity and the White City's gargantuan display of every conceivable application of power. Westinghouse had practically gone bankrupt providing most of the electricity for the fair, which consumed more power than the entire city. He won the contract over GE's bid because he offered to supply power for half the cost. Everywhere one turned, there was an electric light, train, or use of electricity. Edison's phonographs and kinetoscopes, forerunners of the motion picture, featured "peep shows." The fountains were powered by electric pumps. When President Cleveland opened the fair, he kicked it off by pushing a button that lit up 100,000 lightbulbs. L. Frank Baum was so moved by the fair that he used it as the model for his Emerald City in *The Wizard of Oz.*

Tesla's work was featured in the Machinery building along with 12 new 1,000-horsepower Westinghouse generators. Behind the Westinghouse section was an array of electric signs, streetlights, and an Eiffel Tower of lightbulbs. Tesla was the impresario of his own sideshow. An electric sign of his image made of tinfoil and glass looked like he was infused by an aura of lightning. Whenever it was turned on, it produced a deafening noise that startled the crowd and alerted them to Tesla's Olympian accomplishments. Some of the first neon lights were twisted to form the names of his favorite scientists Faraday, Maxwell, and Henry. The exhibit in which Tesla's polyphase system was displayed looked like a monument to a Victorian prince.

As a showman who loved being the center of attention, Tesla himself proved to be worth the price of admission in a unique act. First he would rotate a metal

"Egg of Columbus" to show the effects of a moving magnetic field. As a show-stopper, he would take the stage in a waistcoat and large rubber shoes, passing two million volts through his gaunt body. The electrification caused him to glow and emit electric flames from his slender frame. His performances would gain him international fame and the friendship of Mark Twain, who would later visit him in his laboratory. Tesla's hokey portrayal, however, was more than a freak-ish showcase of the potential of electricity. After the fair, some 80 percent of cities adopted his AC system for power generation, including Insull at Chicago Edison.

A profound turn in the American imagination occurred at the fair. Not only had Americans seen a Chicago-style depiction of the Old World, they had front-row seats at the stage of the New World. They saw the arms of steam engines turn mechanical energy into electrical energy, a conversion of work into power that would completely reshape the world. Henry Adams, who visited the fair in 1893 and recorded his impressions in his classic *Education of Henry Adams,* saw that America was eschewing the horse-drawn world for the electrical age:

> One lingered long among the dynamos, for they were new, and they gave to history a new phase. Men of science could never understand the ignorance and *naiveté* of the historian, who, when he came suddenly on a new power, asked naturally what it was; did it pull or did it push? Was it a screw or thrust? Did it flow or vibrate? Was it a wire or mathematical line? And a score of questions to which he expected answers and expected to get none. . . . Chicago asked for the first time the question whether the American people knew where they were driving. . . . Chicago was the first expression of American thought as a unity; one must start there.[7]

The composer Antonin Dvorak discovered something more sublime at the fair. He heard the music of the Kwakiutl Indians of Vancouver Island. The com-plex rhythms of their singing and drumming influenced his New World Sym-phony, which gave the world the heartbreaking melody that yearned for freedom, which was based on a Negro spiritual. The fair, as much as anything else, attempted to celebrate the diversity of the city and America itself, although no African-Americans were allowed to host official exhibits.

Leaders of the local African-American community, however, were able to present a day of special events. Frederick Douglass addressed "The Race Prob-lem in America." Excerpts from Will Marion Cook's opera *Uncle Tom's Cabin* were presented. Scott Joplin, eager to share his new syncopated ragtime music with the world, pulled together his first band at the fair. Within five years, his *Maple Leaf Rag* would be sweeping the country. An 8,000-square-foot

"Women's Building" featured a mural by the impressionist Mary Cassat (which has been lost). All told, thirty-six nations were represented. During Czech day at the fair, some 30,000 Czechs from the around the country marched in a procession and reveled in Dvorak conducting his own works in the festival hall. The great composer suspected that Chicago would be a nurturing ground for the future of modern music itself, which he suggested would be "founded on Negro melodies."

In sympathy with the founders of the fair, Insull regarded the White City's central promise as a democratic covenant. The dynamos, lights, and labor-saving machines were there for the people, not some privileged elite. All told, 7,000 arc lights and 120,000 incandescent lights illuminated the fair. The more daunting challenge was creating a system that would make the underlying power affordable to everyone from the merchant to the farmer residing far beyond the city. Would the widespread availability of electrical power somehow unite urban and rural America in a powerful partnership? Chicago itself was now an ecological and commercial network that consumed materials and capital within a 600 mile radius. Lumber, iron ore, and ice came in from the North Woods country. Grain came in from the west and south of the Great Plains. Cattle and pigs came in from the west and south to be slaughtered in "Porkopolis" on the South Side. Coal came in from central and southern Illinois and the Appalachian fields. One of Insull's first business arrangements when he came to Chicago was to contract for a steady supply of coal, the fuel for the steam engines that drove Chicago Edison's dynamos. He met with Frank Peabody, the future coal king, to guarantee a low-priced supply. Peabody was so taken with Insull that he suggested that Insull buy a coal mine with him. Insull refused, explaining his conflict in being a customer. This led to a partnership with Peabody to operate mines near Springfield, Illinois, the state capital—and Abraham Lincoln's home at one time—about 150 miles south of the city. Insull would later purchase a railroad to move the coal to his power plants, the first of many ventures he undertook to control an essential leg of his enterprise.

The fair demonstrated to Insull that electricity could be harnessed to illuminate large spaces and could be produced using "large marine-type economical steam engines directly connected to large electric generators." Having seen and ridden in the fair's electric trolley, he also foresaw that such an electric transit system could extend well beyond the city. The White City's triumph in attracting 28 million people and creating a building boom was to be short lived, though. A financial panic spread throughout the country in 1893, a crisis that led to a depression and a scarcity of cash in the absence of a bona fide central bank. Most of the White City, poorly constructed with wooden materials, burned down in 1894. The Midway remained for a few years, part of it the home for Frank Lloyd Wright's Midway Gardens, a sprightly and charming open-air *biergarten* and restaurant that was later demolished.

Undaunted by the Depression, Insull managed to acquire the rival Chicago Arc Light & Power Company in 1893 through the issuance of $2.2 million in debentures paying 6 percent. The takeover rid Chicago Edison of at least one competitor and put Insull on track to build his utility combine through multiple acquisitions. Insull next opened the company's Harrison Street station, producing 16,400 kilowatts. Designed to be the most efficient power plant in the world, the facility was situated on the Chicago River, where ample water was available for steam production. Although technically Harrison Street was the *sine qua non* of steam engine-driven power plants, it had reached the limits of what could be done with that technology. Five-thousand-horsepower dynamos, Insull realized, would not be enough to supply the growing city, so he began his quest for a power system that had never been tried, much less built.

LOVE AND WAR

Insull Marries, the Eve of War

I love the messy vitality of this place, the energy of the city. You do feel the fissures here. All the contradictions in this country, all the paradoxes, are within the boundaries of this city.

—Author Alex Kotlowitz, speaking of Chicago.[1]

Of all of the many novel sights of 1893, there was one image that would not let Insull rest, an arresting vision far more powerful than Tesla, the ferris wheel, hundreds of thousands of lightbulbs, and the millions of fair attendees combined. The luminous visage of 24-year-old Gladys Wallis enchanted him. He had seen her picture in the paper at first. The petite, brown-haired, brown-eyed beauty was playing at the McVicker's Theatre during the fair, only a few blocks from his office. The "pocket Venus," barely five feet tall, specialized in comedic roles and was charm incarnate. Her creamy skin glowed in the footlights. Appearing with established actors John Drew and William Crane in touring productions, she was an ingénue headed for a bright career in theater. Even when critics wanted to write a bad review of the plays she performed in, she always seemed to be spared, as her effervescence captivated audiences. Insull, too, was enraptured, tongue-tied as he watched her walk down Michigan Avenue on her way to the theater.

Born Margaret Anna Bird in 1869, Gladys grew up in an actor's haven. Her mother, Katherine, and father, Douglas, had emigrated from County Sligo in Ireland, to New York in 1867, where her mother opened a boardinghouse for actors. Douglas was rarely around. When he was, he was often drunk and fighting with his wife. He left to go out West in 1875 and the family never heard from him again until Katherine received a report that he had died sometime in 1881. Young Margaret adopted the stage name Gladys at eight, deciding that she, too, was destined for the footlights. Having seen the repugnant behavior of her father and the loose morals of her mother's boarders, she pledged to eschew liquor and sex.

By the age of 15, her talent was winning her lead roles in various productions. She had the ability to light up the stage and make people laugh. Five years later, she was making from $75 to $100 a week, nearly top dollar at the time. Appearing in *The Squire of Dames* in Drew's production, the *New York Journal* critic Frederic McKay wrote:

> It was Miss Gladys Wallis' evening at the Knickerbocker yesterday. Mr. Crane [the lead actor] had his name in much larger type, but Miss Wallis, as a young stage-struck girl, abided her time and in the last act she gave a star performance that is by all odds the best thing of its kind since—well, since Miss Wallis' impersonation of the little girl who cries when she is asked to recite in "The Squire of Dames."[2]

Adept at a number of roles, Gladys refused to be typecast and picked challenging parts to expand her repertoire. Her strong personality shined on stage, as evidenced in this review:

> Miss Wallis, as Juliet, surprised even her most intimate friends. Hitherto she has not essayed tragic parts and when it was announced that she was to play Juliet, some of her friends feared that she would not be up to the task. But last evening's performance shows that she is at home in any part.

As a top player in the John Drew company, Gladys was a major draw up until the time Drew's niece Ethel Barrymore came on the scene. While Gladys maintained a polite friendship with Ethel, she lost leading roles to her and another company actor, Maude Adams. The married Drew was more interested in bedding Gladys than in promoting her career, so she left to appear with the "less respectable" William Frawley company.

As the apparition of Gladys moved Insull to undertake a slow and proper Victorian courtship of her, he turned his sights on obtaining more capital for larger plants and ways of selling power to large customers. He needed a respite, though, as the emotional pressures of the Morgan takeover of Edison General Electric and the headlong charge into Chicago Edison had exhausted him. Even

Edison's business was still following him as he began his tenure in Chicago. For some reason, the Edison Electric Light Company of Europe had not accepted his resignation. In his typical peevish style, Insull sent this letter back to Alfred Tate in New York, emphasizing how he had emotionally severed himself from his New York Edison relationships:

> I would point out to you that my resignation ought to be accepted in the case of all of the [Edison] corporations that I resigned from some eight months ago. I have a great objection to my being retained as a director and in some cases an officer of companies with the management of which I have nothing whatever to do. Please reimburse me for the sum of two (2) dollars paid to the New York State Commissioner for taking my acknowledgement for the two affidavits enclosed.[3]

Insull had no interest in keeping any formal executive connection to GE. He had plenty to deal with in Chicago. In addition to trying to obtain enough financing to make Chicago Edison a viable company, he was up against the avaricious "Gray Wolves" of the city council who were preparing to seize control of the city's most lucrative utility franchises. Mayor John Hopkins and the Democratic boss Arthur Sullivan had set up a dummy corporation in 1895 called the Ogden Gas Company, and deftly persuaded the city council to grant a liberal franchise that undermined the grip of the city's gas monopoly, People's Gas, Light, and Coke Company. The Sullivan-Hopkins company then offered its extortionary offer of $7.33 million to People's Gas for a "buyout," thus indirectly shifting the franchise to People's Gas.

That move did not bother Insull, although the next tactic of Sullivan's forced his hand. Sullivan figured that Insull could be cowed into "protecting" his franchise for several hundred thousand dollars if the Gray Wolves voted to create a 50-year franchise for electrical generating rights. Naturally, the city councilmen would initially control this entity before they sold the rights to Insull at an outrageous price. When presented with the "offer," Insull stormed out of the meeting with the graft-smitten politicians. The city council then passed an ordinance granting a new dummy corporation called Commonwealth Electric the 50-year guaranteed power deal. Insull still would not pay the bribe. What Sullivan and his operators did not know was that Insull had quietly purchased the rights to license every American piece of electrical generating equipment through Chicago Edison. While Sullivan was able to form a company and technically create a monopoly, he could not effectively generate an electron of power without going through Insull to buy the necessary equipment. Insull had gained the upper hand and the Gray Wolves backed off. Insull invited Sullivan over for dinner after the incident and they became friends, a relationship that lasted for the rest of Sullivan's life.

Insull had been going nonstop for nearly a dozen years and was no longer the 22-year-old wunderkind who could keep pace with the most energetic men of his time. Insomnia prevented him from getting any meaningful sleep and his immune system was depleted. His doctor told him he had "nervous prostration" and ordered him to rest to avert one of his many nervous collapses after relentless periods of work. He still had the drive; he just needed to restore his energy. Booking a passage on the steamship *Brittanic*, he was pleasantly surprised when he checked into his stateroom en route to England. Not only had he secured the best berth on the ship—No. 28 was the same room J.P. Morgan had occupied when he crossed the Atlantic—Insull discovered that the room was overflowing with fruit and delicacies, gifts from his friends. An unpleasant surprise was the congregation of ship rats who had also savored the idea of eating all that fruit during one evening. Insull frantically bolted from the room in his pajamas, attracting stares from those attending a concert on the deck. He wondered if Morgan had encountered the same problem.

Upon arriving in London in 1896, the coal-fouled air aggravated his respiratory condition, forcing him to leave the city for the seaside resort of Brighton. The lively little town was the Coney Island of England, home to London vacationers as long as anyone could remember. Never quite able to relax and not interested in swimming, Insull poked around the shops that lined the boardwalk. At first, he was pleased to see that all of the shops had electric lighting. Then he took note of something even more remarkable. The usage of current was being metered. Little globes with dials showed how much electricity the merchants were using so that the power company could charge them based on actual consumption. His mind flashed back to Edison's early installations of lighting. The wizard, lacking a metering system, had no way of knowing how much power was being used by his customers. Customers were charged by the lightbulb, which did not reflect the actual cost of the power consumed. Before him was a solution that Insull had never seen before: a meter invented by an Englishman named Arthur Wright, whom he would later meet and talk into a licensing deal with Chicago Edison.

One of the fundamental economic problems of selling electricity was that, while the producers at the time knew the cost of coal, stringing power lines, building a plant and maintaining it, they had no way of measuring how much power was being consumed. Without a meter, customers could literally use as much power as they wanted for a fixed rate. For end users like Drexel Morgan and the New York newspapers, it was a tremendous deal. Ultimately, though, it was a money loser for the power companies, since the cost of consumption never really covered their fixed costs. As a result, most of the Edison power companies were cash challenged.

With the metering concept enmeshed in Insull's brain, a whole new business strategy emerged. Why not charge customers different rates based on their volume of usage? Large users would get a discount. Small users would pay a higher rate. With a meter, all this was possible. Excited with the possibilities, he headed off to Berlin. Under Henry Villard's tutelage, Insull had already been introduced to the Siemens group of bankers and electrical manufacturers, so he was given a hearty welcome when he visited with the *übermeisters* of German finance and industry. This was a cordial visit, in which Werner von Siemens and Dr. Emil Rathenau generously showed Insull the gems of German technology, which had been on an upward trajectory since the 1870s. Insull also was deeply influenced by the partnership between the German government and industry. Bismarck's pension system seemed like a good idea to him (which could be offered by private employers in the U.S.). He was also interested in the role of the state as a watchdog over businesses like his own.

Revived by his European visit, Insull returned to Chicago early in 1897. Infused with ideas, he campaigned for and won the presidency of his trade association, the National Electric Light Association (NELA), which was composed of local power companies. It is unlikely that the executives—coming from local power companies—had any inkling of what the 38-year-old Insull was going to propose next: state regulation of the power industry. His first major speech to NELA left many of them aghast: "Our business is a natural monopoly. It must be of necessity *regulated* by some form of governmental authority . . . its affairs must be subject to proper governmental authority."

While his industry peers did not entirely understand Insull at first, they came to grasp the logic of his argument. Like many things that are manufactured, the cost of electricity dropped as it was produced in volume. Bigger power plants were simply more efficient than smaller ones. Central power plants made more sense than dozens of dynamos in the basements of each customer's building. One big producer could gain most of the advantages of the economies of scale, hence his view that "massing of production" (later shortened to "mass production" by Henry Ford) made the most economic sense. By extension, one major power producer would hold a "natural monopoly" because less competition made the entire system more efficient. Keenly aware of the rapacious practices of the monopolists of the Gilded Age, Insull also wanted to gain the public's support, not by price-fixing, but by reducing customer rates. Retail costs would drop based on efficiencies gained from ever-larger power production and from gauging consumption patterns. Government regulators filled the role of overseers of electrical rates. Publicly elected or appointed officials would serve as arbiters of what rates were "fair"—so long as the industry was guaranteed a profit in the rate-making process. Yerkes had suggested public regulation of his streetcar lines in exchange for long franchises, but could not completely sell the proposition to lawmakers. Insull knew he could advance the idea further than Yerkes had, and put it forth a year after Yerkes failed.

The whole concept of massing production and natural monopolies, which Insull learned from Villard, was startling in its business logic and was destined to reshape the new industry. As the power began flowing from the new Niagara Falls station along an 11-kilovolt AC line, the world itself was slowly adjusting to the new reality of power. The science of energy and social issues was also advancing. The British physicist James Thompson had discovered the electron. Leading intellectuals were discussing Henry George's single-tax proposal, which sought to eliminate all taxes except those on real estate. George Bernard Shaw and his London group of socialists in the Fabian Society were discussing state control of nearly everything to better everyone's working and living conditions. H.G. Wells was dreaming about a time machine. Edward Amet was manufacturing the "Magniscope," the first true movie projector, in Waukegan, Illinois, where Insull would build one of his largest power stations. His 1898 film *The Battle of Santiago Bay* employed some of the first film special effects.

Edward Bellamy's utopian novel *Looking Backward,* which sold more than 100,000 copies, had provided the impetus in that period for social reforms based on the new industrial realities. Bellamy had seen a dark vision of "humanity hanging from a cross" and provided a stern allegorical warning of the evils of industrial capitalism. Henry Demarest Lloyd, a muckraker who wrote editorials for the *Chicago Tribune,* had laid the journalistic groundwork by attacking robber barons like John D. Rockefeller and the Vanderbilts, calling those American pashas "new social types whose sultanic disregard of their American subjects called for new legal restraints." While the election of pro-business William McKinley in 1896 eased the fears that progressives and populists like William Jennings Bryan would gain power, a new era was at hand. Insull had heard the evangelistic Bryan give his legendary "Cross of Gold" speech when he was nominated in Chicago and was concerned that government might be able to limit the growth of corporations if Bryan's party ever got into power. As the powerful trusts came under public scrutiny and condemnation, another corporate entity seized Insull's imagination and would become popular on a larger scale—the holding company. This new corporate body could control an unlimited number of other companies through the issuance of stock. Like the trusts, it could also be controlled by a select board of directors and was virtually unregulated.

Every facet of society was undergoing revision. John Dewey, teaching at the University of Chicago, was also transforming public education with his book *The School of Society.* In reworking the school system to adapt to the needs of an industrial society, Dewey believed the new democracy would survive only if schools practiced "promotion and efficiency." His curriculum paired moral and intellectual development along with practical skills such as cooking exercises. Frank Lloyd Wright, flourishing in his new private practice building custom homes for suburban businessmen, came up with the idea of graceful horizontal lines for his "Prairie" homes in Oak Park, reportedly after seeing the Ho-o-den Japanese Temple at the Columbian Exposition. In Detroit, a young Edison engineer named Henry Ford had successfully assembled a horseless carriage. And the new century had not even begun.

When he returned from Europe, Insull moved to monopolize the affections of Miss Gladys Wallis. Residing at Helen Windsor's theatrical boarding house in New York with rising luminaries such as Barrymore, Maude Adams, Edna Wallace and Minnie Dupre, Gladys was becoming a star who would lead her own stock company. Insull began to pursue her with all of the fervor of his business affairs. A friend, Eugene Lewis, was engaged to Amy Busby, also an actress and a close friend of Gladys. When he was invited to dinner, Lewis asked Insull if there were other people he should invite. Insull unhesitatingly suggested that Gladys would be a more-than-suitable dinner companion.

Gladys was scintillating at dinner, talking about her many roles and life in the theater. The tiny angel he had seen walking down Michigan Avenue and up on stage was delightful in person. He was consumed and began a stage-door courtship with his new, dear friend. Apart from all the powerful and wealthy people he knew, he did not really have any intimate friends in Chicago. His life consisted of arriving in the office at 7:10 a.m., reading the operating report from the previous day, answering any service complaints personally (a practice continued into the 1920s), scanning the papers for any mention of him or his businesses, and taking care of the business of the day. Meticulous in his note taking, he would keep notes in his rare Pitman shorthand and would only hire secretaries who knew it. Evenings would be occupied with reviewing routes of power lines while riding in his electric car. It was a lonely life, and he yearned for a wife and family as he neared 40.

Courting Gladys was a difficult proposition. He was in Chicago, and she was in New York or on the road most of the time. He frequently wrote her, as often as daily. Plying her with flowers, candy, gloves, and stockings, he refused to let the distance separate him from his beloved. She would reply in kind, no matter how busy or exhausted she was, starting letters with, "My Dearest Sam" or "You are the dearest one I know." She often mentions that she is depressed, which would prompt another thoughtful gift from Insull. If they went three days without a letter, the couple seemed miserable. She was on the road quite a bit, traveling with shows to Philadelphia, Detroit, Cincinnati, Cleveland, New Orleans, Milwaukee, Baltimore, and San Francisco, but the letters did not stop.

Gladys's career was in the ascendancy when the Frawley company offered her a 10-week guarantee, which later became a permanent engagement for $100 a week. Gladys tentatively accepted the offer—and obtained a raise to $125. An actor's ideal position, it would have meant no travel, starring roles, and half the work. Frawley apparently was not sincere. He waited until opening night at the Tivoli Theatre, then fired her, citing her "explosive anger and condescension." Alone, friendless, and broke in the city by the bay, she was bereft. Insull consoled her in every way possible. She was so distressed, however, that she forgot his birthday, which led to a five-page apology:

> Can you forgive me? You always think of me. . . . I am more disgusted with myself. . . . There is no use in writing more about it for I could write indefinitely and not express my feelings. I ought to feel badly for being such a *fool!* I could only ask *humbly* for your forgiveness. My best love (which isn't worth much), Love and Always, Gladys.[4]

Over the course of two years, they exchanged more than 200 letters. She was consistent in replying, mentioning every little detail of her day—rehearsing, traveling, shopping, eating, meeting with friends. Gently reminding him that "faithfulness appeals greatly to girls," she saw him little, yet began to know him intimately by his letters. Insull responded with vignettes of his life and sent gifts regularly, from shopping bags to cash. She loved the gifts and "values his friendship." In February 1898, he went to New York to propose. She accepted, but refused to set a date, on the condition that he understand that marrying him is "not the easy way out." Gladys was still determined to have a career and not ready to be a businessman's wife. She accepted a vacation paid for by Insull and resumed her work in a traveling-company play called *The Circus Girl.*

She had her own life, yet was very much in love. She wrote on April 29, 1899: "I love you absolutely my own dear. You are an ideal darling and I am blessed by your words and having you for all times. I am yours, Gladys."[5]

Gladys's fortunes had improved since the announcement of her engagement. In the fall, she received two acting offers. The Crane company asked her to rejoin it, and she was offered up to $500 a week by another company to appear in a vaudeville review. At this point, she was making about the same compensation as Insull at Chicago Edison. Alarmed at the bawdy nature of vaudeville, though, Insull urged her to take the Crane offer, which she accepted.

They were married at the end of the theater season on May 23, 1899. She decided to give up her acting career for the time being to become the "wife of a Chicago millionaire," according to the society-page headlines.

The nuptials were lavish and well attended by all of the Edison principals. The wedding book, as thick as a modern Manhattan phone directory, was loaded with kind notes from Edison and Villard. On April 12, their son, Samuel, Jr., was born. While Insull was really Samuel Insull the 2nd, no one ever called him "junior." After his son's birth, though, Insull's father agreed to be known as Samuel Insull, Sr. Junior—Insull called him "Chappie,"—would later call his son Samuel Insull III, even though he was really the fourth Samuel Insull. Chappie would have a sparse early relationship with his father, rarely seeing him until the late evening, if at all. Gladys would steep him in poetry, plays, and the arts, while Insull would fill his room with mechanical toys such as steam engines. While his mother saw her son going into the arts, the father was grooming him for a dynasty.

Insull's master plan for massing production became an unwritten rule in the electrical industry around the turn of the century before most of the world understood its far-reaching implications. By 1900, power producers were able to send 60,000 volts on a high-transmission line. The following year, Westinghouse was proposing a 3.5-megawatt turbine at a time when the biggest generator was cranking out 2 megawatts. The heart of the power industry was growing exponentially. Now it required some daring to take it to the next level.

Returning to England in December 1901 to visit his mother, Insull was incapable of just enjoying a leisurely trip with Gladys and Chappie. Charles Coffin had contacted him prior to leaving about inspecting a Curtis steam turbine that was the subject of GE experiments. Insull knew exactly what Coffin was referring to, having seen a steam turbine that was invented by Sir Charles Parsons of Newcastle on one of his earlier trips to England. When he arrived in Europe, Insull visited Frankfurt, Germany, where he could see 2,500-horsepower turbines in action. There was something elegant and graceful about them, not to mention their efficiency. Up until that point, most of the prevailing power-generation technology relied upon two basic components: a steam engine and a dynamo. They were two separate units connected by belts, which resulted in a tremendous loss in energy. Not only were they inefficient, they were limited as to how much power they could produce since the dynamo could turn only so fast in this arrangement. A steam turbine, however, eliminated the engine entirely. A coal-fired boiler would heat water to create a high-pressure stream that would turn the blades in the turbine, whose shaft was directly connected to the dynamo. Instead of being 40 percent efficient in its conversion of heat and motion to electricity, the new unit could be 80 percent efficient. Less coal was needed, the turbine could turn faster and create more power. It was a relatively simple principle that is essentially still in use today in every coal-, gas-, and oil-fired power plant.

Upon returning to Chicago in 1902, Insull commanded his consulting engineer, the legendary power plant designer Fred Sargent, and his vice president Louis Ferguson to retrace his path to Germany and advise him on how Chicago Edison could build a steam-turbine plant. On his end, Insull began negotiations with Coffin to build what he wanted at GE. Sargent and Ferguson gave him conservative advice: start with a small unit and build it in the outmoded Harrison Street station. That was not what Insull wanted to hear. He had just secured the contract to supply power for the Lake Street elevated line to Oak Park from Chicago and was on the verge of obtaining the contract to supply power for the *entire* elevated Chicago transit system. Such a large customer would require a generator that did not exist in the engineer's minds. Insull would not be denied as he envisioned his company supplying power for the entire metropolitan area, something no producer had done before. That was Edison's dream, although the wizard never had the means nor the technology to make that dream come true. Insull did.

"My mind was running upon supplying all the energy in centers of population," Insull told his board of directors. "I realized that this could only be obtained from highly economical power stations resulting in a very low cost of energy, competing against privately owned uneconomical steam plants. The opportunity to get this large power business was right at my threshold and I knew that unless I built the most economical power station possible, that opportunity would be lost."

Coffin must have choked on his coffee when Insull told him that he wanted a five-megawatt turbine, which was more than twice as large as what Westinghouse, the leader in AC turbines, had in operation. It certainly was not sitting in a warehouse in Schenectady waiting to be shipped. Such a thing entailed a great deal of risk, so Insull cut a deal. If Coffin would take the turbine back if it did not work, he would completely cover the installation costs. Both men risked their reputations on the turbine. Insull had essentially promised power he could not deliver if the generator did not work; Coffin would suffer a humiliating loss of engineering prestige and give the Westinghouse camp a good laugh.

The site of where Insull wanted to build his supergenerator was unassuming. Like the Harrison Street station, the flat parcel hugged the turgid Chicago River for a ready supply of water. There were no trees around and only a few blocks north of the pungent Union Stockyards, where thousands of head of cattle awaited their final destination. Fisk Street was a quiet street in an industrial district in an area known as Pilsen, which was Czech at the time and would produce a future mayor in Anton "Tony" Cermak, the boss of the Cook County Democratic organization in the 1930s (the road on which the plant was situated would later be renamed Cermak Road).

Insull and Sargent were skittish about throwing the switch for Unit #1 at the Fisk Street station. Although it had been a little over 20 years since Edison had thrown the switch in J.P Morgan's office to bring Pearl Street on line, now Insull felt as Edison did, only with considerably less of the world's attention focused on him, and certainly not in a white coat with tails. Coffin must have felt the jitters as well. The biggest generator GE had built prior to Fisk Street had been only 600 kilowatts, producing an eighth of the power of the Fisk unit.

The building itself was ornate for a power station, featuring graceful three-story mullioned arched windows and terra cotta ornamentation. Inside the generator room, streetlights lit the cavernous space. The turbine generator itself was a steel octopus, with pipes coming out of the bottom. Looking like something out of a Jules Verne novel, brass railings ringed the top and lower section of the unit. Oval-shaped openings on the turbine made it look like a strange nautical vessel landlocked in the middle of a cathedral of power. Coal could be shipped to the adjacent boiler room, which was separated by a thick fireproof wall for safety. High-sulfur Illinois coal was either barged up the river through the Sanitary and Ship Canal, which fed into the Illinois River, or brought up by train.

The river water was used for cooling. The plant was equipped with eight boilers for the new unit with 40 tons of coal.

On October 2, 1903, the moment had arrived to throw the switch. Sargent asked Insull if he wanted to stay when the unit was engaged.

"Fred, what do you think is going to happen?" Insull asked.

"I don't know, but it might blow up and you better go out," said Sargent with a concerned expression.

"There is just as much reason for *you* leaving here as my leaving here! Is the thing going to blow up?"

"No! My being here is in line with my duty," Sargent said with a military air. "I don't think it's going to blow up, but I don't know."

"Well, I'm going to stay. If you are to be blown up, then I would prefer to be blown up with you as, if the turbine should fail, I should be blown up anyway."

With that, the men winced as the giant generator heaved, made an unearthly noise and generated power. For Insull, the first run was significant because it allowed him to fulfill his promise to the transit system, the largest electrical customer at the time. Both Insull and Sargent knew that the first unit would be one of many because it was not all that efficient and the technology would be refined. Yet what had happened that day was the equivalent of taking a space program from orbiting around the earth to orbiting around the moon. The new unit produced twice as much power as any steam engine ever built— about 11,000 horsepower. From that point on, Chicago was on its way to becoming the most energy-intensive place in the world. Insull immediately ordered two more generators and demanded units that were five times as large, which were well beyond GE's and Westinghouse's engineering prowess in 1903. Such a machine could only be built by Parsons in England. While the 24-megawatt unit became more or less a standard prior to 1910, within a decade Insull was installing 120-megawatt generators. That pitted GE against Siemens and Westinghouse in a constant fight to upgrade efficiency while increasing power output, a battle that is still being waged today.

With the Fisk Street installation, there was no limit to how much power he could sell to any number of customers in factories, offices, stores, and homes. Bigger units would be ordered and built. Now all he had to do was find the money to keep financing expansion and convince customers of all stripes that the future was here and could be piped into every building. The world's largest turbogenerator also ended the reliance on the steam engine to drive turbines. Now the two machines were unified in a powerful whole. While still powered by king coal, at least half of the Steam Age was now history and the modern metropolis was burgeoning along the routes of high-voltage lines.

The concept behind steam turbines is still dominant in the U.S., accounting for more than 60 percent of all power generated. The technology that Insull commissioned is also still very much in use and has been upgraded through thousands of refinements. The present Fisk Street station, operated by Edison International's Midwest Generation LLC, employs a boiler that is fired by low-sulfur coal from the Powder River Basin in Wyoming, the largest coal-producing region in the U.S. The coal is crushed to a powder that has the consistency of flour to improve combustion efficiency, then burned to create steam at the temperature of 2,700 degrees fahrenheit. The steam is then piped to spin the turbines on the generator at speeds of up to 3,600 revolutions per minute. A 550-foot smokestack still sits on top of the plant, which is visible when you drive into the city from the south or southwest. While hardly emitting pristine gases, the plant now burns coal that contains 0.4 percent sulfur, versus 3.5 percent sulfur from the now-unused Illinois coal fields. Coal-fired or "fossil" plants in general became a major source of air pollution in Insull's time and still imperil the health of the industrialized world.

The soaring skyscrapers of downtown are visible from the site, which has become a national engineering landmark. Dignitaries such as Edison and Britain's King George and Queen Mary visited the plant, which was something of a tourist attraction in the first decade of the twentieth century. The plant would be subject to numerous fits and starts involving several shutdowns and repairs. The turbines would often throw off sparks and produce minor explosions. One time a janitor was up on one of the turbines polishing the brass rails when "a rupture took place with a terrific report and a vast cloud of smoke, causing the janitor to scramble from the top of the generator to the floor . . . he issued a general fistic invitation, especially to the switchboard operator, who, he believed, had made him the victim of a practical joke."

While industrial safety has improved dramatically in the past century—some half million workers died in industrial accidents in 1907—seven men have died in the plant since 1938, including a fireman whose ghost is said to haunt the building. The first accidents involved accidental electrocutions in late 1903. The brave workers are memorialized on a garden plaque between the old generator room and an adjacent switch house.

The year that Insull made turbine power a reality on a large scale was an *annus mirabilis* in the history of innovation. Two bicycle mechanics from Ohio completed the first self-propelled airplane flight on Kill Devil Hill in

North Carolina. Orville and Wilbur Wright had been struggling for years, but they joined Henry Ford, who incorporated the Ford Motor Company in 1903 with $28,000 in capital. There were only about 8,000 cars in the entire country at that time and 144 miles of paved road. The average wage was 22 cents an hour, with the average worker making about $400 a year. About 10 percent of the population was illiterate and 95 percent of all births were at home. Oklahoma, Arizona, New Mexico, Alaska, and Hawaii had not been admitted to the union yet. There were 30 people living in a desert village called Las Vegas. The following year, sociologist Max Weber would publish a seminal work entitled *The Protestant Work Ethic and the Spirit of Capitalism* on why people like Edison, Ford, and Insull were so successful.

As it had been with Insull, Ford was inspired and encouraged by Edison, who had dissuaded Ford from starting his business with an electric car. Ford had sketched his idea for a car powered by an internal combustion engine on the back of a restaurant menu during a dinner meeting with the wizard.

"Young man," Edison said, pounding the table. "That's the thing! You have it—the self-contained unit carrying its fuel with it! Keep at it!"

Ford produced his first Model T on his new assembly line and sold it to the public for $400. Ford, like Insull, was interested in firmly controlling his operation, lowering prices, and making his product available to the masses. The two men had met a few times, including at the first dinner at which Ford showed his idea to Edison. Ford and Edison became close friends, even bringing tiremaker Harvey Firestone into their circle as Edison became increasingly interested in developing technologies for the nascent automotive business in the last ten years of his life. Five years later, Insull would forsake his electric cars and buy an automobile—a Buick.

Seizing the momentum of the Fisk Street start-up, Insull now had the power generation capacity to serve a much larger area than downtown Chicago. As Einstein was theorizing the existence of the time-space continuum, divining the nature of light, and explaining how everything was relative in the universe, Insull was harnessing the power of electromagnetism to transform cities into interconnected metropolitan grids.

Five years after opening Fisk, Insull had powered up the new Quarry Street station on the river a few blocks south of Fisk, running with six 24-megawatt turbines. GE's Coffin was on hand to throw the switch. While his power plant

building program continued apace, Insull was buying small power companies
throughout the area. He was heartily backed by Chicago Edison's board of directors, which included the lawyer Robert Todd Lincoln, the son of the president. Lincoln's partner William Beale was also instrumental in writing contracts
and securing financing.

One of Insull's financial innovations was the creation of an open-ended
mortgage. Up until the inception of this vehicle, each project had to be financed
separately through the sale of bonds or stocks. The bond-backed, open-ended
mortgage was like an ever-expanding line of credit with the banks that was not
tied to any one expenditure, so it was flexible. Scouting around Chicago's suburbs, Insull was able to finance the purchase of several power plants that he combined into another company called Commonwealth Electric, which operated
using the open mortgage and had owned the Fisk Street plant.

Local bankers had never seen an open mortgage before, so they were reluctant to deal with Insull in buying his bonds. Using the influence of Beale and
the salesmanship of Chicago Edison director Edward Brewster's brokerage
house, Insull was able to place the bonds. While initially encountering resistance
from the Chicago banking community, Insull also had a difficult time convinc-
ing the Chicago Edison board to extend mortgage financing beyond $6 million.
He needed more money for his expansion plans, so he went to London to secure more capital and somewhat regretted that he had not gone to New York for
funds. The House of Morgan was watching Insull's business grow and was wondering when they would be called to participate in the creation of what was becoming the nation's largest single power producer.

Controlling the entire Chicago metropolitan power supply was now within
Insull's grasp. In 1902 he had consolidated several small power companies in the
northern suburbs to create the North Shore Electric Company. His reach now
extended 30 miles from the city's center and was venturing into the countryside.
He sensed that there was no reason why the power interests of the city should
be any different than those of the country. Defying the conventional wisdom in
his industry that it was foolish to invest in rural power stations, he began what
he called the "Lake County Experiment." The county immediately north of
Cook County, which encompassed Chicago, could be wired for electricity and
serve sparsely populated towns. While the technical means were not at hand yet,
there was no reason to believe that one station could serve a large area that included everything from homes to farms. It was a prescient idea that was later
embraced by Franklin Delano Roosevelt in creating the Tennessee Valley Authority and the Rural Electrification Administration more than 30 years later.

Insull continued his acquisitions of small, rural power companies, reaching as far south as the Ohio River, where he bought two power stations and a trolley line in New Albany and Jeffersonville, Indiana. Insull sent his brother Martin down to run the companies.

Insull knew that farmers and small towns needed power just as much as city people, and wanted it for the same reasons: illumination, public safety, and productivity. As he later told his peers in the utility industry:

> It should be borne in mind that cheap power is as essential to the farmer as it is to the manufacturer. This same policy has brought cheap power within the reach of manufacturing institutions, be they ever so small, established in country districts, and opened up the possibility of the establishment of larger manufacturing businesses in rural communities which would give employment to the families of the farmers adjacent to those communities.[6]

How ironic that Insull the "natural monopoly" power baron was espousing the views of a progressive Democrat a generation before rural electrification would become a well-funded national program. The benefit that electrification bestowed upon exurban communities was enormous. Every indoor farming activity could be done under electric lighting. Milking could be done much more efficiently with electric milking devices. Refrigeration would keep everything from milk to meat fresh for months. Machine tools did not need to be hooked up to awkward belts that were connected to the power takeoffs of tractors. Farmers would have 24-hour power for water pumps, silage fans, and nearly any piece of electrically powered equipment. Smokehouses would no longer be needed to preserve meat. Farmers would not have to wait for the iceman to deliver huge blocks of ice for small ice boxes. Washing and ironing would not take two days. Most farms could not even afford hand-operated clothes wringers, anyway. Ironing consisted of putting a flat "sad" iron on a hot stove and waiting until it warmed up. It was a tedious, hazardous, and time-consuming process that occupied women in endless hours of daily chores. Best of all, with electricity, farmers could throw out dangerous oil and kerosene lamps, which were carried from room to room in the farmhouses and into barns, where they often started catastrophic fires.

Power transported outside of cities gave economic leverage to the country. Cities no longer were the exclusive domains of heavy industry. Manufacturing plants could be located anywhere they could be connected to the power grid, which became a reality a few years after Insull conceived it. It was all about building infrastructure. While someone could have come along to conceive their own version of the Lake County Experiment, it was Insull who believed in it, financed it, and made it happen.

In the city, the Insull plan was hitting some snags. The city council was discussing regulating Insull's utilities while his companies were negotiating to supply power to the fractious trolley lines. His companies were selling power at 16 cents a kilowatt-hour (more than twice the average cost today). Insull was afraid the city would set a flat rate at 10 cents an hour, which would cause his companies to lose $400,000 a year. Rate cutting, though, was always Insull's cudgel against "agitators" who pressed for extensive regulation and municipal ownership. He would consistently argue that private concerns like his were always more efficient than municipal corporations and announce a rate cut whenever political sentiment seemed to be favoring municipal ownership. By 1906 he had already cut rates by 20 percent, and would invoke a rate cut whenever he thought it would gain the company political leverage and good public relations. Rate cutting was also good for business since it brought in new customers. New accounts translated into a greater "load factor" for his power plants. They could run longer and more efficiently if there were more power customers.

In Chicago Edison's burgeoning advertising department, which was started by Insull in 1901, the use of electricity as well as the use of electrical appliances was promoted to increase the load factor and profitability of residential accounts. The company began to send out regular mailers and circulars explaining the advantage of "fans, motors, signs, and other electrical appliances," which are known to be "excellent load builders." Three years later the company invested in a $40,000 direct-mail campaign prepared by the Bates Advertising Company of New York. It was one of the first direct-mail campaigns undertaken by an American utility. The previous year, former newspaperman and Chicago Edison promotional guru John Gilchrist started *Electric City,* a glossy magazine that promoted the lifestyle and workplace advantages of electric power. Gilchrist cleverly placed mahogany distribution cabinets in drugstores in exchange for wiring the retailers for electricity. The magazine continued publishing until 1917, when it was shut down because of high printing costs during World War I. Gilchrist would be the consummate planner of most of Insull's promotional campaigns. He got his start through his plan of installing six free outlets in any home that signed a contract for a year's worth of electricity. Homeowners who felt they got a deal often ended up wiring their entire homes and buying appliances from Chicago Edison. Gilchrist would then follow up by sending trucks and salesmen to the "wired" neighborhoods to either give away or sell fans and irons. Once households had one useful appliance, they craved more. The nascent consumer culture became electrified.

Rampant efficiency improvements at Fisk Street convinced Insull that building and improving the station was "the greatest thing which has happened in our business. In the months of November and December, we produced power at Fisk at a lower cost than any plant I have ever heard of using coal as a basis of power production. Our balance sheets for the year will show up very well."

Seeing the fertile fields and scattered farms of Lake County reminded Insull of his beloved English countryside. It triggered a latent idea inside of him. He could now do something that his father and almost no one in his family had been able to do—become a noble squire and own and manage a country estate. Having the means to purchase land, he bought a farm near Libertyville, Illinois, about 35 miles northwest of Chicago. The farm came with a large, white-framed four-square farmhouse with fringed awnings, wraparound screen porch, and 160 acres of some of the richest soil on the continent.

By 1907, Insull had become landed gentry with his spacious apartment in the city and farm in the country. His family moved into what would be known as "Hawthorn Farm." Bisected by unpaved Milwaukee Avenue and the Elgin, Joliet & Eastern railroad, the farm property was near the Chicago, Milwaukee & St. Paul railroad, also known as the Milwaukee Road. His neighbors consisted of the great "old money" families of Chicago business. Joseph Medill Patterson, whose family founded the *Chicago Tribune*, bordered his property to the south; the Armours and Swifts of the meatpacking fortunes were to the east; the Mc-Cormicks were on the lake; and the Ryersons, who prospered in steel, stayed near the McCormicks.

Insull was enamored of the idea of the farm, but likely spent little time there during the week. It would have taken hours to drive downtown in the absence of major, paved roads, much less expressways, and no direct commuter trains were running yet. Gladys often spent days alone with Chappie and the servants, even when they were residing in their spacious city apartment. For a career woman who had led a cosmopolitan life where she was often the center of attention, it was maddening. In the country the local towns were modest clumps of homes with dirt roads as main streets. During the "mud season" between February and June, the roads were nearly impassable. There were no theaters or restaurants nearby. Libertyville, nestled on several hills where Milwaukee Avenue rolled through the middle of the village, was a market town for central Lake County. Having gone through several name changes from Burlington to Independence Grove, it was once the county seat before the seat was moved to Waukegan to the east. Local legend had it that local Native

Americans had told the French voyageur La Salle that there were magical mineral springs somewhere near the Des Plaines River to the east, which La Salle was exploring in the seventeenth century.

A trip to Europe the following year refreshed Insull's relationship with Gladys somewhat, although living in a farmhouse away from the city was not what she had in mind when she married him. They were becoming estranged. Insull, seizing upon the sentiment that perhaps his wife did not have a home that she could truly call her own, decided to build her a country mansion befitting their stature. He expanded his farm by buying out neighbors, eventually owning 4,000 acres. Now he needed the manor home to go with it, and he set out to find architects who could build a suitable castle.

A viscount of the machine age deserved an enlightened approach to home design and building. "The art of the future will be the expression of the individual artist through the thousand powers of the machine," proclaimed Frank Lloyd Wright in 1900, who was designing every possible use of electricity into his prairie homes. The architect was more than just incorporating artsy lighting fixtures into his commissions. Light became part of an organic whole. Now the incandescent light looked as if it had always been in his homes alongside fireplaces and custom furniture. The fullest expression of Wright's prairie style came to fruition in the house he designed for Frederick Robie, a bicycle and auto parts manufacturer who lived next to the University of Chicago. The 1910 Robie house, reclining on its city lot like a giant chaise lounge, featured cantilevered porches and generous windows. Often said to resemble an abstract steamship, the horizontal house does more than reside on a piece of land, it glides in a suggested motion. It is as fluid as the machine age itself. Inside, the large rooms convey a sense of space and light without sacrificing intimacy. In addition to the Wright-designed furniture and light fixtures, it is equipped with every electrical convenience, including a central vacuum system, a feature that Insull would install in his new home.

Like Insull, Wright was a beguiling self-promoter. As Insull was peddling electricity to the masses through direct-mail pieces, circulars, cards in power bill mailings and magazines, Wright was advertising in the *Ladies Home Journal* in 1907 that he could build "a fireproof house for $5,000," which was a somewhat affordable price for a architect-designed home at the time. Inspired by the Arts and Craft aesthetic that moved Wright in his early years, bungalows and cottage-style homes would blanket Chicago and the suburbs. Insull made sure that they were eventually all wired for electricity. Unlike Wright, who had built nearly all of his first homes for wealthy or upper-middle-class clients, Insull wanted everyone to have power.

While it is not known if Insull ever saw the Robie house or met Wright, they would have known of each other's work. When Wright left his wife and five children in Oak Park for the wife of a client (Mamah Cheney), Wright would turn his practice over to Hermann Valentin von Holst, who would later design buildings for Insull.

The Lake County Experiment took on a life of its own and became a blueprint for acquiring and consolidating other power firms ringing the city. North Shore Electric acquired 11 small power companies nearby, and it occurred to Insull that they all could be connected to create a more efficient producer. He took the experiment into a new phase by seeing if 22 communities in Lake County could be profitably served by one large central station. He shuttered the local power plants that had provided dusk-to-midnight service for towns that generally had populations no larger than 300. All told, he hoped to serve some 23,000 county residents and 125 farms by 1910. He was also serving communities west and south of the city by buying power plants in Joliet, Elmhurst, LaGrange, Oak Park, and Kankakee. By 1911, the large number of small utilities became un-wieldy to manage, so he combined them and put them under the holding company umbrella of his Middle West Utilities, of which Martin Insull was appointed president.

Having captured most of the metropolitan area's electrical territory by 1912, Insull had more operations to manage in every part of the Chicago region, which kept him away even more than during the early days of his marriage when he was only running Chicago Edison and one power plant. Gladys was now considering closing her bedroom door to the mogul, signaling a break from her phantom relationship. Accepting an invitation to visit her friend Mrs. Benjamin Carpenter in Atlantic City, New Jersey, she left for a brief respite, only to be suddenly called back when Chappie was diagnosed with scarlet fever.

Gladys rushed back to find her son near death. Defying the orders of his doctors that she stay away and let a nurse handle the situation—lest she become infected—Gladys rushed into his room at the farm and took charge. Insull obeyed the quarantine, often shouting up to his son's bedroom window to check on his family. Three nurses attempted to pull Chappie back from the brink. There were no modern antibiotics and the disease was generally regarded as a death sentence. Gladys scrubbed his entire room in a vain attempt to eradicate any traces of microbes. Then she scoured the entire house with formaldehyde, the leading antiseptic in 1912. Her hands bled from the caustic liquid and cleaning.

After three months of waiting, cleaning, and nursing, Chappie's fever began to rise without abatement. His heart stopped beating, prompting one of the nurses to pick him up and start frantically pounding his chest. He was revived after he was deemed clinically dead for about a minute and a half. From that point, Chappie began to recover and the quarantine ended within a month. Insull, having tired of occupying his time planting trees and fretting outside the house, was back to work, taking an interest in the electric interurban railroads that were beginning to create commuter suburbs.

The experience of Chappie's illness, compounded by Insull's increasing time spent at work and Gladys's alienation, splintered the Insulls' marriage. After her son's near-death, she declared that Chappie "stopped being Sam's son. He was mine." She then barred Insull from her bedroom, as she had probably never savored the conjugal part of their marriage, or at least what little there was of it. Perhaps she even hated him more for bestowing almost all of his considerable energy and emotion on his businesses. Gladys and Sam had become strangers, and nearly everyone who saw them together seemed to notice.

A much greater conflict was imminent in Europe, though; one that would position Insull in a new role.

A NEW KIND OF POWER

Insull Builds His Image

Power begets wealth; and added wealth opens ever new opportunities for the acquisition of wealth and power.

—Louis Brandeis, *Other People's Money and How the Bankers Use It*[1]

Although coming from a family of Puritans, Insull more than admired the tantalizing soprano Mary Garden and he supported efforts by the Chicago opera company to promote her career. Since she lived to sing and promote her art, no amount of criticism bothered her, as long as she was able to create her roles and deliver to the public the kind of performance that no other artist could render. Her personality was a fortress in an era when the Victorian ethos was being challenged at every turn, particularly in bawdy Chicago. Refused to be tied down through marriage or through her affairs, she proclaimed, "I wanted liberty and went my own way. . . . I had a fondness for men, yes, but very little passion and no need."

With her brooding, deep-set eyes, Olympian posture, and prominent Scottish nose, in appearance Mary could not have been mistaken for anything other than the Hera of the operatic stage, a goddess among mere mortals. Insull was moved because she sang with such conviction, unwavering emotion, and titanic presence. There was no one else who could be compared with her as she glided on the stage, singing operatic roles that she owned so completely that you would forget about every other singer who had performed them. As an independent, unfettered woman, she did as she pleased, traveled when and where she wanted, and never lacked for work. When she took the stage at the Auditorium Theater,

Insull knew that he was not just attending the opera; he was in for a novel experience that tugged at his soul.

Here was a person who had a will and dedication to her business as strong as his own, Insull noted when watching how she handled scandal and wretched reviews and recovered flawlessly to mount her next production. He was learning from her the way he learned from P.T. Barnum, the nineteenth century promoter, lecturer, circus man, and publicity genius. In the middle of his career, Barnum had promoted Jenny Lind, "the Swedish Nightingale," whose voice was so powerful and emotive it made hundreds of thousands weep. Insull had seen and met Barnum in 1878—personally asking him to lecture before his London literary society with a hilarious speech entitled "The World Upside Down." Insull would later follow Barnum's compelling methods of promotion in selling electricity. For Garden and Barnum, there was never such a thing as bad publicity. Insull's stunning march to sell power to the world would advance on reversing negative images of him and his industry at nearly every turn. Mary Garden provided a model, particularly when she rebounded after performances that had been either panned or banned outright.

Insull had been an opera lover since his early days in London as an aspiring clerk. At Convent Garden, he saw the soprano Adelina Patti, who later appeared at the Auditorium for her farewell tour. As someone who wanted to improve himself in every way, Insull read classic literature and listened to good music. A gentleman needed to be able to discuss the latest composers and their operas. A major captain of business needed to go one step further to understand the major players in the arts, travel in their circles, and become a patron himself. Sitting in his center, main floor seat at the Auditorium would not pass muster for Chicago society. To be able to look through the monocles of the McCormicks, Fields, and Pullmans, he needed to take a much more active role, so he joined the opera board, learning the basics of arts management.

By the time of World War I, the "war to end all wars," the Chicago Grand Opera was a struggling organization that needed Insull's management talents. Owing to constant financial problems, there was always the possibility that the company could not pay its performers or staff and the curtain would not rise. There were only a handful of wealthy subscribers, and the season was only two to three weeks depending upon how many patrons there were. Season ticket holders were rare, although Insull was among one of the few stalwarts. The cavernous Auditorium was virtually empty most of the time. In an era in which there was little competition for big entertainment venues—there were no movies, radio, or TV—grand opera was still a musical spectacle to behold. It was (and still is) an art form that combines drama, music, and stagecraft to great effect. With the electrification of the staging process, opera singers and productions with their epic themes of lost love, revolution, and war became bigger than life. Follow spotlights could trace the path of the leading singers as they moved on stage. The dim footlights were replaced by an array of electric stage lighting effects. As the technology developed, entire sets could be moved up and down by electrical and hydraulic means through the stage floor.

While the technology improved steadily, to be an opera singer one still needed a powerful, clear voice to project into the bowels of the opera house and a personality to match. It was not, and still is not, a medium for the meek. Mary Garden was more than an opera singer and diva. She did not merely command the stage, she *commandeered* it. Insull appreciated her ability to mold the audience and public opinion to her ends.

It was Claude Debussy, the poetic impressionist composer, who choose Mary in 1902 to sing Melisande in his opera *Pelleas et Melisande.* Over the protests of the librettist Maurice Maeterlinck—who wanted his mistress cast in the role—Debussy walked Mary Garden through the part by playing the score on a piano with his long, graceful fingers. The music glistened like twilight, rose and fell like the crest of a wave, and conveyed deep emotion. Mary studied the sad story of Melisande, who hastily marries Prince Goulad then falls in love with his half brother Pelleas, triggering a series of tragedies. Although the music managed to capture the light, tone, and chromatic mastery of the French impressionist masters Renoir, Monet, and Degas, it was scandalous music for the time, defying conventional rules of opera and composition.

While Mary tried to master the difficulty and beauty of the score, one professor at the Paris Conservatoire derided it as a "filthy score" riddled with "errors of harmony." Like the impressionist painters, who had a difficult time establishing themselves toward the end of the nineteenth century—Manet's masterpiece *Olympia* was hung so high so that viewers were hard-pressed to see it—Debussy was branded a radical and not given a fair hearing for his luminous score. Although it was finished in 1895, it was not produced until 1902. Mary recalled the first hearing of the score with Debussy at the piano:

When Debussy got to the fourth act, I could no longer look at my score for the tears. It was all very strange and unbearable. I closed my book and just listened to him, and as he played the death of Melisande, I burst into the most awful sobbing.[2]

After rehearsing, Debussy realized that Mary not only was a quick study, she had internalized the nuances of his music. "I have nothing, absolutely nothing, to tell her. In some mysterious way, she knows or senses everything." She continued to refine her role, even traveling to England with the composer of *La Mer* to see Sarah Bernhardt perform in the original play upon which the opera was based. The greatest actress of her age was to have a profound influence on Mary, who would be known internationally for her ability to interpret a role as an actress and singer.

Chicago had nurtured Mary, a native of Aberdeen, Scotland, in a way that her native land could not. Under the patronage of Florence and David Mayer, a wealthy couple whose family was running a leading Chicago department store, Mary was sent to Paris to study opera. Although she had a stormy relationship with the couple, the training transformed her into a world-class soprano. Known to her family as "Molly," Mary was the first of four daughters born to Robert Davidson Garden and Mary Joss. She had changed her birth year to 1877 from 1874 since she was born only a month after her parents were married. As a five-year-old, she was able to sing the folk song "Three Little Redcaps Growing in the Corn." Her father barely made a living in the North Scotland coastal town, so the Gardens moved to America in 1880, settling variously in Brooklyn; Chicopee, Massachusetts; and Chicago. In the Windy City, Robert was able to land a position with Colonel George Pope's bicycle company. The striking, auburn-haired Mary sang for Pope after a dinner at the Garden home. That led to the suggestion that Mary study with Mrs. Robinson Duff, a local opera teacher who had just returned from Paris. After singing difficult Rossini arias in her Chicago debut at the Central Music Hall, she met Florence Mayer, another pupil of Mrs. Duff. When her family moved East so that her father could take another position in Hartford, Connecticut, Mary stayed in Chicago to continue her studies and sing at local recitals until she left for Paris in 1896 with Mrs. Duff.

After her premiere of *Pelleas,* Mary returned to America to take on the most controversial role of the day: Richard Strauss's *Salome.* The original play had been written for Sarah Bernhardt by Oscar Wilde, the *enfant terrible* of the stage who had dared to portray the eroticism of *Salome* through her infamous dance of the seven veils. What would be considered a trifle today was the artistic scandal of the early twentieth century. Sexuality was being examined front and center on the stages of Europe, in the salons of Vienna, and through the naturalism of Chicago writers like Dreiser. The bohemians of Paris, living lascivious, wanton lifestyles in Paris, fueled the revolt against Victorian mores. Freud was contributing to the fray by examining repressed sexual urges in his psychoanalytic theory.

Conveying sexuality on a large stage was a relatively new concept in grand opera. Having the outsized persona and vocal chords was not enough to convince audiences that you were falling in love, dying or leading a charge. You still needed to be able to act, which was not something that opera singers had much training in, since they typically had to concentrate on how to manage their voices above an orchestra and find new ways of adding subtle textures to the music. Sexuality on the stage was limited to embraces, longing stares, and chaste stage kisses—until Mary came along.

In her role as *prima donna assoluta,* the queen of the lyric soprano's repertoire, Mary was the consummate performer. Combining a genuine brilliance for publicity with a voice and acting style that could bring audiences to tears, she was the true innovator in opera in her day. She was to grand opera what Insull was to power plants. This rare and volatile mix of talent, panache, and sheer will must have made Insull realize that he was witnessing a peer, a soul on fire who was changing the world of her art.

Debuting in Oscar Hammerstein's Manhattan Opera House (then the rival to the Metropolitan Opera), there was little Mary left to chance as she gave her *Salome* to New Yorkers in French on January 28, 1909. She carefully studied a Greek version of the dance of the seven veils, sensuously flinging off the layers of her diaphanous costume. The final scene, in which Salome is crushed to death by the shields of Roman soldiers, left Gothamites in stunned silence.

"A conception of incarnate bestiality so powerful had been realized by Miss Garden that it was a dreadful thing to contemplate," the *New York Herald* scowled. Her next show in Philadelphia was greeted by an official protest from local clergy. Rumors made it into the press that she had an illegitimate child in Paris and had lived a life of abandon. Stung by the rumors and embarrassed by her notoriety in *Salome,* the Mayers filed suit to reclaim the $20,000 they spent on her musical training. Mary paid them back in cash and later coldly looked away as Florence Mayer extended her hand in reconciliation in the foyer of the Manhattan Opera House.

When Mary first arrived in Chicago as a full-fledged international star, the Chicago Opera Association was being shepherded by Harold and Edith Rockefeller McCormick, who were the guarantors. As a board member, Insull was observing and formulating a strategy on how to put the opera on a sounder financial footing. He also was studying every move of Mary's as she deftly handled crisis after crisis. After a successful debut in Pelleas in Chicago in 1909, she premiered *Salome* on November 25, 1910, in the second city. Once again, the veils wafted onto the stage with a powerful affect—a "vision of grace but the ferocity of her passion that finally consumed itself was strange and terrible," one review read. The chief of police Leroy Steward had a less diplomatic appraisal: "It was disgusting. . . . Miss Garden wallowed around like a cat in a bed of catnip. I think that the way Miss Garden rolls on the floor with the decapitated and supposedly bloody head [of John the Baptist] is revolting." Edith McCormick shut down *Salome* after two performances, replacing the saucy opera with the less-controversial *Pelleas*. A furious Mary went to Insull, who was on the opera board, for an appeal.

"I'll have to change the performance if you don't get her [McCormick] to permit the fourth performance," Mary told Insull.

"I'll see what I can do," he replied. Insull pleaded with McCormick to change her mind and failed.

"My vibrations were all wrong," McCormick said, crossing her hands on her breast. She would not allow *Salome* to be performed as long as she controlled the purse strings of the opera.

Mary milked the furor over *Salome,* expressing her outrage by protesting to the newspapers that she would never perform *Salome* in Chicago again.

"Some horrid person sent me a package of catnip," she told the papers. "Wasn't *that* disgusting?" Taking *Salome* on the road, the opera was banned in Baltimore and canceled in Toledo when the other cast members refused to perform and Milwaukee was nonplussed. On tour, she had heard that she was being likened to the devil in one of the shows given by evangelist Billy Sunday, the bombastic tent preacher who was known in popular song as the man who "couldn't shut down Chicago." She sat in on one of his sermons, in which he did not mention her. Nevertheless, she walked backstage. It was a blistering summer day and Sunday was soaked with perspiration.

"Mr. Billy Sunday?" Mary asked with authority.

"I don't think I know you, Madam," the preacher said.

"I am Mary Garden." Sunday looked confused then disgusted. He had been ranting for hours about the evils of modern society. "What have you been preaching about me and *Salome?*"

"I'm *not* going to tell you."

"But I *must* know," she insisted. "I'm sure you're telling people lies about me. What have you said about *Salome?*"

"Miss Garden, that's a very sinful opera."

"It's all in the way you take it. Will you stop talking about me and have you got a drink of water?"

"No, but will you come on out and have a drink with me?"

Sunday took Mary to a local drugstore, where they had ice cream sodas and Mary discovered Sunday had a sense of humor. Getting up to leave, she had the last word.

"I'm not afraid of you, Billy Sunday, or *anybody*, and I think the best thing to do when you hear people saying anything against you is to go and face them."

"Miss Garden, I agree, and it's been a pleasure meeting you. I guess I've been hearing a lot of lies about you."[3]

Back in Chicago, Mary had become something of a celebrated martyr and ticket sales boomed for her subsequent productions. She was now "Our Mary" in the Chicago press, which heralded a singing career that became a local institution for the next two decades. At times Chicago seemed like the last refuge on earth for people exiled from other places who held dangerous ideas and exerted strange powers over a restive populace. Deep down, Chicago adored rebels who upset old regimes.

When he was traveling in England on business in 1912, Insull was keenly aware of the European situation and inserted himself into the politics of prewar England. At the time, pacifists dominated the Liberal Party, and like most Americans, the party was not interested in entering into any new European conflicts. Insull had heard discussion of the government taking over the railroads (which were eventually nationalized) with his eye on the ramifications for public ownership of utilities in America. Progressives in the U.S., battling the power of the trusts, had launched some effective, in-depth attacks against the tightly controlled corporate interests, which held huge blocks of stocks in the banks, railroads, steel, and other heavy industries. The concentration of corporate power stifled competition, suppressed unions, and kept wages down. While Insull had almost no problems with his workforce, he was constantly worried about the public takeover of his utilities, which had been debated on and off in the Chicago city council. There were no credible challenges to his power before World War I. It would be another 15 years before the specter of public ownership would rear its head.

A growing chorus of trustbusters, led by Theodore Roosevelt and muckrakers like Ida Tarbell, whose classic study of Standard Oil argued for the breakup of Rockefeller's empire, was gaining momentum and achieving some victories. Roosevelt had taken a stand against the "great malefactors of wealth," a position that was reinforced by his successor William Howard Taft, whose administration prosecuted the trusts, many of which were formed or financed by the Morgan bankers. In the years before World War I, the Progressive Era sounded the alarm against the concentration of wealth. The famous Pujo Committee hearings exposed much of the power structure of the trusts. J.P. Morgan himself spent several hours before the committee. The strain of the appearance was said to lead to his death a year later. The finance giant, with his hideous nose, bloodstone on a chain, glaring eyes, and square-topped derby, formed or consolidated General Electric, U.S. Steel, and countless railroads.

Louis Brandeis, the future Supreme Court justice, discovered another secret of how the trusts controlled a mountain of companies. Interlocking directorates, "the root of many evils" that intimately linked the bankers to the trusts, were "the most potent instrument of the money trust." In his 1914 classic *Other People's Money*, Brandeis showed the connections between the Morgan bank and several railroads, GE, Western Union, American Telephone & Telegraph, and U.S. Steel:

> The prohibition of interlocking directorates, even if applied only to all banks and trust companies, would practically compel the Morgan representatives to resign from the directorates of the 13 banking institutions with which they are connected, or from the directorates of all of the railroads, steamship, public utility, manufacturing, and other corporations which do business with those bank and trust companies. . . . Before the Money Trust can be broken, all these relations must be severed.[4]

As the man who gave the world the phrase "sunlight is the greatest disinfectant," (referring to corporate disclosure), Brandeis not only pushed for greater corporate regulation, he wanted the public to know how much the largest corporations were steered by just a few industrial admirals. As World War I began, Brandeis heralded President Wilson's warning in concluding in *Other People's Money* that "No country can afford to have its prosperity originated by a small controlling class. . . . Every country is renewed out of the ranks of the unknown, not out of the ranks of the already famous and powerful in its control."

The Gilded Age of the trusts, though, was shedding its skin and being transformed into the age of the holding company. Brandeis was already seeing the flaws in the new corporate structure. Holding companies were in many ways new incarnations of the trusts, maintaining their leash of power through crossownership of stock. Brandeis detailed how GE controlled several electric utilities and streetcar companies:

> The General Electric Company holds in the first place all the common stock in three security holding companies: The United Electric Securities Co., the Electrical Securities Corp., and the Electric Bond and Share Co. Directly and through these corporations and their officers the General Electric controls a large part of the water power of the United States. . . . The water power companies subject to General Electric influence control the street railways in at least 16 cities and towns; the electric-light plants in 78 cities and towns; gas

plants in 19 cities and towns; and are affiliated with the electric light and gas plants in other towns.[5]

With GE holding the reins on so many power plants and trolley lines, the company could ensure that it had captive customers for its electrical equipment. This arrangement also stifled competition and allowed the company to maintain high prices. By forming new holding companies and issuing stock, the directors of these entities were able to control a seemingly endless array of businesses. It was a useful model for the utilities business, since it facilitated ownership of thousands of utilities and traction systems. By 1913, Insull was chairman of the People's Gas Company in addition to most of the electrical companies in the Chicago area. He was extending his control through holding companies.

There was little political objection to Insull's ever-wider grip on Midwestern utilities—he now controlled power plants in 100 Chicago suburbs—since he also championed the formation of state utility commissions. With the help of Chicago powerbroker Roger Sullivan, Insull was able to persuade the Illinois legislature to draft a bill that would oversee utilities, although not in an overly restrictive way. That same year, the state's General Assembly approved legislation to create a utility commission, which was granted the power to set rates and monitor service. The state Public Utility Commission became operational in 1914. Unlike a similar law that had passed in Wisconsin, though, the Illinois statute lacked the authority to take over private utilities and put them under municipal control. Two years later, 33 states had utility boards, a movement that Insull had set in motion 20 years earlier when he arrived in Chicago. While progressives were concerned that the new Illinois commission did not promote public ownership of utilities, they saved their energy for future battles with Insull.

Insull also used the holding company structure to acquire hundreds of small power systems from the southeast to the upper Midwest. So long as the holding companies were backed with legitimate securities, physical assets, and positive cash flow, they served as solid receptacles for operating companies, which produced real earnings. When they were backed with securities that declined in value or bank loans, the holding company became precarious. The "pyramiding" of these entities, where a complex chain of companies all own each other, could have catastrophic effects.

Insull was in a delicate situation as the war began. As it was "a penal offense not to be neutral," he wanted to support Britain, yet not appear to be supporting the war itself or advocate that America get involved. Instead, he organized fund-raisers for reservists and volunteers who wanted to join the British forces and their families. He organized a huge bazaar to raise money for this cause.

Turning his intense gaze on what the war would mean to America, Insull prepared to sell the war to Americans without offending them. With his loyalties fixed on helping Britain in any way, he trod carefully in the first two years of the war since most Americans had no interest in joining the European conflict. In most Americans' eyes, this was a skirmish between the Kaiser and the French and English. They had squabbled before, and this dustup would be over in a few months, according to American popular opinion. There was even less sentiment on the part of politicians and civic leaders to antagonize European-Americans in Chicago, where the large German community was a force to be reckoned with as the war became more ideological. While the reasons for the war were tragically obscure, there was no mistaking the Chicago German community's attachment to the fatherland. Local politicians did their best to steer clear of the German-American community's interests, and Insull was sensitive to talking about the war in Chicago. Adding to the complexity of local ethnic tensions, the large Irish population often lodged its sentiments with the Germans—who were fighting their ancient overseers from Britain—and saw the Great War as a fulcrum for Irish independence.

Sidestepping the open promotion of his war aims, Insull worked behind the scenes to peddle pro-British propaganda. His elderly parents were still living in England, and he felt obliged to help his native country. Although his superb salesmanship skills were largely unused during the early Chicago years of consolidation and acquisition, the war provided an opportunity for him to finetune his pitches for Americans to embrace England. Part of this now-insidious campaign was to paint the Germans, or "Huns," as barbarian invaders, less-than-human savages who were bent on destroying civilization. Posters that would later depict the Kaiser's spike-point helmeted soldiers as demons derived their roots from the early propaganda effort. As an appeal to Americans to rely on their justice and mercy for the British people, the early campaigns that Insull secretly supported were sent to 360 American newspapers that were not subscribers to services such as the Associated Press. He also contributed $250,000 toward this effort.

Skirting America's official neutrality, Insull's focus was on *preparing* Americans to be involved in the war. The national economy had slowed down to such an extent that with each year, the country was increasingly concentrating on what it would mean to be drawn into a European war on a scale that the world had never seen. On the heels of a similar event in New York, Insull seized a moment by staging a "preparedness parade" in Chicago that was designed to lobby Congress to "adequately prepare for the defense of national honor and national interests." Nearly 2,500 Edison employees were asked to "volunteer" for the flag-waving rally. All told, nearly 130,000 marched through downtown Chicago in a patriotic fervor.

When America declared war on Germany in April 1917, Insull was ready for the challenge of fund-raising as part of a national effort. He was asked by Governor Frank Lowden to chair the Illinois Council of Defense, a position that he undertook with characteristic zeal. President Wilson hoped that each state council, as part of a National Council of Defense, could monitor the activities of German-Americans and potential spies, which were seen as one and the same during those years. Insull, however, had no intention of alienating his customers, many of whom were German Americans. He assembled a group of businessmen and civic leaders who would promote the moral correctness of the war in every way: patriotic appeals, support for the troops, and extensive fund-raising. Organizing an army of public relations men, speakers, and salesmen of Liberty bonds, Insull was diligent in making sure that Illinoisans were doing their utmost to support the effort. His electric companies alone sent 1,376 men to the front; 23 died, most of them of pneumonia. Sponsoring a financial assistance program for families whose men went off to war, his companies also sold a quarter million dollars in Liberty bonds. Patriotism was the underlying theme of every facet of the campaign.

"We owe a great deal to this country," Insull said in a speech promoting the campaign. "We owe everything to it except birth, and what we all love so much, that liberty, which was given to us by that Mother Country from which we spring. But we owe our opportunities in life to this Country. We do not want to be British-Americans here, nor English-Americans, nor Irish- Americans, nor Scotch-Americans. We want to be Americans."[6]

Insull worked with local leaders such as George Cardinal Mundelein in selling the war. Mary Garden took a more personal approach. On May 5, 1914, she left New York aboard the *Kaiser Wilhelm II* along with Enrico Caruso and Arturo Toscanini (an earlier crossing brought her into contact with Andrew Carnegie). When she arrived in Paris, it had seemed as if the city had shut down. She donated her car as an ambulance and turned her chateau at Suresnes into a refuge for women and children. She would not sing in public for the next two years, working part-time as a Red Cross nurse. She even attempted to enlist in the French Army. When the story leaked out to the newspapers, she dramatically replied, "yes, I *tried* to enlist. Why not? I owe France more than I can ever repay, even by giving her my life, and I am sure that I could fight as well as any *man* if they would let me. I have never failed to subdue every man I have met so far."

While it was not declared as such, Insull's fund-raising was a financial success, prompting many to remark that Insull could have made the entire war profitable. Of the $275,000 it cost to run the state campaign, Insull solicited $100,000 in private donations and the equivalent of $187,000 in donated rent, heat, and light. Other efforts such as a wartime exhibition raised even more money. All told, Insull turned over $442,000 in cash to the federal Committee on Public Information. He even donated his personal yacht to the state. Insull's war efforts resulted in a public relations juggernaut that few Illinois citizens at the time could escape. Governor Lowden wrote him a commendation. The elation that he must have felt from his war campaign was dampened when he traveled to England after the war. His parents, who were invalids during the war years and nursed by his sister Emma, died in the spring of 1918. His father was 87, his mother 84. There was little communication with them during the war years, and they apparently had had little to eat. Insull blamed his inability to get his family food during those years as a reason for Emma's death from heart disease a few years later. Although a man of constricted emotions, his eyes would well up with tears at any mention of his parents.

While he was leading the war effort, though, Insull came under attack for war profiteering. William Hale "Big Bill" Thompson, Chicago's mayor in 1915, had opposed America entering the war. Pandering to the city's large Irish and German communities, he comically threatened to punch the Prince of Wales in the nose if he ever set foot in Chicago. Big Bill had to find another cause in 1917, so he turned on the rising utility rates charged during the war years, which were largely due to inflation. Interest rates had nearly tripled—from three percent to eight percent—from 1914 to 1918, and that made it difficult for utilities to borrow or float bonds. Electrical demand had also soared. At the beginning of the war, Insull's Middle West Utilities company was producing 200 million kilowatt hours of power. Six years later, the demand mushroomed to more than a billion kilowatt-hours. Insull's companies had to keep returning to the new utility commission to obtain the rate hikes.

To counter Thompson's parries, Insull created the Committee on Public Utility Information in 1916. It was modeled after the defense council's public relations arm and was headed up by Bernard "Barney" Mullaney, a publicity wizard who would be Insull's creative director for his many propaganda efforts. Mullaney's entry into the battle with Big Bill may have marked the informal beginning of modern corporate public relations. The energetic flak attack was newly designed to shape public sentiment as well as legislation. Mullaney wrapped his first campaign in the American flag by claiming the utility industry was *patriotic* by obeying Wilson's directive for businesses to be totally candid with the public during the war years. The second part of the thrust to win public support was to link employees and public investors to the company's fortunes. A stock ownership plan was launched at the time to better align the interests of Insull's companies with those who bought the stock of Commonwealth Edison, the main electric company in Chicago. The company's forerunner, Chicago Edison, had a company savings plan since 1909, one of the first in the country. Insull was building loyalty through company stock ownership in tandem with a corporate culture that tied the employees and community directly into the fortunes of the company.

If people owned the stock, earned the dividends, and held onto it, they had a vested interest in seeing the company do well, Insull surmised. They were, in effect, "given a piece of the action." Mullaney's image and stock ownership campaigns defused Thompson's antiutility crusade. When he attacked the utilities, he was now disparaging his electorate—average people who held a few shares, but had a tangible stake in a growing business. Moreover, the expansion of corporate benefits gained employee loyalty in other ways. By giving them a greater stake in their employer, they became ambassadors for the company in the public and private arena. The image of Commonwealth Edison was enhanced by those employees who did not just work for the company, they represented it.

"You represent your company and your community," Insull told his employees. "Be a credit to both."

During the war campaign, Insull's image began to change from rising company executive to public benefactor. When a blizzard prevented coal shipments from reaching Chicago in the winter of 1918, he ordered that coal reserves from his company's power plants be donated to those who needed coal for heating. He gave "Insull awards" to plant workers who exhibited heroism. Whenever letters came to him asking for money from an employee or citizen needing a check to tide them over, Insull wrote a draft on his personal account. Thinking of Chappie, he would often detach stamps from envelopes for his son's collection. Insull had a great model for philanthropy in his peer Julius Rosenwald, the president of Sears Roebuck. Rosenwald and Insull had lunch together often and would share notes on how their donations could do the most good. Both men believed that Chicago should become the nation's banking center and should feature world-class amenities and arts. Insull supported the opera, and Rosenwald donated money to build the Museum of Science and Industry after hearing his son raving about a technology museum in Germany. Both men were sympathetic to the needs of the growing African-American community and gave significant amounts to scholarships and colleges.

Commonwealth Edison employees were expected to show the company's wares at every opportunity. Workers received discounts on power, home wiring, and appliances. The company itself was a major retailer of appliances. Its first electrical shop opened at Michigan and Jackson in 1909. It closed in 1917 during the war. The specialty store featured everything electrical. You could walk into a room filled with nothing but lights and lighting fixtures, then see all of the latest appliances from electric fans to giant washing machines. The company had 12 salesmen in merchandise sales as early as 1912. The enterprising new department sold $1 million in new appliances and lighting devices. When a local merchant complained that Insull's shops were taking business from local department stores, Insull closed his retail outlets, although he maintained a light-bulb discount program for his customers, a plan that was in place two generations after Insull died.

As Insull sought to build a hospitable corporate environment at Commonwealth Edison, he also attempted to make it a familial workplace. Before the U.S. entered the war, Commonwealth Edison had a workforce of about 5,500 employees. When the war ended, Insull insisted on placing returning soldiers on the payroll first, then finding jobs for them. Even when the company had to lay workers off, which was rare, employees could still remain in the company savings plan and earn interest. The culture of Commonwealth Edison was becoming more homelike. Kitchens, dining rooms, showers, and reading areas were added to the gritty power plants. Company picnics took place on the grounds of the Northwest station with giant smokestacks looming in the background. Games such as footraces, pole vaulting, and baseball were highlights of the outings. The company also sponsored bowling, baseball, and basketball leagues. There were Shakespeare and "Edison Players" groups that performed plays, an Edison Inn, and *Edison Roundtable,* an in-house company magazine. Every employee was encouraged to participate in the myriad company events and clubs. Eventually the company bought a lakefront resort and hotel in Wisconsin called Lake Lawn Lodge, where it offered company-subsidized vacations. The rooms only cost a few dollars a night. Christmas parties came complete with entertainment and gifts for the kids. Turkeys given away at the holidays were popular until the company replaced the birds with life insurance policies. Employees preferred the turkeys to the policies and were eventually convinced through a company education program that the insurance offering coverage up to $1,500 was probably more useful over the long term.

Part of the standard Commonwealth Edison package of benefits was a pension or "service annuity" program in which the company made all of the contributions. Started in 1912, the plan paid a full pension for employees age 55 with 30 years of service, or age 60 with 15 years. For those employees who wished to further their education, the company offered night-school scholarships and the Central Station Institute, which trained new employees. Most, if not all, of these benefits were human resource innovations at the time.

The company women's group, called "Electra," merged with the larger Edison club in 1919. The group was active during the war performing charity and welfare work. Before the war, it promoted social activities such as lectures, educational programs, plays, swimming, dancing and cooking. While women were not allowed to stay with the company if they became pregnant, they were encouraged in their prematernal careers. After the World War I, though, they lost some of the upward momentum that they had gained within the progressive company as soldiers returned from the front. Pam Strobel, an executive vice president of Commonwealth Edison's successor Exelon Corporation, recalls that her grandmother Beryl Love came to the company in 1919 "because of the evolving importance of high technology." A researcher in the company's testing department, Love worked for the company for three years. She had been the first woman to graduate from the University of Illinois with a physics degree and would attend lectures at the Electra club entitled "A Debate on the Matrimonial Fitness of Home versus Office Girls."

Cultural groups within the company often performed before the public. A Commonwealth Edison orchestra and glee club were formed in 1914. Conducted by Morgan Eastman, it performed in Orchestra Hall. Discounted seat prices ranged from 25 to 50 cents. The program for the orchestra ran ads for electric washing machines, lights, electrical supplies, and stocks of Insull's companies. Sold through Insull's preferred brokerage house, Russell, Brewster & Co., whose owners were also company directors, the program touted the generous dividends of the Insull company stocks:

—Commonwealth Edison: Quarterly dividends at 8 percent.
—Public Service Company of Northern Illinois: Cumulative preferred stock paying a quarterly dividend of 6 percent.
—Illinois Northern Utilities: 6 percent cumulative preferred stock. At present price nets better than 7 percent.

Not only did the Insull stocks pay regular dividends, they were tax-exempt in Illinois. Every activity that Insull engaged in had some connection to making his employees happy salespeople for electricity. His advertising department's slogan was, "Early to bed and early to rise, work like a dog and advertise!"

Even the way Insull had set up his boardroom suggested a close proximity to his mission control. The heart of the company was in the Edison building. Oak panels and marble floors would instantly signal you were in the executive domain in the Edison building. The boardroom was lined with dark walnut panels. Toward the north end of the room was a fireplace with an electric clock embedded in the wall above the mantel. Behind the fireplace was Insull's office, with an anteroom for his assistants. A phone booth was off to the side. Insull would emerge from his office smoking a cigar and sit at the head of a long, oak table. His brusque manner suggested that he had little time to waste, so executives rarely bothered him with small talk. When one saw him in the hallway, they were expected to say, "Good day, Mr. Insull," or they were fired, the company legend goes. The truth was that Insull rarely fired anyone.

Commonwealth Edison employees were frequent guests at baseball games. In 1918, the Chicago Cubs were in the World Series, playing the Boston Red Sox. Playing in a season shortened by war restrictions, the series featured a powerful young left-handed pitcher named George Herman Ruth, nicknamed "Babe" Ruth by the legendary Chicago sportswriter Ring Lardner. Over the previous three years the pitcher had won 65 games, although in the 1918 season his hitting was gaining notice: he had hit .300 with 11 homers in 317 at bats. Boston won the series in six games, their last world title before they won it again in 2004.

The following year, Ruth went 9 and 5 as a pitcher, but clobbered 29 homers. He went on to become one of the greatest sluggers of all time, albeit with a team in New York. The last time the Cubs won a World Series was in 1908 (as of this writing).

The war council also gave some of Insull's adversaries a public showing of how the utility mogul operated. Harold Ickes was a lawyer working for the state defense board at a salary of $1 a month. During the time Ickes worked for the board, his law partner Donald Richberg was suing Insull over what he deemed to be excessive rates. Ickes and Richberg formed the core of local progressive lawyers who lobbied for publicly owned utilities in Chicago and throughout the country. They were joined by other Chicago progressives such as Clarence Darrow, Harry Booth, and Jane Addams. Insull had little tolerance for this group of agitators. Ickes recalled that Insull used to launch into tirades against Richberg when he was working for the war council and was put in charge of patriotic propaganda:

> Insull acquired the habit of coming into my office when he had nothing else
> to do, especially on Saturday afternoons, and then ripping into Don Richberg
> in vituperative and picturesque language, much to my own and to Don's sub-
> sequent amusement.[7]

The future Secretary of the Interior under Franklin Delano Roosevelt, Ickes had been approached by Insull, who wanted to hire him after World War I. Employing his adversaries was Insull's way of controlling those who opposed him. Mullaney was friends with Ickes until Mullaney took a job with the utilities boss, causing a speechless rift that lasted for years. "Yerkes, [Chicago Mayor] Busse, and Insull helped me sharpen my teeth for Mussolini, Hirohito, and Hitler," Ickes later reflected in his autobiography. Insull could tolerate many things, but he demanded loyalty and was standoffish to all but a few of his most intimate friends. When he could not charm, employ, or buy out his enemies, he used all of the clout at his disposal to fight. Of all the things that he despised, though, personality conflicts took a backseat to bad management.

People's Gas, neglected during the war, had become a financial morass. Employees and customers alike were discouraged. Service was terrible for its 700,000 accounts. For investors, the dividend was suspended, the death knell for utility shareholders. The People's board tapped Insull to reorganize the company. Like thousands of other utility companies, People's Gas was revitalized and given efficient management by Insull. By 1919, the company was in financial distress and in danger of defaulting on its bond payments. Insull persuaded the board to elect him president, and he quickly moved to secure new financing and build a new gas manufacturing plant. Employing some of the public relations techniques he had honed during the war—this time stressing customer service instead of patriotism—Insull split half his workday between Commonwealth Edison and People's Gas during the gas company's rehabilitation period. Within two years of his takeover, People's Gas was profitable and paying a dividend of 5 percent. It was paying its old dividend of 8 percent by 1925. Insull refused to fire a single worker during the transition.

Railroads also held a special place in Insull's sphere of influence because they were huge power consumers. By the end of the war, he was supplying all of the power for the city's entire elevated electric transportation system, and he later owned it outright. Since his electrical system was branching out into the suburbs, it was logical that Insull also acquire the electric interurban railroads as well. Owning the power lines and the plants entitled him to large rights-of-way that cut large swaths through the growing metropolitan area. Insull acquired the bankrupt Chicago & Milwaukee Electric Railroad in 1916, reorganizing it as the Chicago, North Shore & Milwaukee Railroad, or simply the "North Shore Line." He turned the line over to his best rail executive, Britton Budd, and told him to modernize the railroad. Budd needed to negotiate trackage rights into Evanston and the city from the northern suburbs. He finally completed an agreement by 1919. The war years provided some opportunities to promote the line. On February 22, 1917, for example, 1,200 teachers were sent to visit the Great Lakes Naval Training Center in North Chicago. In June of that year, a special "naval recruiting" train festooned with bunting and shaped like submarines was employed to sign up sailors.

The electric interurbans formed an impressive network that connected Chicago with three states. You could take an electric train from Chicago to all of the major outlying cities including Rockford, Joliet, and Aurora. The system extended as far as Janesville and Milwaukee, Wisconsin; South Bend, Indiana; and South Haven, Michigan. Connecting buses would take you even further to other large cities such as Detroit or St. Louis. While the interurban era peaked before World War I, the three lines that Insull bought were fully funded and modernized. Under the capable and efficient Budd, the lines ran faster and provided superior service, often featuring well-appointed dining cars on the longer routes.

Like Insull's electrical grid, the interurbans erased the boundaries between city and suburb, urban area and exurban area. They were the transportation links that shuttled city dwellers to the lovely Ravinia Park in Highland Park, Catholics to the Mundelein Seminary, and carousers to the hooch joints of Howard Street, the border between Chicago and Evanston. Growth along the interurban corridors made the adjacent property more valuable because transportation access made it more likely that someone could live in one place and work in another. Real estate that had been sitting unoccupied for years suddenly exploded in value when Insull's power lines gave rise to the interurban stops and entire wired communities.

Before Insull began construction on an extension of his North Shore Line into Niles Center (now Skokie, Illinois), for example, the adjacent land along the right-of-way was worth $1,000 an acre. After construction began, the value shot up to $6,000 to $7,000 an acre. Long term, property values always appreciated near the electric transportation routes. Along the Wilson Avenue corridor in Chicago, land prices soared by a factor of 8 from 1899 to 1923, increased by a similar factor in Rogers Park from 1907 to 1923, and rose by a factor of 14 in the Ravenswood district over the same period. Part of Insull's pitch to civic leaders was that the prosperity that accompanied electrification and rapid transit was not confined to landowners and his companies. The "customer owners" or 200,000 security holders of his companies, also benefited. The public ownership campaign and expansion of his enterprises, he argued, was good for nearly everyone. Commuter suburbs that sprang up along these routes were now part of the city's expanding network of transportation, power, and jobs. The modern metropolis was mushrooming along Insull's electric commuter lines.

Seeking respite from the relentless pressures of reorganizing People's Gas and running the electric companies, Insull was looking forward to spending more time in his new home at Hawthorn Farm. The modest old farmhouse had been quaint and Midwestern, but it was not what an industrial leader the caliber of a Samuel Insull needed as showpiece of his wealth and power. Designed in 1914, but delayed by a shortage of building materials during the war, the new home was to bespeak of elegant country living and the prestige of a manor house. The Insulls were not able to move in until 1917.

Designed by Benjamin Marshall, the new home was modest in its exterior facade, considering Insull's wealth and stature. Unlike the brown fortress of Morgan's Manhattan abode or the giant French chateau of Vanderbilt's Biltmore estate, Insull's home was more Midwestern Medici. Marshall leaned toward neoclassic designs. His Drake and Edgewater Beach hotels were Old World elegant, yet not triumphant like New York's Plaza. At Hawthorn Farm, Marshall sought to give the Insulls a powerful sense of being influential landowners in a time when only a handful of urban Americans owned much more than a small space. Like Wright, Marshall was vitally interested in the use of light. Most of the home is bathing in light, which is its greatest resource. Unlike Wright, though, Marshall was not the least bit interested in originality. His likely inspiration was Andrea Palladio's sixteenth century Villa Pisani, a classic rectangular design with an interior courtyard popular in the Veneto region.

The landscape architect Jens Jensen, who was to naturalistic landscape architecture what Wright was to modern building design, laid out a serene plan for the ground of the estate. Jensen designed Henry Ford's estate and some of Chicago's most classic parks. He never fought the natural terrain. He used native plants, trees, and shrubs and endeavored to create a harmonious whole that reflected what thrived in the harsh Midwestern climate. Creating a Versailles-like garden would have been anathema to him. The gentleness of Jensen's personality was reflected in his designs—rolling hills, limestone waterfalls, small lakes, prairie plants swooshing in the breeze. Jensen worked to preserve natural vistas. He created open spaces leading up to the lake that can be seen from the dining and summer rooms of Insull's house. Elms lined the half-mile driveway, which later were replaced with maples when the trees succumbed to Dutch elm disease. A tiny, gurgling waterfall was created on the lake. Nothing was out of scale in proportion to the house or property.

A gradual berm rose on either side of the swimming pool and pool house, creating an almost intimate sunken garden for the pool arena. The back door and all of the bedrooms faced an esplanade that had a view of the pool and an amphitheater, where Gladys often performed in the summer. She was able to make a grand entrance through a colonnade and pergola that led to the half-circle grass proscenium. On either side of the rectangular pool area were two rows of alternating apple and cherry trees. The garden embraced the entire western part of the home. When the Insulls looked out of their bedroom windows, they could see the sun set, the glimmering water of the pool, the graceful pergola, the orchard, and garden. A council ring, a Jensen trademark reminiscent of the public circles where Native Americans held powwows, graced a corner of the property, along with lily ponds, perennial grasses, a sunken garden, and meadows. It was all so effortless; it was if it had been there 500 years and echoed the sublime Boboli gardens in Florence. Roman gods such as Pan and Mercury seemed out of place as they stood on pedestals on either side of the esplanade.

The 31,000-square-foot, 32-room home was built to last hundreds of years and designed to look as if it was the home of a Renaissance family. Made of poured concrete that was covered with plaster, for the most part, it could more than survive the unforgiving Chicago winters. When you walk in through the barrel-vaulted vestibule on the travertine floor (porous limestone) and through the massive iron and glass interior door surrounded by stone fruit baskets and satyrs, you do not have a sense of the place until you enter the great hall. Then light pours down on you from the skylight more than 30 feet above. A loft for organ pipes was installed, although no organ was ever built. The ever-leaking skylight opens up in the summer to let a breeze in as the house must have been sweltering with all of that light and heat flooding in during summers that could reach 100 degrees. A primitive air-conditioning system using radiators with cool water are in some of the rooms. In the great hall, it is as if the house opens up and takes a deep breath and you feel like you have been swallowed up by the space. A fountain in the middle of the great hall imitated the great villas of Europe. You have a sense that Gladys would soon come floating down the stone stairway to your left like Gloria Swanson.

A loggia with odd corinthian, ionic, and doric columns separates the hall from the rooms on every side. The doorknobs are brass leaf forms. To your right is a sunroom that leads to a courtyard. To your left is the "ship's room," which Insull used as his office. He had Marshall tear out the dark pine panels from the captain's cabin in a seventeenth-century ship and panel the entire room, which had a nautical feel to it. The panels hid compartments for books and a telephone booth. There is a safe behind his desk and under the stairs. In the dark library, shelves extend from the floor to the 20-foot ceiling. Stained glass in the windows gives the room a medieval feel, although cupids adorn the fireplace mantle. A movie theater is in the back of the house on the way to the garden.

A formal salon with an adjoining ballroom are off to your right. Both of these rooms are relatively simple with grillwork covering the radiators. The ballroom has windows on three sides and opens up to a patio with a view of the lake. A formal salon is next to a butler's pantry where flowers were cut and prepared for Gladys every day. A formal dining room and breakfast room are next to the flower room. The dining room seats 64.

A carved stone frieze, railing, and half-timbered roof give the second floor loggia the feel of a Tudor home. Each room has the standard pull cord to summon the servants, only with Insull's touch apparent. Instead of ringing bells, the pull cords were hooked up to an electrical intercom system that had stations in the kitchen and front vestibule. Insull also installed a central vacuum system and electric clothes drier in the basement, perhaps one of the first in the country. The bus connections in his fully wired home were gold plated. An electric elevator remains one of the oldest operating elevators in the world. Insull kept electric cars charging in his garage until he bought a sedan in the 1920s. His stables were home to brown Swiss cows, hackney ponies, and prize Suffolk punch dray horses, which he had coveted since his youth in Oxfordshire. He had a particular interest in the farm section of his estate since he wanted to introduce science and electricity to every aspect of farming. He fought state officials who had to destroy most of his Swiss herd when the cows contracted foot-and-mouth disease. Managing to spare some calves, he reestablished the herd and set milking records.

It was intentional on the part of Marshall that the symmetry of the home nearly match the proportions of a Medici home such as Michelozzo's Palazzo Medici in Florence. The public spaces, such as the great central hall and formal dining room, convey a sense of baronial power while the private spaces such as the upstairs bedrooms, which all have carved stone or wooden fireplaces, convey intimacy. Insull's walnut, rococo four-poster bed looks more like the Bernini altar columns in St. Peters than a staid Victorian gentleman's bed. The bearded visage of a wild Dionysius stares out from his wooden, carved mantelpiece. All of the bathrooms have gold-plated fixtures, radiators, and commodes that look like wicker chairs. Like an ancient castle, there are several ways of exiting the bedrooms in the event of a peasant uprising or siege. Both Gladys's and Chappie's rooms have sleeping balconies for the sultry summer nights. Fearing that Chappie might be kidnapped, there are steel bars enclosing his porch. Gladys's room was modest, yet features a sit-down porcelain sink and a commode in a closet. A servant intercom button is to the left of the sink. Despite its many amenities, though, the home is less than endearing. It seems to be at odds with the Midwestern landscape that Jensen so lovingly attempted to enhance and put on display. The hue of the home (its current color is a vibrant pink) seems alarmingly out of place in the prairie and meadows, particularly in the winter. The palazzo's interior, though, redeems the garish exterior with its buoyancy and the soaring spirit of its owners.

Chappie was away at Yale in 1919, studying engineering. Gladys wanted him to pursue a career in the arts, but Insull would not hear of it. He wanted his dynasty and was not acquiring all of those companies just for himself. Chappie was torn between his mother's wishes and his father's designs. He wrote from college that he was trying to secure positions and was asking Insull's advice on whom to contact:

> If Medill McCormick [a senator whose family owned the *Chicago Tribune*] is in the East, I could run down to see him and get something on "University Graduates needed in Politics." . . . By telling him whose son I am, I could probably get a word or so from Bowman, the hotel man, on "How to Prepare in College for Business" or some kindred subject. With mother's help, I could probably get a few words from Erlanger or Klaw on "What Makes a Success on Broadway." Lastly, I know it is an imposition to ask you to use your business relations to get me access to big men. . . . So please tell me what can be done.[8]

Gladys and Insull were mostly estranged at this point, yet Insull may have believed that the all-consuming activity of decorating and furnishing a large house would somehow restore her affections. The coming decade would prove challenging to their relationship as the Roaring Twenties would thrust America front and center into modernity.

ALL THAT JAZZ

The 1920s Boom Times

Out of the Twisted Twenties flowered the promise of Chicago as the homeland and heartland of an American renaissance, a place of poets and sculptors yet to come.

—Nelson Algren, *Chicago: City on the Make*[1]

The improvisational genius of the jazz age was entering every electrified home in the form of new and varied technologies. The new vibrations that Insull wanted to sell were powered by his electricity, creating a new polyrhythm within the home, office, and workplace. Appliances and uses for power would take on every size and shape, color and tone. The thudding of rugs being beaten was being replaced by the high-pitched hum of vacuum cleaners. The stifling summers were being eased by the whir of electric fans. And the torment of mishandling and getting burned by a flatiron from a woodstove was being replaced by the predictability of an electric iron. The twin giants GE and Westinghouse looked to sales-oriented moguls like Insull to promote and sell their wares by wiring factories, offices, and homes. The progressive home was becoming the new stage in singing the praises of electricity in everyday life, and Insull was the electrified home's Louis Armstrong, an ambassador, salesman, and chief spokesman for the modern lifestyle.

New housing, as exemplified by the common bungalow, a fixture in Chicago's working-class neighborhoods, was a case in point. Instead of a parlor, it had a small, front living room. The bedrooms were smaller and the bathrooms bigger. It had a basement and an attic, which could be converted into living space. It was designed long and narrow for city lots. The kitchen was half the size of the Victorian kitchen, if not smaller. The kitchen shrank because modern appliances made servants (mostly married African-American women) unnecessary for middle-and upper-middle-class women. Between 1900 and 1920, the number of domestics dropped by half—from 80 per thousand to 39. Modern scientific management techniques, pioneered by Frederick Taylor and employed in Chicago's Western Electric complex, made the layout of the kitchen more efficient. The stove and icebox were much closer together. Gas and electric stoves produced much less exterior heat than their predecessors, so they did not have to be as large. Sinks also shrank.

Women also did not have that much time to cook. The twentieth century gave them more opportunities to work outside the home in offices and factories. By 1900, women worked in nearly every occupation listed in the census. Since health care was improving and women were earning college degrees, family size also fell. The average number of children was less than four per family in the first two decades of the century. As millions moved into the cities, large families were no longer needed to run farms.

Electricity also enhanced home life. More activities could be done at night as homes were wired for lighting. And once homes were hooked up to the power company, any number and combination of appliances was possible. The sales of electrical appliances quadrupled from $23 million in 1915 to $83 million in 1920. By the end of that decade, that number more than doubled. Two years before World War I, only 16 percent of American homes had electric lighting. Nearly every home had electric lighting by the end of the 1920s. Wiring made home life much more convenient because it brought every appliance within reach of the family. Initial hookups provided only lighting fixtures. That meant if you wanted to plug in an appliance, you needed to unscrew a lightbulb and plug it into a fixture. It was awkward and often dangerous. Outlets in every room—particularly the kitchen—made it easier to connect more appliances. Insull's companies constantly promoted wiring deals that linked electricity contracts with home wiring services.

A parade of innovations entered the home through Insull's utility sales campaigns. Vacuum cleaners, steam irons, fans, stoves, and toasters were among the most popular early appliances. Insull's stores sold every appliance that GE made. To a large extent, the wave of appliance selling was keyed to women's political aspirations. One ad pitched an appliance sale as "the Suffrage and the Switch." Seizing upon this theme, marketers like Insull wanted women to believe that his products and services would liberate them from the servitude of housework. In the growing suburbs, electricity was sold as social salve. Yet by the end of World War I, the suburbs were largely an unfulfilled promise. By 1920, more people lived in metropolitan areas than in the country, but there was a housing short-age of some 500,000 units. Less than half of all families owned their own homes. In the suburban ethos, quiet streets and modern homes would make family life easier and more stable. There were no steam trains or trolleys running through outlying neighborhoods. New developments were wired for electricity and streetlights, but also had fewer amenities at first, such as restaurants, grocery stores, butchers, bakeries or delis. The new electrical kitchen offered families much more flexibility in preparing food at home.

As early as 1913, Insull was forging a link between reduced housework and the electrical home, an advertising thread that was interrupted by the war. An ad in Commonwealth Edison's *Electric City* magazine from May of that year was tagged: "Every Day in Every Way Electricity Makes Housework Easier." A serenely smiling woman in an apron is shown in the upper left-hand corner with an electric iron. In the lower half of the ad, the company promotes the virtues of irons, washing machines, and cooking utensils such electric grills, chafing dishes, and coffee makers. For the time, this was the equivalent of advertising the latest high-tech gizmo, only these ads were pitched directly at homemakers who were tired of using flatirons and scrub boards. The ad copy insinuates its message by playing upon a woman's enslavement to long, tedious housework:

> For the modern household, Electricity is at once a servant, a source of heat and light and unfailing convenience that can be enjoyed every day in the year. In any house that is wired for Electric Light, these modern labor savers will be ap-preciated.[2]

Another ad for a rather ugly Westinghouse motor in the same issue takes an economic posture: "Your Washing Done for 1 cent an Hour: Westinghouse Motor Saves Half the Time and All the Backache." This unorthodox use of elec-tricity (who would buy just a motor?) is part of a larger contraption that fits on a large counter. Once the motor was installed, you could run any number of smaller appliances such as an apple and potato parser, dough mixer, coffee grinder, egg beater, ice cream freezer, meat chopper, and polishing wheels for the knives and silver. While running all of these devices from one motor may have been efficient, the "Federal Electric Kitchen Cabinet" was unwieldy and never caught on. To promote the modern kitchen, Insull's Middle West Utilities ran a long Pullman-type train car named the *Electra* that featured the appliances. It is doubtful, though, that many people bought these appliances since so few homes were wired before 1920.

The modern kitchen shrank because space was at a premium. New plumb-ing, wiring, and heating systems required space in walls, and this raised the square footage costs of homes. Rooms became multipurpose. Kitchens, which averaged 120 square feet in bungalows, were also home to breakfast nooks. Victorian-era rooms such as libraries, parlors, sitting rooms, sewing rooms, and guest rooms were eliminated. Dining rooms often flowed into kitchens or living rooms, a design improvement largely attributed to Frank Lloyd Wright. The widespread use of electricity cleaned up the home by its very introduction. Kerosene and gas lamps left pungent odors in homes. Incandescent lamps had no smell at all. The constant soot created by the hydrocarbon illumination necessitated decorating with dark wallpapers. Electric lighting brightened up homes considerably.

Progressives such as Henry Demarest Lloyd saw the marriage of electricity with the more compact home as a sign of social progress:

> Women, released from the economic pressure which has forced them to deny their best nature and compete in the unnatural industry with men, will be re-sexed. . . . Every house will be a center of sunshine and scenery.[3]

Lloyd was reflecting a sentiment earlier expressed by Theodore Roosevelt that the more demanding economic strains of living in cities had forced more women into the workforce, which was perceived as undermining their femininity and roles in the home. A convergence of industrial efficiency techniques, a male-oriented yearning for women to leave the workforce, and a need for homes to become more efficient labor-saving environments created the foundation for the 1920s building boom and embrace of electrification. Sociologist Gwendolyn Wright observed:

> The progressive movement at the turn of the century announced that all classes of Americans needed better homes and asked how science could improve domesticity. Amateurs and professionals analyzed the needs of the rich and poor, working women and housewives, rural and urban households. They asked what should be discarded, what collectivized, what preserved in the modern home. By 1910, the formula for a progressive home resembled the proposal for an efficient factory.[4]

It was not coincidental that Insull's household sales campaigns highlighted the scientific management dogma of labor and cost efficiencies. The more power used, the greater the load factor. That translated into a higher capacity, profit, and efficiency for his power plants. Insull was not just selling appliances, he was selling power and lifestyle enhancement. The more ways he presented of consuming it, the more electrons he could sell. Every washing machine, heater, fan, and iron sold boosted the load during "off-peak" hours for his industrial users.

The electrical appliance campaigns were positive stories that were designed to persuade homeowners into wiring their homes and buying electricity. In many ways, the underlying theme was "keeping up with the Insulls." The first electrical family of Chicago gladly promoted all of the appliances in their homes to their guests, including a 3,000-watt "walk-in" clothes dryer that was as big as a closet. In its 1913 magazine, the utility proudly announced that such a dryer was being used in Comiskey Park by the White Sox. *Electric City* also illustrated industrial, retail, and farm applications of electricity. The Crown Dairy Company of Dubuque, Iowa, was featured as one of the first dairies to use a refrigeration system. Being able to keep milk products cold would revolutionize the dairy industry and also create entirely new businesses for entrepreneurs like Clarence Birdseye, who pioneered frozen foods.

Every aspect of housework was targeted as Insull sought to create new consumers for his product. Insull's Electric Shops sold electric sewing machines for $16. The GE irons that Commonwealth Edison sold were guaranteed and "if not abused, will last a lifetime. It more than pays for the electricity it uses by lessening the wear and tear on clothes and doing the work in one-third less time." The popular GE fan promised "four hours [of operation] at a Cost of One Cent." Insull was not above larding on guilt in his advertising, either. A famous ad that appeared in the 1920s was entitled, "How Long Should a Wife Live?" It was an advertorial by Bruce Barton that extolled the virtues of electricity in prolonging—and saving—the lives of women:

> How Long Should a Wife Live? The answer in the old days was "not very long." The homes of those days [prior to electricity] had two or three mothers and no motors. The home of the future will lay all of its tiresome, routine burdens on the shoulders of electrical machines, freeing mothers for their real work, which is motherhood. The mothers of the future will live to a good old age and keep their youth and beauty to the end.[5]

Insull's sales and advertising department reached homeowners in every possible way. They would mail, visit, and service homes while offering maintenance plans and attractive purchase plans. Not even the holidays were to be ignored. Commonwealth Edison was one of the first utilities to "electrify" Christmas by promoting appliances for gifts and lighting. A Santa Claus with an outstretched hand pointing to the slogan "Give Something Electrical" heralded the company's Christmas cheer.

Electricity also made good business sense for landlords to wire their rental properties. Commonwealth Edison claimed that a wired house could rent for

$10 more a month ($45 versus $35 for the unwired house), netting a gain of 28.5 percent and an increase in property value of $2,000. The slogan for industrial users was even more powerful: "Modern Efficiency Means Electricity: Turn out More Work During Dark Hours." The company had a staff of "illuminating engineers" who would call on factory owners to discuss the productivity gains of converting to electric lighting. One powerful industrial claim was that 28 percent of the company's new customers found that their costs were reduced and output increased. A "no first cost" installation program promised per worker output gains from 2 to 10 percent. The factory owner would then keep the lighting fixtures with the agreement that Commonwealth Edison would "maintain" what it installed. Motors in factories were installed to make every facet of production more efficient. Only 10 percent of factories in 1905 used electric motors. By the end of the 1920s, 80 percent of plants used them, eliminating the incredibly inefficient overhead pulley systems that had been in use since Edison's early days. The company documented efficiency improvements ranging from metalworking to letter sorting.

In the public sector, Insull was promoting electricity as a public safety benefit. New electrical lighting and traffic signals were reducing accidents. After a signal system was installed in New York City, serious traffic accidents declined by 12 percent. Even though there was little traffic relative to today, more than 32,000 traffic accidents took more lives and created more monetary losses than all of the crimes put together in 1921.

Insull was proud to promote his company's advertising and promotion techniques to the National Electric Light Association. As an innovator in selling electricity, the entire industry was observing and copying what he was doing during the 1920s. The campaigns were effective in increasing sales and positioned the company as a friend of the homeowner. By 1925, the company's sales volume of electrical merchandise increased by a factor of ten over the previous decade. The 111,000 electrical items sold in 1925 alone represented $1.4 million in additional Commonwealth Edison sales. The top-selling appliances were irons (42,843), haircurling irons (10,292), electric heaters and radiators (9,994), and electric coffeepots (9,835). To boost sales, Insull sent out electric-powered trucks outfitted with the latest fixtures and appliances. The salesman were trained to "replace inadequate household fixtures" such as outlets and kitchen units.

By the middle of the 1920s, Chicago was *the* electric city. Insull had transformed the city into the highest per capita user of electricity in the world. Insull's metropolitan system was distributed through five plants and 99 substations through 30,000 miles of conductors to 811,366 customers. This "power pool unequalled in the world," the company boasted to NELA, produced more than a billion kilowatt hours in 1924 alone.

Power companies all over the world adopted Insull's marketing techniques. Although two thirds of all American homes lacked electrical wiring in 1920, a decade later, 80 percent of all homes would be electrified. More wired homes stimulated the production of appliances, which caused prices to drop dramatically during the 1920s. While only a handful of households had electrical appliances in the first two decades of the century, by 1930 nearly 80 percent had electric irons, 52 percent had washing machines or refrigerators, and 47 percent had vacuum cleaners.

The advertised promise of unshackling women from housework did not materialize, however. Yet the time required to do the most time-consuming chores was reduced and made more convenient. It was not quite the realization of the Progressive movement's dream of mating technology with women's liberation, as electrical appliances created cleaner, brighter homes while raising expectations. Because homemakers had vacuums, washing machines, and dryers, women were expected to keep the house cleaner and do even more chores. For households that could now afford washing machines instead of sending the wash out to commercial laundries, there was a marked *increase* in labor.

Using the argument that the new appliances reduced their wives' burdens, men stopped assisting in mundane tasks like beating rugs (they did not offer to take up vacuuming). In fact, in addition to the new mode of housework using appliances, more household income was needed to pay for the new devices, sending women in increasing numbers back into the workforce.

Gladys refused to be marginalized as Insull escalated his all-consuming affair with his business. She was active in charities during the war and wanted to make her presence known. Insull employees knew to stay out of her way when she was around, yet when she made a request, they were to act as if she was running the company. When she needed a staff for the Allied Charities Bazaar, she handpicked her own staff from Edison employees, who "volunteered" to help with the boss's favorite *cause du jour*. Insull trusted Gladys and let her manage his people, even though it led to conflicts as to their (the employees') loyalties. Gladys found a young bookkeeper that she liked by the name of Philip McEnroe. When the war ended, she put in a good word for him.

"Sam, there's a nice young man in the bookkeeping department who worked at the bazaar," Gladys purred. "I don't know his name, but he has honest eyes and he is very nice. You'd better have him in your office." Without a hint of jealousy, Insull promoted McEnroe to become his personal bookkeeper. He would be entrusted with keeping track of Insull's growing fortune.

Despite their joint efforts during the war, Gladys was growing even further apart from her husband. She was not as interested in society as much as he was and avoided most of the Gold Coast matrons who would have gladly anointed her the queen of Chicago society—had she made the effort to show up to half of their soirees. Edith McCormick, the domineering and beautiful daughter of John D. Rockefeller and guiding light of the opera company, was in a marriage that was dissolving. While she held sway over all of the balls and opera matters, when her husband Harold divorced her for a young opera singer, she retreated temporarily from social life. Gladys certainly had the charm and graces to fill in the void, yet she found the wives to be "shallow and pretentious fools." Perhaps out of spite for Insull leaving her alone so often, she never choose to be the queen of the upper register.

Insull, however, was undaunted by his wife's disdain of her peers. He continued to raise money from Chicago society the way a general would muster troops, treating this elite group as if they were underlings. Somewhat unpopular campaigns to fund the education of African-American doctors, the Chinese YMCA, and other groups not affiliated with Chicago's upper crust succeeded because Insull bullied them through his club and dinner circuit. When Insull donated the land and $50,000 to build Condell Memorial Hospital in Libertyville, all he needed was a few phone calls to raise additional funds. Nobody dared resist him. Along with Julius Rosenwald and Richard Shedd from Sears, Stanley Field of the department store fortune, the McCormicks, and Medill-Pattersons, he was one of the city's key powerbrokers and financiers. If you needed money for a worthy project—and could get through to him—Insull was your man. In the private salons of Chicago's Gold Coast, though, the Insulls were not well liked. They did not abide by the old money rules of the game. Gladys was not a regular at high teas, and Insull had few intimates. He would often be seen in his clubs, puffing away at a cigar, alone. He also had a genuine empathy for those that society traditionally ignored, which alienated many of his upper-class peers.

Insull filled company positions with African-Americans when white employees left for the war. When the war ended, Insull refused to fire his African-American employees. He reassigned them to be meter readers on the South Side. The city was experiencing a tremendous migration from the south at the time as local African-American newspapers such as the *Chicago Defender* and leading journalists such as Ida B. Wells encouraged the exodus from the Jim Crow south. The South Side had produced Jack "Lil' Artha" Johnson, who became heavyweight champion of the world from 1908 to 1915. Johnson ran a tavern on the South Side and was generally reviled by racist whites for his bravado, intelligence in the ring, and preference for white women. At the height of his fame, his flamboyant lifestyle was costing him $20,000 a week. He was convicted for violating the Mann Act (which also gave Frank Lloyd Wright legal problems) and died in a car accident at the age of 68.

Although the end of the war led to a recession (compounded by a global influenza pandemic that killed perhaps 50 million people), millions of factory jobs would be created during the 1920s. At the end of the war, 50,000 African-Americans streamed into Chicago; another 100,000 came north during the 1920s. Men like Frank Lumpkin, who earned money in barefisted boxing throughout the South, could put his mind and hands to work in steel mills, where he could earn a decent union wage and a pension.

As African-Americans began to arrive from the South, catastrophic tensions led to violence. A five-day race riot broke out in 1919 on the South Side that left 23 African-Americans dead and more than 300 wounded. The largely segregated city was evolving into a metropolis that could provide jobs for all, yet equality would be a hard-fought struggle beginning with the self-reliance movement of the early 1920s to the Civil Rights era of the 1960s.

The Illinois Central railroad, which linked Chicago to New Orleans, was the main conduit for families moving north. During the migration, intoxicating new sounds floated up from the delta region. New clubs and the prospect of recording contracts lured musicians such as King Oliver and Louis Armstrong into Chicago. While New York may have been the center of recording and Tin Pan Alley of songwriting, Chicago was the mecca for performers. Jazz and blues artists found a lively and welcoming home and spawned "race" record labels such as Okeh, Vocalian, and Chess.

Studs Terkel, the Chicago author, radio personality, and "poet of the tape recorder" recalled hearing jazz for the first time as a young man in the 1920s. "I was waiting for my brother outside of ballrooms, where he was trying to pick up girls. *What* a sound." Terkel interviewed many of the great jazz artists over the years such as Louis Armstrong and Earl "Fatha" Hines and noted that they came to Chicago first to perform before leaving for New York, where they gained international fame.

As the naturalistic school of poets and novelists had flourished in Chicago during the past 20 years, now it was the musicians who thrived in the city's underground cultural scene. The lead curtain of the Volstead Act after the war did little to dampen Chicago's lust for drink, music, dancing, and bawdiness. The clubs became speakeasies, and the Sicilian, Irish, and German gangs took over the liquor distribution business. While Insull continued to acquire more power companies, gangsters like "Big Jim" Colosimo took over the rackets by force. The other Big Jim—Mayor Thompson—a "wet" mayor at heart, mostly looked the other way.

The stage in the Auditorium was crackling with excitement as Mary Garden entered the studio of Station KYW on November 14, 1921. She had been asked by Insull to test a new radio transmitter that was perched on top of the Edison building at 72 West Adams. The Westinghouse Company had licensed the station, stringing a line to the theater where Mary and her company were ready to perform selections from *Madama Butterfly* under the baton of maestro Giorgio Polacco. For some reason, the stage light was a single, dangling lightbulb as Mary entered the area where the massive microphone was placed.

"My God but it's dark in here," she complained, unaware that the station was already broadcasting live. With a director frantically waving his arms, Mary then proceeded to introduce the cast, and the orchestra began with arias from the opera. There were only 1,300 radio sets in the entire city when Mary stepped in front of the microphone. Programming that year consisted of most of the opera company's season and nothing else. Serge Prokofiev's *Love of Three Oranges,* an opera in the modern idiom that Garden championed and Insull disliked, was presented in its world premiere. The thud of soprano Marguerite D'Alvarez could be heard by the listeners as she fell climbing a stage staircase in *Samson and Delilah.* Whether or not the audience loved opera, they were treated to live broadcast music that did not involve buying a ticket. Insull sold more electricity and Chicago had its first radio station. By the end of the season, there were 20,000 radios in the city.

Radio was a new medium emerging from electricity that would unify the nation. City and country dwellers shared a common experience through national and regional programming. While there were only a handful of radios in use in 1920 (the first commercial radio broadcast was November 1920), over the next 20 years, the wireless would become the nation's ears as more than 40 million Americans tuned in. Always interested in how new technology could promote the use of electricity, Insull not only started his own radio station, he sat on the board of the Marconi Company.

Insull's station was later sold to Colonel Robert McCormick, the publisher of the *Chicago Tribune*. McCormick, who dominated his newspaper as much as Insull lorded over his businesses, proudly renamed the station "WGN," initials for the "World's Greatest Newspaper." Later in the decade, the colonel employed the station to promote his paper in a unique way. He would have announcer Quin Ryan halt all programming if a crime was in progress. Donating radios to police squad cars, they would receive instructions from Ryan like, "Attention all squads! Drug store held up at East 57th Street. Watch for three men in a Buick." This was high drama in the 1920s that actually resulted in a few arrests. Those within a 100-mile radius of the Edison building were tuned into crime stopping at its most entertaining.

Although they traveled in the same social circles, Insull and McCormick despised each other. McCormick had run afoul of Insull when he was president of the Sanitary District Board in 1909. As an entity that produced its own power, the district was able to sell excess power at the time. McCormick contracted with City Hall and other municipal buildings for a fraction of what Insull could charge. Then the colonel advertised that he could save Chicagoans $1 million a year by tapping into more of the excess capacity of the district. This infuriated Insull, who wanted no competition with large municipal power producers. Insull sent out his lawyer William Beale to defend his interests; Beale charged McCormick with the "rank confiscation" of Illinois' streams and rivers. McCormick retaliated by cowriting a *Tribune* editorial condemning Insull's virtual monopoly. The two men would never reconcile their differences. The colonel, who had an unpleasant experience during his schooling in England, abhorred anything English and opposed America's entry into both World Wars. It was natural that he also hate the London-born Insull, who did everything in his power to rally state citizens to the defense of England. The venom continued to flow during the 1920s. At one point, McCormick supposedly received a call from a thug named Big Tim Murphy that he was coming over to kill him, so the colonel hid a revolver among a stack of books in his office. He waited, but Murphy never showed up.

"If he [Murphy] would have come through the door, I would have shot him," the colonel later boasted. "I wouldn't have had any conversation with him at all. But he didn't come. He was killed later, but he killed a lot of people first." Some of Murphy's victims, he insinuated, were murdered by orders of Insull. It was not true, but it reflected the seething enmity he held for the most powerful businessman in the city. As a savvy executive himself, McCormick built the *Tribune* to be the most powerful newspaper in the Midwest. He modernized printing plants, lowered the cost of newsprint through smart acquisitions of

Canadian forests and pulp mills, and boosted circulation. His Cantigny estate west of the city reflected his love of martial display, later becoming something of a war museum complete with tanks and howitzers on the grounds.

Insull and McCormick would later have a common enemy in Franklin Delano Roosevelt. Insull opposed Roosevelt because he favored municipal and public control of electricity. McCormick, an arch-conservative Republican whose views were emblazoned on the front page of his paper, distrusted Roosevelt because of his progressive reforms and his later declaration of war on Germany and Japan.

Chappie was ready to enter the real world now that he was done with Yale. Still undecided about his future, he was cajoled into taking a grand tour of Europe with Gladys, who did not want him starting graduate work just yet. Gladys wanted to show Chappie all of the hallmarks of European civilization—the cities and the salons and museums of the Old World. Insull reluctantly agreed to let Chappie see the continent on one condition: that in addition to visiting museums, he call on every important European electric company and executive. Gladys rolled her eyes at the request, still hoping that her son would pursue a career in the arts.

Insull doted on Chappie when he was a boy, often bringing home the latest electrical toy. One of his first playthings was an erector set and Insull barely let the boy play with it. When his son put together something incorrectly, Insull would lean over and say, "no, no Chappie, do it this way." When Insull had three breakdowns from the tremendous stress he was under, he would bring Chappie with him to Europe. They often ended up relaxing in the quiet English countryside. The only photographs Insull liked having taken were him sitting with his son and wife. As a short man, he was uncomfortable with the way he looked. By 1920, his hair and wide mustache were completely white, his cheeks ruddy, and his belly prominent. Wearing his trademark homburg or boater made him look somewhat taller, but he would always growl when news photographers came by. He had an official mug shot and oil painting commissioned. Both made him look like a menacing—but taller—robber baron.

Prior to Chappie's postcollege European respite, Gladys had spent her days decorating, furnishing, and landscaping their pink palazzo. While Insull usually kept maniacal control over everything in his life, Gladys felt free to order changes to the estate on a whim. Insull gave her a yearly allowance of five figures for clothing and no limits on jewelry. None of these token gestures ended her emotional isolation from the city's business titan. When Insull was out of town, she ordered that a group of newly planted trees at their estate be uprooted, rearranged, and replanted. She found their original placement to be tasteless.

When Insull returned, he thundered to the groundskeeper, "who the hell moved my trees?"

"Mrs. Insull told us to," the man sheepishly replied.

"Oh," said the magnate in resignation.

"Shall we put them back?"

"Of course not. If Mrs. Insull told you to put them upside down, you do it."

Such power plays were unusual in the Insull house, though. Gladys generally played the dutiful wife when they were together with guests. Even though he was a teetotaler, he kept a fully stocked wine cellar for guests. She was not known to imbibe excessively, but she likely kept her distance from him in the mansion as if he were an alcoholic. Her abiding passion at home was performing for guests. She would act a scene from a play or sing a song. Making a dramatic entrance onto the grassy stage behind the pool, with her costumes flapping in the breeze, she appeared as a middle-aged Venus among the statues of the gods. This was the woman Insull had fallen in love with, and still he adored her, particularly when she was the center of attention.

In London the following year, Insull was talking with British leaders and financiers about war debts. As a leading Anglo-American financier, he was regularly consulted by British and American politicians. He had personally met with presidents Theodore Roosevelt, Taft, and Coolidge. His advice was so sought after that Taft sent an apology that he could not meet with Insull when he was in Washington one time visiting with Chappie. Invited to meet with a group called "The Other Club," he dined with Winston Churchill and other dignitaries. Insull advocated forgiving the war debts to the U.S. on the part of the every other nation, but not forgiving the English debt to the U.S. His one consolation was lowering the interest on the loans and reducing the principal. The English noblemen grumbled about the idea with reserved indignation. Insull asserted that he thought the arrangement would ensure that London would remain a financial center, "following the old rule that a creditor is always interested in the prosperity of the debtor." He doubted whether the other nations would repay their war debts and was confident England was in the best position.

The British leaders were suitably impressed with Insull and asked him if he could run a national power system for them. While politely declining, he freely offered his advice on the subject and was courted for his knowledge in every visit to London. Insull also regularly met with bankers while he was in London. Like Villard, he consciously avoided visiting Wall Street when he needed the kind of financing that Chicago bankers were unable to provide. New York financiers were clearly taking note of his absence from their boardrooms.

Insull was well known among English royalty. In London for an international power conference, he was invited to Buckingham Palace for a reception for 1,500 people. All of the leading politicians, courtiers, and industry executives were there. Insull strolled through the reception line to meet the king and queen with Gladys on his arm, who was bedazzled. The kindly looking King George, upon meeting Insull, recalled members of his family, most likely his uncle the mason, who had worked for him. Insull was touched by the king's thoughtful memory: "He looks about like any other English gentleman, and you feel at ease the moment you meet him. I would say of the two, Queen Mary has more the air of a queen than her husband has of a king, and that he exudes 'with the milk of human kindness.'"

The Roaring Twenties was shaping up to be Insull's decade as Mullaney's publicity machine gained momentum. Having learned how to reach people directly through the war campaign apparatus, Mullaney wanted to position Insull and his many operations as items of great public interest. Insull was no longer the Chicago utility executive; he would be the main spokesman for private utility management, business as a way of life, and the wonders of having electricity in every home. Mullaney would be Insull's P.T. Barnum, sending him on lectures, ensuring that his speeches were widely distributed and that everyone knew how incredibly brilliant and successful Insull had become. Nearly every speech would include how central station power made everyone's life better, created jobs, paid taxes, and made the U.S. a great place to live. Insull was being transformed from the power baron into the public benefactor, an icon of a higher standard of living.

Mullaney and Insull borrowed heavily from Barnum's powerful strategy. The circus promoter's classic 1855 autobiography and manual on humbuggery *The Life of Phineas T. Barnum, Written by Himself,* was the bible for Mullaney's all-out campaign to make Insull as prominent as the president of the U.S. Insull had clearly abided by several of Barnum's principles ever since his New York tenure with Edison, following closely what Barnum espoused in his "Rules for Success:"

- *Select the Kind of business that suits your natural inclinations and temperament.* Some men are naturally mechanics; others have a strong aversion to any thing like machinery, and so on; one man has a natural taste for one occupation, and another for another.
- *Let your pledged word ever be sacred.* Never promise to do a thing without performing it with the most rigid promptness.
- *Whatever You Do, do with All of Your Might.* Ambition, energy, industry, perseverance, are indispensable requisites for success in business.
- *Sobriety.* The use of intoxicating drinks as a beverage is as much an infatuation as is the smoking of opium by the Chinese, and the former is quite as destructive to the success of the business as the latter.
- *Let Hope Predominate, but be not too visionary.* Many persons are always kept poor, because they are too visionary.
- *Do Not Scatter Your Powers.* Engage in one type of business only, and stick to it faithfully until you succeed, or until you conclude to abandon it.
- *Engage Proper Employees.* Never employ a man of bad habits, when one whose habits are good can be found to fill his situation.
- *Advertise Your Business. Do Not Hide Your Light Under a Bushel.* Whatever your occupation or calling may be, if it needs support from the public, *advertise* it thoroughly and efficiently, in some shape or other, that will arrest public attention.[6]

As a fellow teetotaler and nonconformist Protestant, Insull adopted Barnum's sobriety guidelines, or at least he told everyone he did. Insull also had an obsession with keeping his word. Part of that bond was that if his customers were not getting the best service—or there were service interruptions—he would often rectify the problem personally. He had a special phone line installed in his Hawthorn Farm home to take such calls. While he could have been successful in nearly any business venture, he concentrated his considerable energy on central station service throughout his career and delegated authority for running railroads, retail sales, and his other ventures to his underlings, who were chosen for their competence, energy, and dedication. Like Insull, his captains were required to know their business thoroughly and expected to make a profit. His railroad chief Britton Budd, for example, an upright, bland, and diligent performer, knew what Insull expected and ran his railroads the way Insull would. Insull's overall vision and ability to advertise it were simply defined: get people to buy more power in myriad new ways. Mullaney and John Gilchrist were in charge of this aspect of Insull's operation and rarely failed in delivering the Insull sermon in hundreds of thousands of messages.

In the 1920s, Insull's gospel was straightforward and everyone in his companies understood it: promote power consumption while offering superior customer service. As the main preacher of the gospel of consumption, Insull never failed to remind the public that he was one of the godfathers of the electrical age, starting with his humble beginnings as a telephone operator to Edison's right-hand man. By 1921, Insull controlled power companies in 15 states representing more than a half a billion dollars of investment. He constantly sought to embellish the image of private ownership of utilities and waged separate propaganda campaigns to put himself and his enterprises in a glowing public light. Inveighing against the progressives' publicly owned utility movement, he took to the lecture circuit to convince his audiences how public utility ownership could hurt them:

> The total investment in the public utility services of Illinois is $1.25 billion. . . . The properties created in Illinois by this investment are owned not by a few "bloated capitalists" who "fatten on the necessities of the people," as pictured by the demagogue, but by upwards of 400,000 citizens of Illinois who have invested in the stocks of bonds of the state's public utility companies. . . . With their families, they constitute practically one-third of the state's population—all having a direct ownership interest in public utilities."[7]

Bolstered by Mullaney's stock sales campaigns before and after the war, Insull turned his attack on the progressives into a defense of the growing investor class. After all, Insull reasoned, how could one assault private ownership of utilities without insulting the thousands of wage-earning stockholders who were the real owners of these companies? He also was likely referring to "the demagogue" William Jennings Bryan's many jabs at big business and his industry. In the same speech, delivered before the Peoria Area Chamber of Commerce, Insull extolled the benefits of electrification to industry and agriculture. He acerbically lumped the public utility reformers with Luddites, calling them "the smashers of weaving machinery in the earliest textile mills and the mobs that stoned railroad trains when the steam locomotive was young."

Insull had a much larger agenda in reaching out to the public. In the early 1920s, the nation was being transformed from a country of cities connected only by telegraph, telephone, and rail lines into a network of interconnected power systems. The emerging model for a coast-to-coast power grid was called "Superpower" and had been endorsed by the U.S. Interior Department. At the time of the Peoria speech, Insull's system alone was 110 miles short of connecting a network that spanned from Minneapolis in the north to St. Louis and Louisville in the south. Chicago was the hub, using the rail system as a model. Coal was shipped north to feed Insull's power plants, and the electricity supplied much of the Midwest. Insull opposed the Interior Department's overall plan, which would have given local communities "home rule" power over utilities. The mogul believed that large, privately run plants could supply power more efficiently if they were centrally located and distributed power into the grid. He was right about the economics, though he did not accept the politics involved. While he boasted that 10,000 Illinois farmers had power in the early 1920s, the vast majority of the countryside did not. They had no way of getting power unless a power company came along and built a power plant or brought a high-tension line into town. Small towns had no ability to finance efficient plants and only benefited if they had access to hydropower, which meant that they had to be near a river and dam. That worked fairly well in the Tennessee Valley and the Pacific Northwest—as future public projects would demonstrate. But in areas in between the great rivers, there was a profound power gap.

Whatever new operation Insull acquired, it was given "the Insull treatment." The formula was drummed into his executives as if they were marine recruits. The process began with the physical upgrading of the property. Money was poured into the property to bring it up to date and efficient. Then it was relaunched as the latest new Insull project and given every possible promotional and advertising boost. Using the People's Gas turnaround model, Insull used his capital wisely. He bought properties like the Chicago elevated system to protect his power franchise. Customers on el trains were—or could be—customers for power in their workplaces or homes. Insull's acquisitions of three interurban electric rail lines not only expanded his customer base outside of the city, they created new markets more than 100 miles from the center of Chicago.

The North Shore Line, which Insull bought from receivership, was resurrected to great effect. The North Shore project, shepherded by Budd, took the line beyond the original goals of attracting new power customers. Inspired by the posters promoting the London Underground and French railways, Budd hired the best commercial artists of the time to create artistic posters that would promote the destinations and lifestyle afforded by Insull's rail lines. The posters did not just tell people to ride Insull trains because they would get to their stop quickly. The campaign promised glamour, excitement, recreation, comfort, and beauty. Two aficionados of the 1920s poster campaigns were John Gruber and J.J. Sedelmaier, who observed:

Nothing quite like them had been seen before. Commuters waiting at stations noticed them mounted on platform boards, large as life. They were simple, straightforward statements about local museums, parks, streets, sports and resorts, lithographed in full color. With a minimum of type, they stood in sharp contrast to the busy, garish, ugly products of most other advertisers. It was 1922, and the Chicago electric railroads had taken a new approach to poster art.[8]

All told, Budd had more than 200 posters created. They trumpeted a 300-mile arc of metropolis from southern Wisconsin lakes to the pristine Indiana dunes southeast of the city, all of which were accessible by Insull's train system. The power of advertising, which was coming into its own in the 1920s, was producing results. The Chicago Field Museum approved a railroad poster with an illustrated seahorse. Within three weeks, attendance had tripled. The museum, which had never advertised before, complained when the poster was removed. Some of the more famous posters, now favored by art collectors, featured Notre Dame football, polo matches, and special events in Milwaukee. Some posters were as simple as a single painted image such as a fish, while others appealed directly to commuters. Featuring the work of artists such as Oscar Rabe Hanson, Otto Brennemann, Carroll Berry, and Arthur Johnson, the posters highlighted their destinations in bright colors and striking images. They drew you into an idealized world of where you wanted to be once you left the city and the train.

Through increased advertising, ridership and service on the North Shore Line increased dramatically. By the mid-1920s, the line was running 160 daily trains, including 44 limited trains between Chicago and Milwaukee. As ridership rose, Budd built handsome new stations that resembled arts and crafts cottages or English country houses. Motor coaches were added in 1922 to extend service beyond the end of the line. The line had attracted national attention for its service and growth. In 1923, the line won the first annual Charles Coffin medal. Named after the first General Electric president (ironically the man who displaced Insull in Schenectady), the award recognized the electric railroad that had "done most to popularize electric railway services." Connecting with other trains also was part of the system's graces. A Milwaukee resident could catch the 9:55 a.m. train to downtown Chicago and then pick up the New York Central's *20th Century Limited* to New York City. Some of the many service improvements that Insull added consisted of full-course diners and observation cars. The food was inexpensive and the views, especially going through Wisconsin and northwest Indiana along the lake, were splendid. The dining cars were serving about 80,000 meals a day by 1925.

Since the tracks and grade crossings were well maintained, the trains could hurtle along at up to 100 miles per hour. They were relatively quiet and mostly

ran on time. From 1915 to 1923, Insull's trains were carrying ⬡
lion passengers a year, up from 7 million when he acquired his
North Shore was doing so well that Insull offered stock in th⬡
public in 1924. The railroad expanded further the following ye⬡
five miles north into what became known as the Skokie Valley route from the
city's northern terminus at Howard Street. Like most Insull railroads, the new
line simply used the right-of-way under his power lines. Budd placed new Span-
ish-style bungalow stations every three miles along the new route. Ridership rose
to nearly 20 million by 1926.

As the train stops were built, real estate development soared. The new villages of Niles Center (later Skokie), Mundelein, and Westchester thrived because their residents could buy relatively inexpensive tract homes and work in
downtown Chicago. The elements of cheap, efficient, and reliable transportation combined with electrified homes and businesses made these suburbs
working realities. Along with the Chicago, Aurora & Elgin, and South Shore
lines, Insull's trains reached out in every possible direction to embrace the
growing metropolis. Even at the end of the line, connecting motor coaches
would link you to other destinations as far as 250 miles away from Chicago.
With the electrification of the Illinois Central in 1926—the only large railroad Insull did not own in Chicago—the use of steam locomotives for com-
muting was mostly over (some lines continued to use steam engines into the
1950s). While cities were still far from pristine, given the enormous traffic
problems created by the growing use of the automobile, residents no longer
had to suffer steam engines belching smoke in the Loop area bounded by the
city's electric transit lines.

There was not a single Insull railroad that did not benefit from his takeovers
and promotion. The South Shore Line, which ran from Chicago to Michigan
City, Indiana, received a $6.5 million capital infusion by Insull. His Midland
Utilities acquired the route in 1925. Service was increased from 35 to 81 trains
daily by 1928. Ridership on the line went from 1.5 million passengers in 1925
to 3 million in 1928, with passenger revenues rising by 200 percent. Freight revenues rose by a factor of five in the same period. Budd flatly declared in 1927
that "well located interurban lines, instead of being obsolete, are in reality entering upon the period of their greatest usefulness." Insull constantly told his audiences on the lecture circuit how much he was spending on his operations and
what results were achieved. In highlighting his takeover of the North Shore
Line, for example, he said that by doubling his investment in the railroad from
$14 million to $31 million, passenger receipts rose 113 percent from $3 million
to nearly $7 million from 1919 to 1925. Insull was not afraid to spend money

to make his operations efficient, nor was he shy in telling the public how the expenditures were paying off. The goal was to convince the public that his brand of capitalism was the highest form of public service.

Insull was always pressing for better performance for his railroads, though. On one trip on the South Shore Line, Insull's special train of two motor cars and a parlor was racing back to Chicago from South Bend around 11 p.m. Summoning the line's traffic manager R.E. Jamieson into his cabin, Insull barked, "can't you make this damn train go any faster?" The train was doing 90 miles an hour at the time. Jamieson took the request to the motorman, who released some air from the braking system, producing noticeable vibration. Insull seemed pleased, even though the train was actually moving 15 miles per hour *slower*.

The South Shore and North Shore consistently vied for the title of fastest interurbans in America. The railroads took turns in capturing the industry's Electric Traction speed trophy, the Academy Award of interurbans. Speed awards boosted the egos of the men running the trains, but Insull had grander plans. From the early days of the trolleys, new communities sprouted up along the transportation routes. It had been an established practice in real estate circles that speculators could make a fortune if they knew where to buy land based on new trolley or train stations. New routes and stops were guaranteed ways of promoting development. Insull actively promoted a spur that took the South Shore Line into the Indiana Dunes Park (now a National Lakeshore park operated by the U.S. Department of the Interior). The South Shore's "Outing and Recreation Bureau" advertised the amenities of the park, which included a hotel and bathhouse, partially funded with a $25,000 gift from the railroad. According to the South Shore's famous advertising campaigns, the dunes became "Chicago's Favorite Playground Where Wilderness Is King." Real estate developers quickly capitalized on the campaign and the subdivisions of Beverly Shores, Lake Shore, North Shore Beach, and South Shore Acres made up one of the largest lakeshore developments in the Chicago area (most of Chicago's lakefront was declared off limits to developers thanks to Aaron Montgomery Ward and Daniel Burnham). These communities benefited directly from two, new $15,000 South Shore stations that were located adjacent to the dunes park. Home sales were supported through the railroads' "Own Your Own Home Bureau" and poster campaign. Again, the theme of bright images and simple, pleasant messages dominated the posters. "The New North Shore Where Homes Are Homes," advertised the North Shore Line. In that poster, a man was walking a dog under the fall colors of a maple trees on long avenues.

Insull's restoration and expansion of the interurbans led to tremendous industrial growth as well. Supplied with relatively cheap power and natural gas, northwest Indiana, also known as the Calumet region, became one of the world's largest steel-producing areas on the planet. U.S. Steel was one of the first major steelmakers in the area, establishing itself in Gary, Indiana. The nation's largest steelmaker also had plants in South Chicago, Waukegan, and Joliet (all but the Gary facility have since closed). Iron ore from northern Minnesota or the upper peninsula of Michigan could be delivered right to the mills, most of which occupied lakefront property on the southern shore of Lake Michigan. Bethlehem, Jones & Laughlin, Youngstown, Republic, and National Steel also had plants in the area. Long after most of the mills had converted to either basic oxygen or electric arc furnaces from the highly inefficient open-hearth process, the industry benefited from Insull's utilities. As a booster of industry, Insull publicly proclaimed that the day would come when the Calumet region would become the nation's leading steel-producing region. He certainly knew how much power the mills consumed in the mid-1920s: about 300,000 kilowatts or roughly 400,000 horsepower. With his power plants supplying only 11.5 percent of the power (the plants largely produced their own power), he was looking for a greater share of the power production. The 39 blast furnaces in the region also used a tremendous amount of gas—3 billion cubic feet every day. The Insull campaigns furthered industrial development through its "Come See the Workshop of America" promotions. By the end of the 1920s, 15 new industries were being served by the South Shore Line.

Coasting on the success of Insull's rail takeovers, power business, and public persona as the man who could make any business go, Mullaney was transforming Insull into a business icon during the mid-1920s. From the wild dance craze of the Charleston to the thriving business of the speakeasies, the 1920s demanded dynamic, larger-than-life figures. While the newly liberated class of young Americans poured bathtub gin down their throats courtesy of Al Capone and his minions, the business of America, in the words of Calvin Coolidge, *was* business. Every form of enterprise from advertising to typewriter sales was booming. Corporate cultures were blossoming as wide-eyed country girls and boys entered the city, looking for a jazzy lifestyle and a career. They all needed someone who could be a model to them as they plied the exciting new world of commerce. Mullaney realized that Chicago truly needed a role model like Insull, a man who had come to America with a funny accent and nothing in his pocket but prospered through hard work and intelligence. Turning Insull's stump speeches into hagiographic pamphlets, Mullaney started out with dull diatribes like *The Principles of Public Utility Management.* Despite the off-putting title, Mullaney had condensed Insullisms for general consumption. More than just excerpts from his speeches, they were guideposts to becoming a successful businessperson and citizen:

- Honesty and Punctuality. Punctuality is one of the first rules of business. . . . For the man in the highest position and the man in the lowest position, they are the first essential elements.
- A Creed of Publicity. I believe in presenting the facts to the employees, whose interest is just as vital as that of the managers, to the citizens of the state who are owners of the properties, to every customer of a gas company, an electric light and power company or street railway.
- Advantage of Cooperation. No matter how much ability may be displayed by the higher officials of a corporation, unless there is close cooperation all down the line, it is impossible to bring success.
- Courtesy to the Public. Courtesy to the public and the best possible service constitute the fundamental cornerstone of our policy.
- All the Cards on the Table. Take the public into your confidence, not as a favor to them, but as their right.
- Responsibilities of Citizenship. I believe that every man and every woman should take his or her part in the affairs of the community in which he or she lives.[9]

As the face of modern business, Insull was developing a highly visible public persona as the businessman with integrity, effectively laying to rest the monstrous image of the robber baron rapaciously preying upon the public and his competition. The persona would be enhanced by his role as patron of the arts, promoter of religion, real estate developer, virtual banker, and public benefactor. There was little that Insull could not touch and turn into gold, yet his overriding need for complete control of his operations was becoming his prime obsession.

MANAGING THE SPECTACLE

Mid-1920s Scandals

I've long respected President Calvin Coolidge. He knew when not to talk and what not to say.

—Charles Walgreen, founder of the drugstore chain.[1]

Tired of ossifying at home as Mrs. Samuel Insull, Gladys wanted to revive her career. Chappie was fulfilling his role as Samuel Insull, Jr., and learning the basics of his father's business. Simply known as "Junior" now, he no longer had an interest in an arts career and was seduced by the utilities industry. Insull had a place for him and few questioned that he would inherit the throne. Engaged to Adelaide Pierce, he would officially be out of the nest by July 15, 1926. Gladys was ready to reenter the theater world.

For her reemergence onto the stage, Gladys chose Richard Brinsley Sheridan's comedy *School for Scandal*. No longer burdened by the necessity of auditions, contracts, or ticket sales, she had the enthusiastic backing of her husband, who leased the Illinois Theater in downtown Chicago for the production. Gladys had the luxury of knowing that the run would not end prematurely, the house would be full on opening night and few papers dared to give her a bad review, based on the stature and fearsome nature of the producer. She was giddy about the prospect of doing what she loved again. She did not have to travel, could go to sleep in her own bed after the performance, and was free to mount the production as she pleased.

The one slight drawback was that she was now 56 and chose the role of an 18-year-old country maiden named Lady Teazle. Not fearing that the director would recast her, she rehearsed with zeal. Her skin still had a whipped-cream tone to it and her figure was still relatively petite. She had been acting for years on the backyard Hawthorn Farm stage, so she was not entirely divorced from theatrical presentation. The first night the house was packed. Insull had called in every one of his associates, business connections, politicians, and society denizens. Few dared to miss the premiere because it doubled as a benefit for St. Luke's Hospital.

As the innocent country girl who marries a man old enough to be her grandfather, Gladys was lively and charming, if not noticeably miscast. As she had in her New York acting days, she beguiled her audience and the papers deemed the play a critical success. The night also was a financial success as Insull netted nearly $138,000 for the hospital.

The typically vitriolic *Herald & Examiner* critic Arthur Meeker, Jr., who said 30 years later he thought Gladys was awful, wrote a gushing review:

> I have seen Ellen van Volkenburg, Mary Young and Ethel Barrymore [as Lady Teazle], but none of them could approach Mrs. Insull for delicacy of touch and humor. It is not only that she is the most beautiful of them all; she read the lines with so much archness and grace, and interpreted the varying moods of the character with such a fine sense of values that . . . it was the most charming and exquisite and distinguished high comedy performance I've ever seen![2]

Whether he, too, was intimidated by the daunting prospect of panning Insull's wife or was told by his boss Hearst to go lightly on Gladys, Meeker's praise was excessive, even for a charity performance. She would not find the same gleeful local boosterism, however, when she took the show on tour to New York. An aspiring playwright named Herman Mankiewicz was assigned to review Gladys's production by drama editor and comic genius George S. Kaufman at *The New York Times*. Mankiewicz saw the play, got drunk, came back to the newsroom and started to write a venomous review. Then he passed out on his typewriter before finishing it. Kaufman came by, read the drivel in the typewriter, and fumed. He refused to print it. Instead he ran a humiliating item saying that the play would be reviewed in tomorrow's paper. Mankiewicz's wife Sara was summoned to take him home; she assumed he was fired. The critic returned to the paper the next day, though, still employed, but penned an unsigned review that was watered down to the point of blandness:

> As Lady Teazle, Mrs. Insull is as pretty as she is diminutive, with a clear smile and dainty gestures. There is a charming grace in her bearing that makes for excellent deportment. But this Lady Teazle seems much too innocent, too

thoroughly the country lass that Joseph terms her, to lend credit to her part in the play.[3]

It would have been impossible for "Mank" to separate Gladys the actress from what he knew about her reputation in Chicago's upper circles. Mankiewicz worked as an overseas correspondent for Colonel McCormick's *Tribune* in 1921. He knew about Insull's involvement in the opera and the reputation Gladys had acquired—she was "notorious for her discordant twitter and petty dissatisfaction with everything."

Mankiewicz went off to Hollywood in 1927 and started luring some of his literary friends from New York to the movie capital. Luminaries such as Dorothy Parker followed. Holding various studio jobs, Mankiewicz got the writing offer of a lifetime 13 years later when the wunderkind Orson Welles asked him to write a film about a newspaper mogul—*Citizen Kane*. His Chicago experiences came back to him while shaping the character of Susan Alexander, Kane's mistress. Gladys was the partial inspiration, although she was not a singer. The Kane character was a composite of William Randolph Hearst, Colonel McCormick, and Insull. Welles, who had once performed on the stage of the Chicago Opera as the lovechild of Madama Butterfly, was fascinated with Insull's story (Insull died three years before the movie was written, though Hearst was still alive). Mankiewicz worked Insull's involvement with the opera into the screenplay as Kane's obsession with buying operatic venues for Susan Alexander, who is an awful singer. Welles also instructed his makeup artist Maurice Siederman to make him look like Insull in the 1930s—he literally handed him a photograph of Insull—complete with brush moustache. Hearst was also part of the composite character. For his part, Mankiewicz injected autobiography into the screenplay. The scene in the movie where the Joseph Cotton character comes back to the newsroom drunk and falls asleep on his typewriter while panning Susan Alexander's performance was no fiction. Gladys's *School for Scandal* performance was his likely inspiration.

Encouraged by the audience reaction and ignoring her lukewarm reception in Gotham, Gladys went on to found an acting company in Chicago and attempted to land other acting jobs. A young newspaperman and aspiring writer named Ben Hecht was starting his own theater company at the same time and auditioned Gladys. Hecht was interviewing Insull for a newspaper story when the subject of his theatrical freelancing somehow came up:

> At the time of my casting call, Mr. Insull was an employer of thousands and a man of millions. Yes, said the puissant financier, he had a greatly talented and beautiful actress to offer our Player's Workshop—his young wife. Mrs. Insull

became one of our players. I have no memory of her work, except as a gifted seller of tickets.[4]

Gladys's theatrical career sputtered and concluded shortly after her engagement with Hecht. The playwright went to Hollywood and wrote more than 140 screenplays. His classic work included *The Front Page,* about his ribald days as a Chicago newspaperman; *Gone with the Wind* (uncredited after several screenwriters were fired); *Notorious,* starring Ingrid Bergman; *Cleopatra,* starring Elizabeth Taylor and Richard Burton; *Mutiny on the Bounty* and *Guys and Dolls,* starring Marlon Brando; *The Man with the Golden Arm,* starring Frank Sinatra; and *Gilda,* starring Rita Hayworth.

After Gladys left the theater for the second time, she took up studying Napoleon Bonaparte as a serious hobby. Insull, who had read a few books on the little corporal, bristled at the idea of concentrating one's time on a single subject. Gladys had another insight: "Sam, you should learn about that man, and about what happened to him. If you don't, that's what's going to happen to you."

Insull found it essential to control the debate on whether his businesses were operating in the public interest. His venom was usually directed at the city's progressives, although he was cautious to avoid battling city politicians by name in the open. Usually supporting Republican candidates, he supported Mayor Thompson even though Big Bill wanted to make Chicago "as wet as the ocean" and attacked Insull's utility rates during the World War I. On the national level, Insull generally favored internationalist candidates who often held imperialist stances. Presidents McKinley and Theodore Roosevelt, both of whom he knew, were two of his favorites. Never forgetting a sleight, in politics, Insull backed the candidate who least interfered with his business.

Frank L. Smith was running for senator against utility owner William McKinley (no relation to the slain president) in 1926. Smith was the chairman of the Illinois Commerce Commission, the agency that Insull lobbied for beginning in 1898. As a fair-minded man, Smith was hardly in Insull's pocket, yet he was not his direct adversary, either. In his term as the commission's chairman, Smith had blocked all of Insull's rate increases and ordered or approved five rate cuts totaling $42 million. McKinley, on the other hand, became Insull's bitter enemy after McKinley refused to sell his downstate utility properties to Insull's companies. Owners with utility properties to sell rarely refused Insull. Those who did not take Insull's offer wished they had—if they later faced Insull as a competitor. Upon leaving the country for another trip abroad, Insull gave his brother Martin carte blanche to fund Smith's campaign and to generate propaganda against the World Court, an international judicial body backed by McKinley, which Insull opposed. Martin opened up the Insull accounts and recklessly wrote more than $150,000 in checks directly or indirectly to Smith's campaign, a staggering sum for a Senate race at the time. Fearing that Insull's role in the election would embarrass the Chicago business community, Julius Rosenwald offered Smith $550,000 to get out of the race, which he refused. McKinley spent more than $500,000 of his own money during the campaign.

Smith was elected, but the integrity of the Senate was besmirched, and the body refused to seat Smith and nullified the election because of Insull's "purchase" of his seat. Senator James Reed, a Democrat from Missouri who had his eye on the presidential nomination, held a hearing into the Insull contributions in 1928. Presidential candidate and progressive Robert LaFollette also had a deep interest in the utility baron's political financing scheme. Insull was brought in for questioning before Reed's committee.

At first, Insull was defiant and refused to answer any questions concerning his donations to local candidates. With the municipal elections looming, he did not want to hurt his candidates. Then Insull candidly admitted to financing Smith's campaign, showing no remorse. Insull was cited for contempt of Congress for refusing to provide details on his local political war chest, yet avoided prosecution when he provided the information after the city elections. Testimony by Allen Moore, Smith's manager, showed that it was Insull who freely offered envelopes of cash containing up to $125,000 from his desk drawer to finance the campaign. One senator on Reed's panel wanted to know if "there were persons in the contest who would fix the taxes upon the public utilities."

> "Oh, undoubtedly," Insull replied matter-of-factly. "But the public utilities are owned by 40,000 stockholders . . . of whom I am one, and I put up $237,000 in this whole campaign. Would I put that up to influence the taxes for a corporation? I did it because of reasons that I have not told you and do not intend to tell you, because it involves a dead man [McKinley died after the election], and other reasons, because I am very much interested in politics generally."[5]

Insull had another reason to support Smith. The utilities commissioner was backed by the Anti-Saloon League, a prohibitionist concern. Nevertheless, the scandal tarred Insull across the country, although he was not asked to resign from any of his companies. The Hearst newspapers were now emblazoning their front pages with headlines about the "power trust," a pejorative phrase that rekindled the bad old days of Gould, Rockefeller, and Morgan. Hearst, who was a friend of Insull's, called the utilities baron to insist that nothing personal was meant by his newspapers' campaigns. Hearst's business was selling newspapers, and Insull understood that all too well.

The progressives, though, now were emboldened by the Hearst broadsides to hound Insull and the other major private utility interests. While Senator Robert La Follette of Wisconsin had failed in his 1924 presidential bid, the Chicago progressives were reenergized by the Insull folly. One of La Follette's planks had been the creation of a "national super-waterpower system." Progressive Senator George Norris of Nebraska saw the Insull affair as another sound reason to promote publicly owned utilities. Paul Douglas, a professor of economics at the University of Chicago (and future U.S. Senator), saw Insull as the source of corrupt management in private utilities. Donald Richberg and Harold Ickes continued their crusade against the Insull concerns, claiming that Insull's monopolistic control was depriving Chicagoans of lower utility rates. David Lilienthal, a lawyer who would later play a large role at the Tennessee Valley Authority in the 1930s, sided with Richberg, Ickes, and Douglas. And the governor of New York, Franklin Delano Roosevelt, was waiting in the wings.

Insull's brother, the pugnacious Martin, whose leaked correspondence to one senator showed he was trying to curry favor for his industry, lashed out at his critics on national radio:

> I have never seen a goblin, and . . . I don't believe that you can recall in any news dispatch, speech or editorial, a real effort to explain what the *power trust* is. The power trust must therefore remain a myth until the politicians, professors and editors who talk about it so glibly condescend to give more definite information about it."[6]

Martin had a patrician air and cared little about fine-tuned public relations. Often seen around the city in riding boots, he never became an American citizen and benefited from a college education at Cornell that his brother had financed. Having even less social cachet than Insull, he was often a loose cannon. While following the Insull management dictums of profitability and sensible management, he was soundly disliked by his employees and did not travel well in political circles.

Taking on some of the roles that Insull had adopted when he first came to Chicago, Martin was an active propagandist for the utility industry, particularly when lambasting the public ownership movement. On this front, he had some powerful allies. In a speech before the National Electric Light Association, he quoted President Coolidge's Inaugural Address reference to the industry's "ownership and control of their property, not in the government, but in their own hands." Insull and Martin were touching a deep nerve in American history when they spoke about private ownership of their industry. Before the time of the Revolution, colonists had come to the New World to assert their property rights and to be free of capricious confiscation of their land, a political right articulated by the philosopher John Locke and every political radical who seeded the revolt against imperial power. Public ownership, in the Insull interpretation, was nothing less than government confiscation of private property. The business-oriented presidents McKinley, Harding, Coolidge, and (eventually) Hoover all tapped into the business community's animus toward government control. After all, the Insulls argued, their industry exhibited good citizenship and was a benefit to society, an *ownership* society based on the number of share- and bondholders of their companies.

Martin reminded the public that "$7 billion dollars of the savings of the people" were invested in his industry, serving 17 million customers and "doing the work of eight million horses every hour to carry on the industrial and social life of the nation." Moreover, the industry paid $135 million in state, local, and federal taxes every year, "to say nothing of the taxes paid by the investors." The powerful argument that was the locus of the Insull propaganda effort was subtle: Government takeover of the utilities industry was *un-American*.

Few people understood the Insull line better than the brilliant former mining engineer and commerce secretary Herbert Hoover. In 1925, Hoover was the heir apparent to the White House. A likable yet commanding presence with a sharp mind and compassionate reputation, Hoover backed the business community wholeheartedly in the McKinley Republican tradition. The man who was given 32 honorary degrees had organized a massive program to feed Europe after World War I, was well respected, and was an expert promoter of his ideas. At the 49th convention of the National Electric Light Association, he was the keynote speaker and was introduced by Martin.

Hoover was an enthusiastic backer of Insull's superpower vision, the idea that private utilities should be able to build a large, national system and be under minimal or no federal regulation as they expanded across state lines. He knew the history of the industry, its struggles with regulation, and Insull's role in promoting it. It also helped that he opposed further (national) regulation or government ownership. Hoover also understood the progressives' opposition to what they called "Giant Power" and was bent on defusing their public power movement. His speech described the industry's prowess in prosaic terms and left the industry with what it wanted to hear from the future president:

You deliver your energy with the same delicacy of feeling as the dentist's hammer and the boiler maker, and you relieve a lot of human sweat. Our people now substitute for muscle an average of 3,300 kilowatt hours per year per family instead of 250 kilowatt hours but 10 years ago—although they mostly do not know what a kilowatt hour is, they know what to do with it . . . I do not agree with the conclusion that federal regulation is necessary.[7]

Hoover went on to tilt at the industry's tiny foe—municipally owned power plants—which only had 3.5 percent of the nation's total generating capacity at the time. On every point, Hoover was on board with what the Insulls were proposing: free flow of power across state lines, no federal regulation of power (the state commissions were enough), and the increased movement toward "customer" ownership and the unfettered selling of utilities stocks. If the industry had a greater national political friend than Hoover, Martin was hard-pressed to name him. Hoover concluded his speech with the nobility of purpose the Insulls wanted to convey: "The electrical industries, through their methods of organization, may be the bearers of a new gift to sorely tried men, greater even than the energy they supply," Hoover finished, then received rapturous applause.

The Hoover address was hardly a turning point in national public policy. Yet it spelled out in clear terms what the industry could expect from him as president. His hands-off attitude was like an insurance policy that would virtually guarantee that the White House would leave them alone to conduct their business as they saw fit and continue to grab smaller operators across state lines while building holding companies and selling stock.

With his public image tarnished by the Smith affair, Insull had suffered a serious public relations blow, the first of many as the decade came to a close. Undaunted, Mullaney kept him on the lecture circuit, where the utilities magnate specialized in tirades against government inference in his business. Every speech took a new twist on the "big government is bad" theme, even invoking the "slippery slope" argument:

Political ownership [of utilities] once seriously undertaken in any industry will soon extend to the factory and the farm; it will become *political* ownership of all business and industry, including the colleges and universities that play with the idea. Municipal and political ownership proposals are not new, and their failure to make more headway in this country has not been due to sinister opposition from the so-called "capitalistic interests," as alleged by the soap-box orators. It has been due to their impracticality and their inherent economic implications.[8]

In that same speech, Insull also put his spin on the term "holding companies." He preferred the term "investment" companies, rightly claiming that a holding company is a misnomer because "they don't hold anything." He characterized the entities as conduits that "facilitate the investment of capital for the specific purpose of fostering development, and supplying high-grade service to communities and territories which otherwise would have only inefficient service, or none at all."

Once again, Insull invoked his cause in the name of his 200,000 employee-investors, his 2.5 million customers, and 220 million railroad passengers. In 1925, almost no one else in the world could make that claim. As with every Insull address of that period, he was quick to promote the idea of superpower. Citing his history of massing power at central stations and transmitting high-voltage current throughout the Midwest, Insull was positioning himself to be the logical *capo di capo* of a national utility concern. His empire was to stretch from Maine to Texas and those who did not subscribe to his vision were against progress and sound economics, or "supplying energy in the greatest possible volume at the lowest possible cost." He was quick to laud his own efforts, saying that building his system resulted in the "lowest selling price (of power) . . . in any large center anywhere in the world." That claim was partially true. Electricity prices were generally lowest in areas where hydropower was dominant—largely unpopulated areas where the raw material for creating power was free.

In every industry speech of the mid- to late 1920s, there was some defensive reference to time and human toil saved through electricity, the number of people who benefited from central station power, and the overall societal gain. The electric metropolis was a growing utopia in Insull's view, a land where people worked less and reclaimed their time for better things. And this great boon to civilization was dropping in cost as his operations became more efficient and everyone became richer because of it:

> What electricity has meant in terms of national wealth is shown by the fact that electric motors throughout the country are doing every day as much work as could be accomplished by 170 million men [the U.S. population was 116 million in 1925]. . . . Not even political agitators have been able to challenge the fact that our industry, working under State Regulation, needing vast amounts of capital for development, working with narrow margins of profit and slow turnover of invested capital, nevertheless has made electric light and power among the cheapest, if not the cheapest of all commodities in daily use.[9]

Noting that "since 1920, the investment in electric light and power stations and their transmission lines has equaled the total capital provided [to the industry] in the previous 39 years," Insull urged his industry to continue its mission despite the growing voice of the progressives.

While Gladys was finished with the theater, Insull was just beginning to assert his full control over the opera. As a member of the opera's board, he had always pushed for austerity measures, yet was always met with opposition from the free-spending, stage-loving egos of the McCormicks and Mary Garden. The McCormicks, who had been the financial mainstay of the opera through 1922, were headed for divorce. Harold McCormick was having an affair with the young soprano Ganna Walska, who was married to New York millionaire Alexander Smith Cochran. The opera always ran deficits, but the McCormicks had always opened their checkbooks to cover salaries, scenery construction, and the many other costly details of grand opera. Insull was never happy with such financial abandon. In his view, an opera could be run as efficiently as a business, with costs controlled and the proper marketing to sell subscriptions.

Mary Garden had been the unofficial executive running the opera since the beginning of the 1921 season because of the abrupt resignation of Gino Marinuzzi, the artistic director. In addition to the approval of the McCormicks, she had the backing of J. Odgen Armour, the meatpacking king, whose fortune was estimated at $100 million. While she never openly admitted she had an affair with Armour, she certainly loved the handsome, kindhearted civic leader. Armour once followed her to Kansas City and had invited her to lunch at his club, his house north of the city, and his London apartment. Coincidentally, Insull also regularly stayed in London, had a country home only a few miles from Armour's, and had direct dealings with Mary, who likely met him at his clubs. (Mary was coy about her secret admirer in her autobiography and never mentions her lover by name.) Finally named the director of the Chicago Opera Association, although she insisted on being called the *directa*, she immediately announced who would be singing for her and the breakdown of operas performed: 50 percent Italian, 35 percent French, and 15 percent in English. Insull battled with her over the exclusion of German operas, noting that there were far more citizens of German descent in the city than French.

Working with Harold McCormick and Insull, Mary moved to democratize the association's membership by soliciting 500 guarantors of $1,000 each for five years. She vacationed in the Riviera with the Cole Porters that summer and returned to Chicago to discover that the McCormicks had separated. She told reporters, "That doesn't mean anything. Why, if *I* had a husband, *I'd* live under a separate roof, and only let him come around when *I* wanted him." She sang *Salome* later in the year and was again pelted with a barrage of insults and death threats, including a package that contained a pistol and hollow-pointed bullets. Once again the critics blasted her performance as "vulgar, obscene and immoral." The press called for her resignation the following year, but Insull, who was now head of the governing Civic Opera Association, fully supported her. Tenor Lucien Muratore had resigned in protest, also enlisting chief conductor Giorgio Polacco, who refused to conduct her farewell performance for that season. Polacco's revolt was said to be retribution for an earlier row with Mary over his unsatisfactory conducting of her treasured *Pelleas* earlier that year. Mary reportedly punched the maestro repeatedly and told him to leave. In April of that year she resigned as director (she had forgone her salary), leaving a $1 million loss in her wake. Insull asked her to stay on for another season. Despite attendance records being broken, she retreated to Europe, taking the time to nurture new singers and play the tables at Monte Carlo, where she won 80,000 francs. She needed a break from the conflagration of egos, particularly from Muratore, who she often called either a "pretty boy" or simply a "pig."

"If she had been a *man,* I would have killed her to defend my honor," Muratore bravely crowed after Mary left Chicago.

Insull had another view and expressed nothing but admiration. "Her conduct in the past year had been 'manly'—that's the only word that describes it."

Now the president of the newly constituted Civic Opera Association, Insull brought in his allies to shore up the opera's finances. He recruited Stanley Field, the cousin of Marshall Field, to be secretary and treasurer of the association. Charles Dawes, who was also serving as President Harding's chief of the National Bureau of the Budget at the time, was Insull's chief cost cutter. Every expense was to be scrutinized, justified, or eliminated under the Insull regime.

"I am not in any sense an authority on grand opera, except as to what it costs," Insull told reporters. The former London office boy who had forsaken meals to buy a sixpenny seat in the nosebleed seats of Convent Garden was trying to rein in costs while presenting a variety of operas. By 1925, Insull had boosted attendance, raised ticket prices, and trimmed the budget. The ruling elite, though, were grumbling, since some of the higher-priced singers were being lured away by the Metropolitan Opera. Soprano Amelita Galli-Curci was one of the defectors, which gave the colonel at the *Tribune* an editorial opening to dig at Insull's management:

Mr. Insull lost Galli-Curci, just lost her, and didn't get a penny when New York took her. It's all wrong and Chicago's out $40,000 in a season which never had a chance. . . . Opera, as it is, requires a subsidy whether it gets it from mad citizens or mad kings. . . . The Civic Opera isn't civic and it isn't grand.[10]

Under attack by the critics, the *Tribune,* the social register, and the artists, Insull stiffened his resolve. The shortfalls were becoming smaller while receipts rose. The attendance also increased, despite growing competition from radio and cinema. The annual deficits were now averaging about $200,000. Seeing a means to provide permanent financial underpinning to the opera, Insull launched a bold concept that no one contemplated in the days when the wealthy were seen as the sole benefactors of the arts. On December 9, 1925, Insull told a meeting of the Chicago Association of Commerce that he was going to construct a new building to house the opera company. The skyscraper would provide generous space for a grand hall and foyer, rehearsal and storage space, and offices whose rents would cover the operating expenses of the opera. Occupying the first six floors of the 45-story building, the opera would have a new home situated on the Chicago River on Wacker Drive.

While a few civic savants gave faint praise to the idea, others were appalled. The Chicago River at the time was past the western boundary of the Loop, closer to a grimy warehouse district. The river usually stank, and others feared that barges would ram the building. The psychological impact of moving from the venerable Auditorium on elegant Michigan Avenue was akin to a blunt trauma for many society matrons. Insull used the pending demolition of the Auditorium as an excuse to build the new opera house. In reality, the Auditorium, which was as solid as a mountain, had no structural problems and only suffered from a relatively small, cavelike foyer. Its acoustics then, and now, were unrivaled. Once again Insull had inflamed the sensibilities of Chicago's elite. As he had done in the past, he would solider on and ignore what the fur-laden crowd was saying. This was the 1920s and anything could be accomplished.

Although still sneered at by his society peers for his brusque manner and apparent disregard for their refined tastes, Insull was still the first man in Chicago you contacted if you wanted action on a large project. George Cardinal Mundelein placed such a call to Insull in 1925. As the leader of the city's growing Catholic community, the cardinal was a talented organizer, builder, and financier in his own right. He had arrived in Chicago in 1916 upon appointment of the Pope to steer one of the most fractious archdioceses in the country. Growing immigrant populations were constantly wrestling for influence within the city's church. Poles, Italians, Germans, and Irish each had their established neighborhoods. When the population of those fiefdoms expanded, as was the case in the first three decades of the twentieth century, new pressure would be put on the archdiocese to create a new parish, a new church, and a school. Compounding the needs of the burgeoning Catholic population was the growing demand for new priests to serve in the parishes. Any archbishop would be flummoxed by the complex politics among the ethnic groups, each jostling for its own parish. Mundelein was not an ordinary cleric, however. He was a deft practitioner of big-city politics and could bring rival groups together with lay businessmen to build what he needed. In many ways the equal of Insull in his own sphere, Mundelein also understood the sophisticated ways of financing construction.

Mundelein was close friends with Harold Stuart of the firm of Stuart-Halsey. Stuart was the sales wizard behind Insull's numerous bond sales and one of the reasons Insull did not need to court New York bankers when he was floating a new bond issue. Mundelein met both Stuart and Insull during the Liberty bond campaign of World War I. The cardinal proved to be as adept at selling Liberty Bonds to his flock as the Insull team had been, and consequently earned the respect of the two businessmen. Mundelein learned quickly from the city's financiers and was able to do his own bond sales. He became so fluent in the arcane world of bonds that the city's business community mused that the cardinal "missed his calling" by becoming a priest. It was an enormous compliment.

Mundelein carefully cultivated his relationship with the business community, particularly with Stuart and Insull. Like Insull, Mundelein insisted on large-scale projects with a vision. St. Mary of the Lake was like few seminaries in the country, for the cardinal wanted his priests to have the best. Designed in colonial style, the buildings of the seminary looked more like a New England college, highlighted by Georgian details such as neoclassic corinthian columns. The main chapel, reminiscent of London's St. Martin in the Fields, is at the end of an esplanade that ends in a peristyle on a wooded lake. The cardinal modeled it after a congregational meeting house he had seen in Old Lyme, Connecticut, where he had vacationed as a boy. A boathouse is cleverly concealed in the middle of a balcony. The scope and feel of the grounds, though, are Roman. One feels a sense of walking from St. Peter's—there is a statue of the saint on a three-story column—to the Tiber down the esplanade. The cardinal's villa, also Georgian, was a fairly close copy of George Washington's Mt. Vernon. Insull, who also contributed money to the building of the seminary, was a frequent dinner guest in the cardinal's home, as his Hawthorn Farm was only a few miles away. Most of the $10 to $20 million in funds to build the seminary was donated by Chicago businessmen such as Edward Hines, who owned a lumber company and managed to have his son (who died from pneumonia in the World War I) buried above the boathouse. The 1,000-acre seminary was a self-sufficient complex with its own power plant, library, and gymnasium. It was so well known by the Vatican that Mundelein would later suggest that the Holy See relocate to the seminary during World War II. Proud of what he had accomplished, Mundelein insisted that out-of-town visitors take the grand tour of the seminary. To many critics, though, the seminary was needlessly lavish and was derided as "the enchanted forest." Nevertheless, the cardinal knew that the serene setting with its four miles of walks through the woods and around the lake would make a splendid, spiritual setting.

Mundelein learned so much at the feet of Stuart and Insull that later in the decade he was chosen by the Vatican to lend his advice in financing the pontifical college on Janiculum Hill in Rome. The College of Cardinals was preparing to raise the money before they built the school. Mundelein, however, suggested they borrow the money, something the Vatican had not done since 1870. Using archdiocesan property as collateral, Mundelein floated $1.5 million in bonds through Halsey-Stuart. The financing was not a gift, though. Mundelein stipulated that the bonds be repaid through Vatican revenues.

Unlike Insull, Mundelein relished pomp and ceremony. Upon his arrival in Chicago in 1916, he choreographed a special train containing 63 priests that came to New York to "escort" him to his new city. After being installed by the papal legate Archbishop John Bonzano, Mundelein was the guest of honor at three receptions, the third event being a mass levee at the Auditorium. One reception, in which 300 civic leaders were invited to the University of Chicago Club, nearly ended in tragedy. A deranged anarchist kitchen employee poisoned the soup with arsenic. While most of the guests were sickened, none died since another cook had diluted the soup when he detected a foul taste. Mundelein did not touch his soup that evening.

Upon being elevated to cardinal in 1924, Mundelein was planning another event that would bring greater visibility to his archdiocese, now the second largest in America behind New York. At the time it was rare for American archbishops to wear the red berretta, as most of the cardinals were predominantly European. By the mid-1920s, though, American money was largely supporting the financial operations of the Vatican and American bishops were gaining ever greater influence in Rome. Mundelein made a bold move, offering to host the

28th Annual Eucharistic Congress in Chicago in 1926. The devotional event, which would attract pilgrims all over the world, had never come to the U.S. Its only North American venue had been Montreal in 1910. By holding the Congress in Chicago, Mundelein was showing Rome that American Catholics were deserving of recognition.

Although he was not Catholic, Insull was asked by Mundelein to become one of the event's main organizers. Logistics would be the main dilemma as hundreds of thousands would be streaming into Chicago for a mass at Solider Field, and a final procession would be so large that most public spaces in the city would not be able to handle the crowds. When the Congress was held in London in 1908, the government banned the procession altogether. The seminary grounds were favored by Mundelein since they were on private property and no governmental permission was needed. The main logjam would be getting people by car or train from Chicago to Area (since renamed Mundelein), the town adjacent to the seminary, which was 40 miles to the north.

Insull was the ideal man to put in charge of the logistics between Chicago and the seminary. His North Shore Line had just completed a $10 million extension of its Skokie Valley route that went right into Area. It was more than a coincidence that the massive transportation needs of the Congress coincided with Insull's plan to promote the new line. The North Shore spur, which extended the line close to his Hawthorn Farm estate, allowed Insull to serve areas west of the North Shore communities where he had bought power plants nearly 20 years earlier. The railroad would pioneer the use of "piggyback" and refrigerated freight cars and two streamlined *Electroliners* that were some of the most elegant trains of their day. Fill from a lake that was dug on his farm property was used in the North Shore's construction. While he was building the railroad spur, Insull purchased two banks in the Libertyville area and some land for real estate development. His estate was now spanning 4,000 acres and he was anxious to see how the North Shore Line would fuel growth. Local residents joked that they bought their electricity and gas from Insull, banked at his banks, went to his hospital, and rode his railroad.

In New York, Mayor Jimmy Walker and Governor Al Smith greeted the 49 cardinals who stepped off the ship from Rome. They accompanied them through the streets to the train station, where a special, red-painted train whisked them to Chicago. Upon their arrival in Chicago, the cardinals and their party were feted at the Coliseum, a large convention hall. Insull was asked to give the opening address to officially welcome the delegation. It was one of the more memorable speeches he ever gave. More the speech of a diplomat, it was gracious and offered a unique perspective on the importance of Chicago for the event. As a tribute to the city, his guests, and Mundelein, it was devoid of his jibes against his usual adversaries and made no reference to utilities:

> By reason of its youth, its situation, and the special character of its development, our city especially typifies the purely industrial and commercial forces that now play so large a part in human affairs. Industry and commerce have their place, along with the benign influence of religious teaching and the cultural effects of Art and Literature, in the promotion of civilization, as the word Civilization is commonly interpreted in this 20th century . . . it is apparent that the spiritual needs of man's nature have not been subordinated to material concerns. Everywhere amongst us the church, the school, the library, the Art Museum and the University are neighbors to the agencies of industry and commerce.[11]

Insull was host to nine of the prelates, who stayed at Hawthorn Farm. He moved into the farmhouse for the duration of the Congress and told his servants to accommodate his guests in every way. Gladys, who originally had removed most of the Italian furniture that Insull had bought for the villa, found a few pieces and brought them into the house to make her European guests feel more at home. Cardinal Dubois, the archbishop of Paris, was particularly impressed with Insull's wine cellar and a small chapel he had built on a sunporch.

"I have two questions about your house," the cardinal asked Insull before he left. "First, what is a Protestant doing with a beautiful chapel in his home? Second, what is a teetotaler doing with the best wine cellar I've ever had use of?"

Insull replied that he kept a well-stocked wine selection to entertain guests. The cellar included a rare 1855 Madeira and dry whiskey.

On the first three days of the Congress (June 20 through 23), the weather was perfect. An estimated one million people came into the city for the services and not one incident was reported. There were no reported anti-Catholic demonstrations against the "Romanists," although a rumor was spreading out East that the Pope was preparing an invasion.

On the final day, some 600,000 made their way by car and train to the seminary—a crowd equivalent to the entire population of Philadelphia. The North Shore Line performed flawlessly, as trains arrived in Chicago every 40 seconds. By 10 a.m. of the final day, some 130,000 people had arrived at the seminary via 820 trains and 5,216 cars.

The cultural world was gyrating along with the rhythm of the 1920s. Prosperity, the booming stock market, and higher wages were propelling young people out into the workplace, the theaters, the cinemas, and the speakeasies. It was a time for celebration, sexual liberation, dancing, and song. George Gerswhin was conquering Broadway with his musicals and injecting jazz into his impressionistic piano pieces like *Rhapsody in Blue,* a piece the critics gave a lukewarm reception to when it premiered in 1924. The Tin Pan Alley tunesmith had become an innovative composer and the world was not moving in his direction fast enough. *Strike Up the Band* and *Oh, Kay!* were pleasant enough, yet there was more to come. The prolific composer, working with his clever lyricist brother Ira, would pen *S'Wonderful, She Loves and He Loves,* and *How Long Has This Been Going On?* Jerome Kern was breaking new ground by introducing racial themes to Broadway by writing the music to Chicagoan Edna Ferber's *Showboat,* featuring the immortal *Old Man River.* Irving Berlin, Cole Porter, and Irving Caesar rounded out a decade that celebrated the popular song through piano rolls, sheet music, recordings, and live performances. Never had music been available to so many in such mass distribution. Popular music no longer was relegated to amorous or patriotic themes, it was branching out into politics and heading to new horizons. Al Jolson's *California Here I Come* was as much about the discovery of the New West and Hollywood, where he made the first talking motion picture *The Jazz Singer,* as it was about the runaway exuberance of a country on the move.

The world of literature was adjusting to the new reality of fiction. Sinclair Lewis had turned his piercing gaze onto Middle America in *Babbitt,* a runaway bestseller in 1924, before it had been displaced by F. Scott Fitzgerald's *The Great Gatsby* in 1925, the defining novel of the jazz age. While Lewis exposed the hypocrisy of middle-class mores, Fitzgerald went full throttle after tycoons and the new meaning of money. Wealth was no longer just status and power; it became a narcotic state of isolation and disillusionment. As Scott and Zelda Fitzgerald were getting bombed and dancing in fountains, America was dancing right along with them. Lewis, Fitzgerald (who, like Lewis, was also from Minnesota), and later Hemingway, represented a triumvirate of critical midwestern voices. This heartland contingent of the "Lost Generation" emerged world-weary out of World War I wanting more out of life and they challenged everything about American culture.

Nearly every literary figure seemed to pass through Chicago en route to fame. Future Nobel Prize winner Lewis, stopping in town for a dinner in his honor in 1925, was feted by the enlightened Dr. Morris Fishbein, editor of the *Journal of the American Medical Association.* The swashbuckling actor Douglas Fairbanks was in attendance, as was Carl Sandburg, biographer of Lincoln, poet laureate of Chicago, and emerging folksinger. Sandburg, who had been collecting every

known type of American folk song for his renowned *American Song Bag,* was asked
to sing a ballad. After someone handed him a guitar, he gave a rough rendition of
The Buffalo Skinners, a heartbreaking story of starvation, Indian fighting, being
cheated out of meager wages—and murder. When Sandburg finished, Lewis was
sobbing. "That's the America I came home to. That's it," Lewis said.

Culture was being broadcast every day through the burgeoning medium of
radio. In keeping with large companies getting into the business first to promote
their product, Sears Roebuck started radio station WLS in Chicago in 1924.
The call letters stood for "World's Largest Store," imitating the braggadocio of
Colonel McCormick's "World's Greatest Newspaper" (WGN). An old-time
country music show called *The National Barn Dance* was a hit. Almost two years
later, WSM in Nashville launched *The Grand Old Opry.*

For the first time in history, electricity allowed radio to air the great questions of the ages, in addition to everyday music, news, sports, and weather. Insull's opera broadcast had opened the door at the beginning of the decade. By
1925, nearly everything was being questioned as America grappled with its fundamental nature. Throughout the country, conservative forces were resisting the
tide of the 1920s with its free-living ways and open challenges to the Victorian
prohibitionists. Aimee Semple McPherson and Father John Coughlin had their
own radio shows to bluster against sin. Tent shows featuring evangelists were as
popular outside the cities as bathtub gin was inside. The Ku Klux Klan, with its
racist, anti-Catholic, anti-Semitic, pseudo-Christian dogma of protecting the
white "race," was thriving throughout the South and extended its tentacles as far
north as Indiana. The time produced flashpoints when the secular, scientific civilization born of the Enlightenment collided with the fundamentalist, Bible-
centered beliefs of the preindustrial world.

Clarence Darrow was a secularist and a progressive who had as much passion as an evangelist and a sense of justice that riveted courtrooms. Having come
to Chicago from Ohio, he specialized in defending the indefensible. His law
partner, Edgar Lee Masters, was a poet, having penned *Spoon River Anthology*
about a group of souls in Central Illinois. In 1924, Darrow took on the case of
Nathan Leopold, Jr., and Richard Loeb, two teenagers from wealthy families
who confessed to the kidnapping and murder of a 14-year-old boy named
Bobby Franks for the apparent thrill of it. The murderers, who were 17 and 18
respectively, were also brilliant college students. Leopold was the youngest graduate of the University of Chicago and Loeb was on his way to graduating from
the University of Michigan. While there was little doubt of their guilt, Darrow's
mission was to save them from execution, no easy feat considering the public
outcry for their deaths. Darrow had a reputation for long closing statements and

this trial would be no exception. It was a titanic feat of rhetoric, poetry, mercy, and pleading that took 12 hours to complete. When he was finished, the courtroom sat in stunned silence and the judge was in tears. The boys then received life sentences and avoided the gallows.

Nearly a year later, Darrow took on an even higher profile case that attracted national attention. He defended Thomas Scopes, a 24-year-old Tennessee high school teacher who defied the state's "anti-evolution" law to teach Charles Darwin. The man who lobbied for the law—William Jennings Bryan—was virtually retired in Florida, but volunteered to assist the prosecution. Bringing the trial to a huge audience was Chicago radio station WGN, which had set up a special hookup to broadcast the trial live. The "Scopes Monkey Trial" attracted more than 3,000 in the tiny town of Dayton, Tennessee, and hundreds of thousands of listeners around the country. The trial was one of the century's first media events. Outside the sweltering courtroom, there were hotdog and lemonade vendors, revivalists, labor activists, anarchists, and more than 100 newspapermen, including critic H.L. Mencken. Western Union installed 22 telegraph lines to accommodate the scribes.

In the torrid heat, the jury of church-going Tennesseans heard expert testimony from Harvard professors to biblical scholars. The trial climaxed when Darrow called Bryan to the stand and the "Great Commoner," secretary of state, and presidential candidate sat in the witness chair without a coat, his sleeves rolled up, collar tucked in, and fanning himself with a palm leaf. The often hilarious repartee between Darrow and Bryan lasted for an entire day and featured exchanges like this:

Darrow: How long ago was the Flood [of Noah] Mr. Bryan?
Bryan: Let me see Usher's calculations about it.
D: Surely. (hands Bryan a bible)
B: It is given here as 2348 years B.C.
D: Well, 2348 years B.C. You believe that all the living things that were not contained in the ark were destroyed?
B: I think the fish may have lived.
D: Outside of the fish?
B: I cannot say.
D: You cannot say?
B: No, except that just as it is, I have no proof to the contrary.
D: I am asking you whether you believe.
B: I do.
D: That all living things outside of the fish were destroyed?
B: What I say about the fish was a matter of humor.
D: I understand.[12]

The judge ruled that Bryan's testimony be stricken from the record. With that, Darrow asked that the jury be brought in to return a *guilty* verdict. Scopes was fined $100 and court costs, but won on appeal in the state supreme court. Bryan died a few days after the trial. Darrow quipped that "a man who for years fought excessive drinking, now lies dead from indigestion caused by overeating."

The Monkey Trial marked one of the early highlights in the media age. Newspapers and radio would be joined by newsreels, movies, television, and the Internet as the world tried to keep up with the electricity-fueled appetite for information and entertainment.

As Insull ruled the business world in Chicago, Capone and his henchmen ruled the underworld. There was plenty of money flowing through the economy of the mid-1920s, and Capone was there to keep the booze flowing and his competition in line by the deft application of brass knuckles and Thompson submachine guns. Crime was as much a part of the diffuse 1920s as high culture and electricity. In 1924, the nation's largest train robbery was committed within a few miles of Insull's Hawthorn Farm at a junction of railroad tracks named Rondout. A group of Texans named the Newton Boys robbed a mail train of $3 million in cash, bonds, and jewelry. Employing a mail inspector as the "inside" man to set up the heist, the robbery involved accomplices from Kansas City and Oklahoma. Postal inspectors tracked one of their own, William Fahy, to the saloons, where he was spending $300 a night—a month's salary at the time. Fahy was arrested some two months after the robbery and helped investigators track down the other culprits and all but $1 million of the loot, which, to this day, has not been recovered.

Capone held tight control of his rackets in downtown Chicago, west suburban Cicero, south suburban Chicago Heights, and the North Side. Capone traveled around his territory in a seven-ton bulletproof car with gun ports. Fearing being kidnapped or assassinated—Insull had been fired on before while riding with Gladys in his limo—Insull turned to the one man who perfectly understood his dilemma. Capone offered to provide security services if Insull agreed to pay the mobsters' salaries and benefits. Insull not only did not like the price of Capone's services, he did not want to be seen with men sporting wide-brimmed fedoras, pinstripes, and tommy guns, so he refused Capone. There is no record of the discussion between the two men, other than an account by Capone's biographer Laurence Bergreen:

Beyond the need for security, the *modus operandi* of both men had much in common, for Insull and Capone were determined to build monopolies and control their product. Insull contributed $100,000 to [Mayor Big Bill] Thompson's campaign, almost as much as Capone had, but few bothered to criticize Insull for doing so or to divine sinister motives. As Capone knew, people outdid themselves to worship the wealthy, as long as they did not have Italian surnames.[13]

Insull instead turned to his own employees to form a squad of security men and ordered an armor-plated car. He knew they would be more attentive and probably did not have to pay them as much as Capone's thugs. They might even be more loyal in times of distress. Chicagoans of that era would not have blanched at the idea of Insull and Capone meeting. They were both celebrities, although only one of them would emerge from that time with greater infamy.

ATTACK FROM ALL SIDES

The Crash, Failure, and Opera

Instead of the saloon, which had troubled the conscience of moral Chicago for many years, there was arising the empire of illicit drink, with Al Capone as the masterful wielder of its scepter. This powerful state within a state in no way interfered with the despotism of Samuel Insull. In fact, Al Capone and Insull had more in common than people imagined, or than people unaccustomed to analyze realities could see.

—Edgar Lee Masters, *The Tale of Chicago*[1]

Not even Barney Mullaney, with his adroit positioning of Insull as the savior of free enterprise, vanguard against communism, and preserver of cultural institutions, could stop the latest, more ominous threat against Insull. A Cleveland financier named Cyrus Eaton in 1928 was buying up large blocks of the common stock of Commonwealth Edison, People's Gas, and Middle West Utilities. Eaton was an ex-Baptist minister turned stock promoter. Eaton incorporated his Continental Shares in 1926 for the sole purpose of speculating in the stock of other companies. His founding investors capitalized his company with $1.3 million in common and $3 million in preferred shares. Imbued with a genuine talent for salesmanship, Eaton was able to raise $45 million in capital in a few years and control nearly $120 million in investments.

Normally Insull did not mind if local investors bought into his companies. They were usually banks, brokerage houses, or groups of employees. Eaton, though, was from Cleveland, well outside the pale of Insull's influence. While Insull knew of Eaton's utility interests, he did not know whom he represented or where he was getting his financing. That alarmed him. The specter of losing control over his companies to largely unknown investors loomed, which was one of his greatest fears. Eaton was in league with Alfred Loewenstein, a Belgian investor who, along with Eaton, was speculating in the Insull stocks. Both men knew of Insull's weakness for maintaining absolute control, and were engaging in a greenmail scheme where they would eventually sell back their shares to Insull at a future date for an exorbitant price. Like a shepherd dog smelling a wolf at the perimeter of his flock, Insull began to frantically circle around his holdings. He once again turned to the most durable tool at his disposal, the holding company:

> I had no idea whatever, prior to this movement, of trying in any way to get control of the various companies, except by an appeal to the stockholders from year to year for their proxies, but when I found out what was going on [with Eaton] I came to the conclusion that the best thing for me to do would be to form an investment [holding] company to hold the securities of the four companies in question owned by my family and myself, and to acquire additional stock by purchase in the market.[2]

A defensive vehicle called Insull Utility Investments was formed to buy the stock of the main gas and electric companies. Insull, his brother Martin, and Junior were the main shareholders and directors. Since he stacked the board of the holding company with family and associates, Insull felt he did not need to obtain voting control of the company. Once he had control of the boards, the voting shares were a moot point. The transaction creating the holding company, which was a shell entity that the Insulls controlled, was complicated.

Insull also owned companies called Insull, Son & Co. in New York, and Insull, Son & Co., Ltd. in London. They had been established for the sole purpose of selling securities in the other Insull companies. The mogul had aspirations that these two firms would eventually become investment banking houses in their own right, entities designed to compete with the Morgan interests, but based in Chicago. He reluctantly sold the virtual banks because he "did not want anyone to get the impression that I was trying personally, either for myself or for members of my family, to make money through the use of a separate concern." In creating the new holding company, Insull effectively sold securities he owned to Utility Investments, giving that entity a tighter rein over his operating companies—at least on paper. The holding company then gave Insull and his family 764,000 common shares and $4 million in preferred shares. Insull also contracted with the holding company to buy 250,000 shares of common at $12 a share (an incredible bargain). All of the Insulls' transactions put

$3 million in the coffers of the new company. Insull then distributed the new shares among his friends and family. To compensate his family for "the low rate of return that we accepted for the first five years on the $4 million in preferred stock, and for the services of myself, my brother, and my son, as we served as officers and directors without compensation," Insull received an option from the holding company to buy 200,000 shares of common at $15 a share.

The holding company financing was nothing less than a sweetheart deal designed to keep the operating companies (People's Gas, Commonwealth Edison, and Middle West) under the control of the Insull family. The holding company could also operate across state lines and largely escape state regulation. While it was blatantly self-serving, in the era before the New Deal securities laws, holding-company manipulation was all perfectly legal. The Electric Bond & Share combine controlled by the Morgan bank and General Electric had done the same thing, as had several other utilities. In the 1920s, holding companies were as popular as bobbed hair, dance marathons, and flagpole sitting, if not more so as utility executives discovered their merits. Between 1919 and 1928, more than 4,000 utilities were tucked into holding companies. States like Delaware rewrote their corporate chartering laws to become havens for the entities. A single building in Wilmington, Delaware, could hold up to 10,000 corporate registrations on one floor. Better yet, holding companies that operated in several states were exempt from some state utility commission rules. Insull had a sound reason to thunder against federal or local regulation of his companies: he had more freedom to run and finance his holding companies without regulation. Except for modest state utility commission oversight, the entire industry was virtually unfettered on the corporate level.

Through the power of leverage—borrowing to buy securities—Insull could control large holding companies with relatively little capital. The typical holding company would be capitalized with $250 million in bonds, $150 million in nonvoting preferred shares, and $100 million in common stock. The common was the most prized asset for Insull and the other holding company operators, since it had voting rights. Insull only had to invest slightly more than $50 million to control a $500 million company. Since banks were tripping over themselves to lend him money in the 1920s, he had easy access to capital. The newspapers often reported during that frenzied time that whenever one saw a banker talking to Insull in public that was "worth a million dollars." The pyramid worked so effectively that one holding company could control 10 operating companies with $5 billion in real assets. If those companies returned a 7 percent annual profit, the gross profit for the holding company would be $350 million on a $500 million investment. It was similar to holding real estate. If you could buy a $1 million home with $100,000, your gains would be magnified if the property value went up. If your home value goes up 10 percent, you double your principal. With holding companies, the power of leverage works only if profits and the stock market value of the underlying stock increases. If the stock value declines, the bankers and brokers demand collateral in the form of cash or other securities.

Few financiers or utility executives prior to 1929 believed that the market would decline to the extent that they would have to pony up assets for bankers, who were also speculating heavily in the holding companies themselves. Insull Utilities Investment alone had soared from $12 at its creation to $150 by 1929. Electrical output was breaking new records every year as "juice" was the one commodity nearly every prosperous household wanted in the jazz age. Even the debacle of 1929 did not stop the insatiable desire for everything electrical, as noted by the historian Harold Platt:

> The effects of electrification on the lives of Chicagoans were often subtle, barely noticeable changes that gradually transformed domestic routines into an energy-intensive style of life. . . . During the 1920s, the growing demand for energy became so powerful that even the Great Depression failed to halt the increase of residential consumption. Despite the economic crisis, the average Chicagoan continued to use more electricity in the home, setting yearly records until the oil embargo of the mid-1970s. . . . In the home, shop and factory, Chicagoans had created a world based on the intensive use of energy.[3]

The holding companies also provided a primary bulwark against takeovers. In order to control the operating companies—the entities that were actually producing something—a financier often had to buy the stock of the holding companies since these entities had cross-ownership of the power plants, train lines, and gas company. The more holding companies, the more barriers there were in front of the real moneymaking entity. Rather than expose the operating companies to the swift takeovers and consolidations of the Morgan era, where it was a simple matter to buy up large blocks of stock, the holding companies enabled a few financiers to hold on to other companies through issuance of stock and friendly boards of directors. Contemporary critics charged that Insull's leveraging and stacking the holding company boards was nothing less than racketeering. The comparison that Insull's contemporaries made between him and Capone was a bit unfair, although both men wanted an undisputed grip on their enterprises. While Insull certainly set up his holding companies to keep his hands on the companies he created, he also was aggressively selling stock to his associates, employees, and the public. If Insull did not want to share the wealth, he would not have let Mullaney loose with his public stock ownership campaigns.

The complexity of the holding company relationships was befuddling and would come back to haunt Insull. By 1929, he had added yet another holding company to the mix: the Corporation Securities Company. Insull wanted another layer of protection from outsiders' gaining control. The stock sales of Insull Utilities alerted him to the fact that Eaton had figured out his strategy and was buying into his holding companies. The last tier of Insull's pyramid was to prove a meager defense against Eaton.

Backed by the relentless campaigns of Mullaney and the rest of the industry, Insull was confident that the public was on his side with regard to private ownership—and buying his stocks. The ballyhoo was working well because the propaganda was so pervasive. Throughout the 1920s, Mullaney and the various industry trade groups such as the Electric Light Association and the American Gas Association circulated 25 million pieces of literature. Insull's propaganda guru was not above red-baiting the opposition, either. Mullaney had even managed to tie in "the Bolshevik idea" of public utility ownership with those candidates for office who dared to suggest that private utilities be under federal or more stringent state control. He even blacklisted organizations that he believed were opposed to private utilities. They included the American Farm Bureau Federation, the Quakers, and the Women's Christian Temperance Union.

More than 30 state agencies of the industry's propaganda machine succeeded in placing fake news "bulletins" in newspapers all over the country. The faux headlines read, "People Themselves Now Own Utilities," "Holding Company Renders Service," "Customer Owners Double Since War," "Customers This Year Are Buying Utility Securities at the Rate of a Million Dollars Every Business Day." Mullaney's tent show encompassed every medium at the time. There were pamphlets, fliers in electrical bills, a radio show featuring "The Old Counselor" extolling the safety of utility stocks, speeches, and advertisements in every conceivable publication.

H.L. Mencken's *American Mercury*, the premier intellectual journal of its day, ran an advertisement for Commonwealth Edison in which it was noted that "the company has paid 156 consecutive dividends to its stockholders." American Water Works & Electric Company took out a full page ad proclaiming that it is an "industry that never shuts down." The *Mercury* issue also featured a critical piece by Rudolph Weissman on investment trusts, an early form of mutual funds that would cause so much financial distress after 1929. The latest books by Carl Sandburg (*Good Morning America*), Lytton Strachey (*Elizabeth and Essex: A Tragic History*), and Virginia Woolf (*Orlando*) were also advertised.

The reliable dividends and limitless growth of his companies were prime selling points for Insull, as he peddled his securities to the public. By the end of the decade, Middle West and its subsidiaries had more than 275,000 shareholders and 160,000 bondholders. Employees were urged to sell Insull stocks to friends and family. Even the meter reader was selling shares. The man who Edison said was "always looking at the dollar angle" could do no wrong in the eyes of the public, outside of the progressives. His stocks were popular because you could see Insull's mark everywhere from streetlights to elevated trains. His companies spanned half a continent, and his advice was sought from London to San Francisco.

Insull wanted more. He had paid premium prices for utilities and his $2.5 billion empire was expanding every year as the holding companies continued to swallow up smaller utilities. A buyout of National Electric Power gave him a presence from Maine to Florida along the east coast. The New York bankers and investors in holding companies like Electric Bond & Share raised their eyebrows over the encroachment on their territory. Commonwealth Light & Power and United Public Service followed as other Insull buys. At the height of his power, Insull grew his portfolio from 2,064 community companies in 1927 to 4,405 by the end of the decade. All told, he was serving a population of 6.3 million. Gross earnings were $162 million.

The market, particularly the Chicago Stock Exchange, on which all of the Insull stocks were listed, was ecstatic about any Insull publicity. It was siren song whose chorus grew louder as each day passed in the jazzy decade. From 1918 to 1922, Commonwealth Edison sold in a tight range between $100 and $119 a share. It was seen as a staid security that paid a solid dividend and offered predictable growth. As Insull accelerated his stock ownership and acquisition programs, the combination of the aggressive sales of the stock and the mania of the times created a frenzy. The stock's range rose from $126 to $136 in 1924, from $132 to $141 in 1925, from $135 to $145 in 1926, and from $138 to $173 in 1927. By 1929, Commonwealth Edison topped out at nearly $450 a share.

Insull refused to tout the stock throughout this period. As early as 1922, he told reporters "I will not say one word that will send that stock a point higher. It is too high now and more than the stock is worth." Seven years later, after more than tripling, he flatly stated that Commonwealth Edison "was not overpriced in comparison with other public utility stocks of similar type and similar earning capacity." Investors from Commonwealth Edison linemen to Chicago bankers were convinced of Insull's genius and could not imagine what could derail his enterprises. Their ever-growing margin accounts, in which they borrowed money to buy more shares, were an article of faith that Insull was piloting the most secure investment in the country.

While benefiting from his stakes in all of his holding and operating companies, Insull had no control over the market's mania. If investors were willing to bid up the prices of his stocks, he was willing to accept that. His companies had legitimate earnings and ran legitimate businesses. He was not making money under false pretenses, yet he did not want to be charged with overselling his stocks, either. His public stock ownership campaigns were designed largely to deflect criticism that private utilities were not operated in the public interest. Stock speculation was something else entirely. Promoting the interests of the industry was something he had consistently done since the 1890s. If investors overvalued his stocks, they were also inflating the values of other stocks as well. There was no deception on his part. He had a powerful sense of what it was like to be wrongly accused and wanted no part of it. As an office boy in London, he had been accused of stealing stamps from a cash box and was grilled by the police. When it became apparent that he was not guilty, the detective asked him who he thought was guilty. The teenager replied, "I'll not answer. Finding him isn't my job. And I know how it feels to be accused unjustly."

Senators Norris and Reed, however, were incensed by the industry's public relations juggernaut and its ability to snatch up power companies at will. They wanted some answers as to how private utilities were spending their money. The Federal Trade Commission was authorized to begin a second comprehensive probe of the industry (an earlier investigation ended in 1927). Within a few weeks of the formation of Insull Utility Investments, an ambitious state senator from New York began to dent the industry's armor. For a quarter century, Franklin Delano Roosevelt believed that it was in his state's public interest to develop hydroelectric power on the St. Lawrence River and provide low-cost power to its residents. Having wrested the rights from one of Andrew Mellon's companies, he had a much larger vision that the entire country could benefit from publicly owned power companies.

The only refuge for Insull in the Chicago area was Hawthorn Farm. Junior was now comfortably residing in his own home at Red Top Farm, which was down the street from his father's estate. Insull had bought Red Top from Chicago restaurateur John Thompson, who had erected a white mansion with a colonial two-story portico and Cape Cod gables. Also buying a summer house on Scilly Island in Countryside Lake a few miles away, Junior was now a country gentleman like his father. Gladys, who was never really fond of the country, often could be seen driving a horse-drawn surrey between the properties.

Insull had transformed Hawthorn Farm into a showpiece of modern agriculture. Electric pumps supplied water to all corners of the property, including a remodeled schoolhouse that served as the home of his English butler. It even had its own railroad siding for the transportation of Insull's award-winning livestock to county fairs. Insull constantly pushed his farm manager to experiment with new farming techniques and machines. As with his electrical operations, Insull wanted the best, most efficient technology on his farm. He did not just want to be a passive gentleman farmer, he wanted to be an innovator and promoter of the latest farm implements. Despite his interest in the newest and best, Insull had a soft spot for the past. When he had the time, he would take a horse-drawn carriage to the local train station, even after he had bought several cars.

Around the time of his troubles with Eaton, Insull established an 80-acre model farm west of his property. Situated on the highest land in the area, the project was officially called the "Model Farm of the Public Service Company of Northern Illinois." It was to serve a public relations role in showing the world how Insull intended to modernize agricultural areas and electrify the family farm. Like Hawthorn Farm, it promoted the most advanced farming techniques and everything to do with electrical appliances and implements. Insull was direct about the purpose of the farm when he opened it on August 11, 1928. The "semi-educational institution" was set up to sell electrical and gas service to the 30,000 farmers who lived within the Public Service Company's territory:

> We believe that if we can show the farmer how to use electricity and gas advantageously in his home and on his farm, get him to attend meetings now and then on our Model Farm, and have him listen to addresses by agricultural experts, we may be able to help his situation. Incidentally, we may make him a good customer of our Company, which means making him a good friend of ours.[4]

As in his other myriad pitches to sell his services, Insull was promoting a personal relationship with his customers. The model farm became something of a private farm bureau, only with the sole purpose of getting farmers hooked up to Insull utilities. He was selling more than his product; he wanted to electrify the farm. The corollary benefits were that more efficient farmers would use less labor and be more productive. That would ultimately "increase their purchasing power." The model farm, if successful, would be the first of three, each in a different outlying area of Chicago.

The farmhouse itself was a working stage for Insull's marketing plan. Not a kerosene lantern was in sight, a standard appliance in most unelectrified houses. Inside the house were an electric washer and wringer, a gas dryer, a refrigerator, and gas and electric ranges. Every room had wall outlets for vacuum cleaners. The dairy barns featured electric milking machines, the supreme labor-saving tool for dairy farmers.

In keeping with his larger agenda, Insull gave his pitch to the farmers at the opening of the farm. They would all be connected to the growing superpower grid. The economies of scale would be passed on to them from huge power plants he was building in Waukegan, Peoria, and on the state line with Indiana. All of the plants would be interconnected to pool power. Ultimately, the availability of cheap power translated to "the upbuilding of the state and an increase in the wealth and comfort of its citizenship."

Electricity and the railroads were the two arms of the growing infrastructure that dissolved the boundaries between city and country. No longer was there was dividing line that marked a "farming town" from a suburb. Where Insull's interurban lines had stopped, that is where the commuters wanted to live. No place was a better example of how electricity transformed a rural area into an extension of the metropolis than Libertyville, where Hawthorn Farm was located (the site of Insull's former estate today, however, is not within the corporate boundaries of Libertyville, having since been annexed to Vernon Hills). Insull had organized a bank in the town in 1925 called Libertyville Trust and Savings Bank, which would lend mortgages to residents who could access the city from his newly extended North Shore Line. In the Libertyville area, Insull had the reputation of a kindly benefactor. He had donated land and raised money for a hospital and contributed land for Hawthorn School. Known for his generosity and frankness, the town of 2,500 was anxious to work with him to develop the area, which was dotted with farms, recreational lakes, and the estates of Chicago's old money—families such as the Armours and the McCormicks.

With his usual prescience, Insull saw the region becoming an integral part of a metropolis of some 15 million (an overestimate by about 6 million as of the 2000 Census). Aware that Lake County was also a well-known refuge for mobsters' roadhouses and brothels, Insull did not skirt the issue before the Waukegan Chamber of Commerce and Lion's Club: "You have some disadvantages, naturally," he told the group of local businessman, who regarded him as a celebrity. "You are a summer resort of Chicago, and crooks find your territory a ripe field. One-half of your crime in the liquor business is rooted in Chicago."

The year before he spoke before the civic groups, three subdivisions had sprouted up near his North Shore Line. Luke Grant, publicity manager for the railroad, endorsed Insull's view that growth would come to the area because the North Shore shuttled residents from the area to downtown in about an hour, "making it the most attractive residential section within easy distance of the great metropolis by the lake." Selling the virtues of the area not only was good for bringing riders to the railroad; it sold more power. A few miles east of Libertyville, Insull had built the 250,000 kilowatt Waukegan plant, the largest in the world in the mid-1920s. It produced 50 times more power than the first turbogenerator in the Fisk Street station in 1903 and would send it throughout the area on 132,000-volt power lines that straddled the right-of-way for the North Shore railroad.

Insull's companies were in position to marshal the growth. His Lake County Land Company and Libertyville Construction Company worked in concert with his banks to buy land, build homes, and sell mortgages. Not wanting to repeat the mistakes of Pullman, Insull did everything except own the homes he was building. Once the citizens of Libertyville built their homes, they would commute on the North Shore and buy power and appliances from him. He had an indelible presence in the center of town, where he built his "Public Service" building. Architect Hermann Von Holst gave the charming building a Bavarian look, perhaps appealing to the many German immigrants in the area. Holst worked for Insull for nearly 30 years as his chief designer, and was known for his mostly derivative styles, even though he had bought Frank Lloyd Wright's practice and was friends with most of the Prairie School architects.

Festooned with two Teutonic cupolas and copper awnings, the Service building bore the initials of the Public Service Company (which, if you are not looking closely, appear to be Insull's initial's "SI"). Constructed at a cost of $250,000, it was completed on May 3, 1928, and was an aesthetic gift to downtown Libertyville, which was graced by the nineteenth-century Cook mansion across the street and several nineteenth-century frame buildings. When the building was dedicated, 3,000 people turned out, with ladies handing out roses and cigars as souvenirs. Local newspapers devoted entire issues to the opening. The town had been so receptive to Insull that it widened the street (Milwaukee Avenue) some 80 feet. At the time, it was the largest single-unit building in the county, so city fathers did all they could to accommodate Insull.

The building was a glossy monument to public relations with its white facade, open arcade, courtyard, sunken garden, and street-level stores. In keeping with Insull's total marketing policy, the structure was a billboard for the utopian virtues of electricity, flavored by a heavy dose of nostalgia. The building contained elements of Moorish, Asian, Spanish, and Tudor styles. Slate, stone, wood, stucco, and copper are used throughout. The mélange of ornate architectural idioms—reflecting nearly every housing style of the time—was the polar opposite of the Prairie School. The courtyard garden featured colored electric lights. A battery of 12 floodlights illuminated the building from across the street.

The Public Service store on the first floor was the main showroom of the building, aside from a small auto dealership. The large display and salesroom was flanked by a women's washroom and Insull's bank. In the middle of the sales space was a miniature kitchen where tiny electrical appliances were placed. On the second floor, the electric show continued with modern apartments furnished with electric refrigerators and ranges.

With the bank, railroad, power lines, real estate, and construction company in place, all Insull needed were homebuyers. A tract of 6,000 acres that the *Chicago Daily News* called "Insullvania" awaited the arrival of the bulldozers. The model for such an electrically wired, transit-oriented development had already been executed two years earlier by developer William Zelosky in Westchester, about 25 miles southwest of Libertyville. When Insull extended his elevated train line to the suburb, development proceeded quickly in "America's Model Suburb." Weekly passes on the 24-hour electric train sold for $2. Zelosky had come to Chicago from the Texas range during the world's fair of 1893. He distinguished himself by building subdivisions and 22 unique "community centers." The suburb took advantage of enlightened zoning that established districts with single-family homes, small apartments, and small businesses. Unlike the city, manufacturing was not permitted next to residential zones. A library and community center would make the town more family-friendly. Zelosky's companies emphasized that public transportation created wealth, noting that property values near the elevated lines increased by a factor of eight from 1900 to 1923.

The keystone of Insull's strategy to link electrification and transportation with real estate development had succeeded throughout the country, leading to the mushrooming of every metropolitan area in the world. As the 1920s hurtled into stratospheric heights for the stock market and business profits, Insull continued to remind the world that it was he who had taken a risk on a new technology called a turbogenerator more than a quarter century ago.

In addition to its many benefits, the age of the roaring electron revolutionized the way people ate. Food did not have to be bought every day for fear of spoilage or contamination. Iceboxes were slowly being replaced by refrigerators. The food processing industry was burgeoning to meet the demand for frozen and canned foods. New production techniques, aided by the widespread employment of efficient electric motors, created an entire realm of food that was free from bacterial contamination. By the end of the 1920s, the food industry was the largest sector in the American economy. Frozen or refrigerated "convenience" foods could be eaten any time. The advertising business eventually created fictional housewives like "Betty Crocker" to help peddle the new foods. Corner bakeries, which had been a fixture in urban neighborhoods, were fast disappearing as high-volume, commercial bakeries dominated.

Most of the major "white goods" appliances such as refrigerators, though, remained out of reach for most middle-class households in the 1920s. Ironically, refrigerator sales did not really grow significantly until the 1930s, when more of the units were mass-produced and prices dropped. Even so, on the eve of World War II, only half of American households had refrigerators. Much as the appliance makers and electric industry associations tried, the economics of home refrigeration were difficult to dispute. In the mid-1920s, NELA issued a piece of propaganda showing that operating an electric refrigerator cost only $131 a year versus $122 for an icebox (was not the convenience worth the extra $9?). Few households believed this fiction since refrigerators alone cost about $200 and you could buy an icebox from Sears for $50 or less. Ice was a relatively cheap commodity to produce and deliver. Before electrification, the infrastructure was simple: ice was cut from lakes in northern states and stored in well-insulated icehouses until the iceman came to your door. It cost nothing to freeze the water. The rest of the cost was labor, storage, and transportation. You did not have to wire your house or pay for electricity. NELA would later reorganize its refrigeration campaign into the "Electric Refrigeration Bureau," an effort it began well into the Depression.

NELA, through Insull's early publicity efforts from 1898 onward, developed a powerful publicity department that was instrumental in selling appliances and boosting power consumption. By 1928, customers were paying $555 million for electricity to power appliances alone, a figure that had been negligible at the outset of the decade. In keeping with the campaign to appeal directly to women that had been started before World War I, companies tied appliance use into home economics and the sense that women could become more independent. "Mature women with dignity and poise" were hired to lecture housewives on the merits of electric appliances. They worked with builders, and hosted pageants, parties, and fairs. The utilities knew how to exploit the merging of scientific management with household efficiency measures since they had been doing it since the turn of the century. Electrical appliances became the domestic tools of the modern age that were sold to conquer the dreariness of housework once and for all. In the 1920s, this concept of modernity was constantly reinforced by the surging advertising industry. As historian David Nye observed:

> Neither "the machine" [Frank Lloyd Wright's view] nor the corporation deter-
> mined that most Americans could live in electrified suburban houses; rather,
> the decision was the consequence of a centuries-old preference for single-
> family dwellings, reinforced by the home-economics movement. Electrical ap-
> pliances did not replace servants; rather they filled a void created by the
> servants' departure for better-paying work. Electrification did not reduce the
> hours of housework but rather was used to redefine it, and Mrs. Modern
> Woman worked just as many hours as her mother, for Bob Modern Boy and
> his father seldom used the new appliances.[5]

Next to lights, electric fans and irons were the most popular appliances, mostly because of their low cost and because no new space was needed for their installation. Lighting was the universal appliance and provided the opening for other electrical products. The improvement in lighting quality began in public institutions. Schools were the first to upgrade. New standards were set for schools after the 1920s. While millions of homes still had gas illumination in the 1920s, the conversion to electricity encouraged more nighttime activities, particularly reading. Libraries, bookstores, and the direct marketing of books became more popular (hence the "Book of the Month Club" and other imitators).

Lighting had a profound effect on the psychology of time. Scarcely 20 years earlier, most private spaces did not have reliable, high-intensity lighting. Except in areas with streetlights, neighborhoods were mostly bathed in darkness. The new wave of illumination in the jazz age thwarted the darkness and marked a new level of status and civilization, Nye observed. F. Scott Fitzgerald's Jay Gatsby lights his house "from tower to cellar" in an effort to attract Daisy. Gatsby turns his Long Island mansion into a beacon of power, virility, and wealth. Hemingway's short story, "A Clean, Well-Lighted Place," uses light as a symbol of civilization in a Spanish café. Sinclair Lewis's *Babbitt* mocks the residents of Floral Heights as they keep up with each other in their status-seeking purchases of the latest electrical appliances.

Not only did Americans have more illumination in the 1920s, they had dramatically more personal mobility. A boom in automobile sales put millions of Americans on the road. While streets were not keeping pace with the amount of new traffic, the installation of streetlights and traffic signals was making a difference. The first signal lights were put up in New York City in 1923. The familiar red, yellow, and green lights were adopted from railroad signals. Despite the safety improvements, traffic deaths nationally rose from 5,400 in 1919 to 9,800 in 1924 as the automobilization of the world marked a profound change in transportation. Ford's $350 Model T, which ceased production in 1927, accounted for half of all cars sold. The former Edison engineer and wandering mechanic had created a craze for manure-free carriages and was producing a Model T every 10 seconds by 1925. An estimated 20 percent of discretionary income spent by consumers was on automobile-related expenses. The independence of the internal combustion engine and the infrastructure of oil refineries in most urban areas had nearly displaced the electric cars and trucks Insull was promoting. Electric cars ran on batteries and could go only a few hours. While they were excellent promotional vehicles for Insull, often hauling hundreds of electric irons for giveaways in newly electrified neighborhoods, their utility was limited because of the relatively short charge time of their batteries.

In the decades prior to the 1920s, horses had been the prime movers in getting people and goods from place to place. In New York City alone, some 80 percent of residents suffered from some sort of infection, a great deal of it traced to the overwhelming presence of horse manure. The nearly 18 million vehicles that were on the road by 1924 presented new problems, such as traffic jams, exhaust fumes, and parking shortages. Road building also consumed more and more tax dollars as the dirt thoroughfares needed to be paved and major highways needed to be created.

The nascent auto culture raced alongside the new electric age. Popular language incorporated "being taken for a ride" or having an "electrifying" experience. One could be a "real spark plug" or "light up a room." The auto and electrified buildings made it possible to enjoy the latest crazes at any hour of the day. You could drive your Model T to the latest dance marathon, jazz club, speakeasy, flagpole sitting, or mah-jongg game. Crossword puzzles kept people up all night under the glare of their new, dependable lighting fixtures.

There was little debate among the progressives that Insull was most vulnerable to criticism on his utility rates. While his companies were technically under state supervision by the utilities commission, disclosure on how he came up with his rates was murky. In fact, few people outside of his business in the late 1920s knew the byzantine accounting principles employed to "write up" (inflate the value of) company assets to sweeten the financing terms of the holding companies. A University of Chicago economics professor and future senator named Paul Douglas was the one who came closest to peeling away the layers of Insull's many corporate onions. A Quaker with a compassionate heart and sharp mind who loved the city, he was friends with Jane Addams and Donald Richberg. Douglas hailed from a young university that had already been an academic garden for John Dewey, Thorstein Veblen, Albert Michelson, and Robert Millikan. The university was laying a deep and strong foundation for its future dominance in physics and economics. Douglas emerged to be one of the most credible challengers of Insull. Douglas became an expert on utility rates and formed the core of what would become the Utility Consumers League (and a progenitor to modern citizen utility boards), one of the first consumer groups to openly take on the powerful private utilities.

After conducting extensive research, Douglas discovered that public electricity companies such as the municipal power station in the North Shore community of Winnetka charged 1/2 cent per kilowatt-hour for power, while the private producers charged more than 8 times that rate. While the municipal plants had dramatically lower overhead—no advertising or propaganda campaigns—the progressives believed that Insull was routinely overcharging his customers. Acting as special counsel for the city of Chicago, Richberg had also established a case that People's Gas overstated its expenses and was charging exorbitant rates for gas. Douglas further discovered that the operating efficiencies that the Insull companies achieved during the 1920s were not being passed along to consumers in the form of lower rates. Douglas suspected that the Insull operating company profits were being channeled to support the holding companies. Moreover, his research showed that Insull likely overstated the value of the surface streetcar lines to the city when it was proposed that they be consolidated and put under Insull's control in 1927. Insull, who had proposed to reorganize and refinance the lines (at least one had gone into receivership), had already owned the elevated lines. The deal would give the city complete control of the proposed subway and turn over the surface and elevated lines to a private company operating the system at cost and regulated by a public commission. Douglas, though, under the auspices of the progressives' "People's Traction League," estimated that $135 million of the total $264 million stated value was fabricated. According to Douglas's analysis, such an overvaluation would boost the value of the securities financing the surface and elevated lines. Undaunted and employing the clout at his disposal, Insull instructed his lawyer to draw up bills in the state legislature that would allow Insull to merge the lines into one company. If passed by the legislature, city council and popular referendum, Insull then would have undisputed management control over the entire Chicago traction system. When Insull was told that several legislators were demanding bribes to pass the enabling legislation, he was furious. Among his many qualities, Insull refused to pay outright graft. The legislation failed. Two years later, Federal judge James Wilkerson would appoint a "Citizen's Traction Settlement Committee" headed by Insull's friend James Simpson of Marshall Field to come to terms on the traction deal. The committee's final report in 1929 basically mimicked the legislation that Insull had proposed two years earlier and was friendly to his aims of controlling the entire system. A city commission would regulate the new entity and extensions. A subway would be added at a later date.

As most of the utility disputes led to complaints before the commerce commission, the People's Traction League was energized largely to oppose any further expansion of Insull's interests. Ickes, who still felt slighted by being denied a larger role in Insull's World War I fundraising committee, was chairman of the league. The Hearst papers gave their backing to the consumer group and began to editorialize against the Insull terms for the streetcar takeover. Former reformist mayors Carter Harrison and Edward Dunne signed onto the league to lend support. Throughout the summer of 1929, Douglas testified before the city council and state legislature while Ickes, suffering recurring hemorrhages, curtailed his campaign. The group of progressives led by Douglas and Ickes put some teeth into enabling legislation for the traction settlement and Insull was temporarily thwarted, at least in their view.

While Eaton continued to buy stock in the Insull companies, the stock market seemed to know no ceiling. Insull Utilities stock started 1929 at $25 a share, rose to $80 by the end of spring and was at more than $150 by the end of summer. Middle West was hovering above $500 a share. That summer, the market found new ways of redefining its hypermania. During one 50-day period, Insull securities appreciated at the rate of $7,000 *per minute* as all of the collective energy of the time seemed to be focused on the stock market. Insull was personally worth more than $150 million by September ($1.7 billion in 2005 dollars).

"My God," he said. "A hundred and fifty million dollars! Do you know what I'm going to do? I'm going to buy me an ocean liner!" Insull instead formed another holding company and sold more shares to the public. Insull's companies were not the only object of the market's unquenchable desire. Three-million-share days on the New York Stock Exchange were common, which was double the volume from a decade earlier. From 1926 to 1929, the average daily top price for the 25 leading industrial stocks climbed from $186 to $470, a 250 percent increase. That kind of capital appreciation, not based on earnings growth, but on pure, insane optimism, brought 3 million Americans into the stock market. A third of the market players got into the market on margin. They only needed from 10 to 15 percent in cash to buy securities; the remainder was lent by the brokers. So long as prices went up, credit was easy and the brokers continued to push stocks like ice cream cones in August. Brokers' loans to investors totaled some $8.5 billion in 1929 at a time when the national debt was about $17 billion. How could it be that investors were in hock to their brokers for roughly half of the nation's total indebtedness? Brokers, bankers, and politicians were selling the idea of infinite prosperity, that no one factor could possibly derail the miraculous American economy, fueled by cheap coal, plentiful oil, and widely available electricity. This bubble of speculation, which extended into real estate as well, was inflated by the marketing of investment trusts, which neatly packaged companies for investors. Investment trusts were being formed at the rate of one a day, and there were more than 500 of them by the end of 1929. Even the cautious Ickes had invested in Insull securities.

Insull was incredulous at the market's breathless ascent, but he still had Eaton on his heels. He wanted to vanquish the Cleveland marauder so that he could go on with his business. He reluctantly proposed to buy out Eaton for $56 million, even though he did not have the cash on hand. Middle West Utilities then floated $50 million in notes, so his investors would effectively pay Insull to rid him of Eaton. The remainder Insull borrowed from the banks and his other holding companies. If the market continued to rise, the loans would pose no problem as the debts could be repaid with appreciated stock. The price Insull wanted to pay Eaton, however, was $6 million above market value at a time when stocks were at an all-time high. Insull intuitively sensed that this could be by far the worst deal he ever struck—and he still had not concluded his business with the pesky financier.

With the stock market exceeding all expectations, Insull immersed himself in the building and opening of the new opera house, which was on a hectic 22-month schedule for completion. He engaged the firm of Graham, Anderson, Probst & White to create something that did not exist anywhere, a truly "democratic" space for opera goers. The architectural firm had already established its reputation by designing the neoclassic Continental Bank and Field Museum of Natural History, both of which looked like monolithic versions of the Parthenon. The firm's elegant white Wrigley Building and (in the 1930s) art deco masterpiece Merchandise Mart were more befitting the time in which they were built. Insull commissioned lead partner Ernest Graham to go and visit the great opera houses of Europe and design a superior opera house without any of the European pretension and class distinctions.

As a London office boy sitting in the cheap seats, Insull longed to see an opera house designed for *everyone* in the hall, affording a decent view of the stage no matter where you sat. Opera houses typically were dominated by the "golden horseshoe" of box seats practically hugging the stage. If you were under or above this section, the acoustics and the sight lines were impaired. His opera house would have no such obstructions in gracious surroundings.

Insull also wanted to avoid the perennial problem of constantly begging for money from rich patrons every season. Opera had always been an expensive undertaking. Every new season required new scenery, costumes, and talent. Nobody wanted to see last year's production of *Aida* or *Tosca*. Opera was always part spectacle and drama buoyed by the music. Hundreds of people were needed to produce an opera, and they all needed to get paid competitive wages every season. After all, there were millionaires sitting up in those boxes and they could afford to pay top dollar. The only kind of investment that really could keep up with the inflationary pressures of opera production was real estate. Insull's plan was to use the income from rents (which could be raised) to cover the opera's operating costs. In order for his idea to succeed, the building had to be desirable for tenants and served by all of the most modern electrical conveniences and amenities.

When Insull considered the idea of moving the opera from the Auditorium, his first consideration was not a monument to himself, as his critics later claimed. The Auditorium building was in financial trouble. The owners had converted much of the first few floors into a "European plan" hotel. That meant going down the hall to the shared bathroom, where it was difficult to get anything but cold water. All of the modern hotels, such as the Stevens (which became the Conrad Hilton Hotel, the largest hotel in the world during its heyday), built a few blocks south on Michigan Avenue, had private bathrooms. If the Auditorium building went into bankruptcy, the sets and theatrical equipment could be seized by the banks. There was also speculation that the building would be closed because of "structural deficiencies," even though the building was sturdier than a Norman castle. In addition to those shortcomings, the opera company did not own its space, so it would be hostage to the financial health of its landlord. It was far easier for Insull to procure the financing for a new building than it was for him to rescue a building he did not own. To capitalize the Civic Opera building, he sold $10 million in first mortgage bonds to the Metropolitan Life Insurance Company and $10 million in preferred stock. Insull donated $300,000 of his own utility stock to seed the financing. Rentals from the building would cover the interest on the bond and leave plenty of cash to keep the opera afloat, the business plan specified. It was a unique proposition for an arts organization at the time and one that sought to secure the opera's financial independence well into the future.

The last performance of the Chicago Civic Opera in the Auditorium was on January 26, 1929. The opera company then moved into the Civic Opera House at 20 North Wacker, which observers quickly dubbed "Insull's Throne," since the west facade of the building appeared to be like a giant chair with a 45-story tower and 22-story wings. McCormick's *Tribune* ridiculed Insull's role in the new building in a famous editorial cartoon by John McCutcheon entitled "Mr. Insull's Seat of the Opera." It showed Insull imperiously seated as a giant in the new building's chairlike embrace, an image that the colonel probably personally endorsed. Multiple rumors circulated as to why Insull built the opera house to face west, making it appear that the seat of the building was sitting on the edge of the pungent Chicago River and turning its back on the bustling downtown. Local financial reporters believed it was from Insull's distrust and disdain of New York bankers in the East. Gossip said that he had built the opera house for Mary Garden or some other diva with whom he had a liaison. A less cynical interpretation was that Insull simply was facing west because that is where the opportunity was—he already owned utilities from the Atlantic to the Gulf coast. Now he was out to conquer the Wild West. Another more aesthetic explanation was that the open center of the river side complemented the art deco lounge-chair look of the Daily News building across the river. As seen from the Madison Street bridge, the two buildings look like bookends.

The colonnaded portico that ran along Wacker Drive gave those entering the building a European sense of scale, instead of conveying that another Chicago skyscraper was overwhelming you. Inspired by the Paris Opera House design of Jean Louis-Charles Garnier, a combination of art deco and art nouveau elements portray masks of comedy and tragedy and a cornucopia of instruments. On the south end of the building, large bronze doors open up into a long, grand foyer with gilt cornices. The space immediately reminds you of entering the Wizard of Oz's hall in the Emerald City, only that it is illuminated by Austrian crystal chandeliers. Insull spared no expense in the details. The floor and wainscoting was pink and gray Tennessee marble. The columns and pilasters were fluted Roman travertine—the same material used in his pink palazzo. A double staircase gracefully leads to the mezzanine foyer. There was a smaller Civic Theatre on the north end of the building (where Tennessee Williams's *A Glass Menagerie* would later premiere). A dramatic fire curtain featuring Jules Guerin's racy depiction of *Aida* in the parade scene is bathed in gold, pink, salmon, and bronze. All told, there were more than 3,500 seats and only 21 boxes, none of which blocked the view of the other patrons. The total cost of the building was more than $23 million. Insull took out a second mortgage from Continental Bank for $3.4 million to cover the shortfall of the original financing and personally guaranteed the loan.

Mary Garden, who had been in Chicago off and on since she left the management of the company, did not leave on good terms with Insull and harshly criticized Insull's handling of the company. Neither was she happy with the layout or acoustics of the new building: "When I looked into that long, black hole I said "Oh, no!" It was no real opera house at all, more like a convention hall. We had absolutely no communication with the audience."

While the new opera house did not have the Auditorium's crisp conveyance of sound from the stage to the farthest reaches of the gallery—where you could (and still can) hear ballet dancers walk out on stage from the second balcony—it was ideal for opera productions. The backstage area allowed for the easy movement of huge sets through the means of hydraulic lifts. The theater and stage area itself is so large it occupied 16 stories. Moreover, there was generous storage space for the sets, something the nineteenth-century Auditorium lacked.

With the opera serving as the building's *raison d'etre,* Insull strived to give the structure even more cachet. For years, he had been a member of a group called the "Electric Club" that met in various downtown buildings. Largely made up of his fellow Commonwealth Edison executives and members of two other clubs called the Jovian League and the Electrigists, it was a quiet place where you could smoke a cigar and enjoy a relatively inexpensive yet well-prepared meal. Dues were $125 a year. When the opera building opened in the fall of 1929, Insull moved the Electric Club to the opera building with his personal office and apartment occupying the penthouse on the penultimate 44th floor (mechanicals were on the top floor). A half-sized personal elevator took him to his lair.

The Electric Club, with "membership restricted to a number that can be comfortably accommodated," was less a monument to Insull's ego and more a nostalgic statement. It combined the look of an English pub and country inn with interior half timbers and leaded-glass windows. Insull had furnished the club himself with antiques he had acquired from all over Europe. Scenes from English country sports (such as bear baiting) adorned the walls. An incense burner and brass samovar sat on carved pine chests next to telephone booths. English landscapes, engravings of Bartolozzi (after Hans Holbein portraits), and hunting-themed seventeenth-century tapestries greeted you in a long hallway between meeting rooms. The scale is very Elizabethan, with generous dark panels, gothic arches, stained glass, low ceilings, and white stucco. Cigar smoke was the permanent fragrance of every room. An ursine Shild grandfather clock stares at you as you walk in from the elevator and enter the waiting room. The food was said to be above average and reasonably priced. You could start with "perfect" tomato or sauerkraut juice for 20 cents, followed by steamed "Haddie" for $1.85. Dessert was a boysenberry or lemon fluff pie. It was a comfortable, informal place to eat, drink, talk, and smoke. The space reflected Insull's personality when he let his white hair down. Old English with proper manners, yet somehow ever so manipulating—in a yeoman's way.

The opening of the opera house came at one of the most inauspicious times in American history. The stock market had crashed 11 days earlier. The city was being ravaged by mobsters vying for the unquenchable liquor trade, and no one was quite sure what the future held. In February, Chicago was the site of the notorious St. Valentine's Day Massacre, in which Capone was believed to have ordered six members of "Bugs" Moran's gang machine-gunned in a garage on the city's North Side. Only a year before, Hoover had been elected with the slogan "a chicken in every pot" and FDR became governor of New York. William Faulkner published the stream-of-conscious novel *The Sound and the Fury*, while Hemingway released *A Farewell to Arms*. A "talkie" based on Shakespeare's *Taming of the Shrew* starred the dashing Douglas Fairbanks and the plucky Mary Pickford.

The popular songs that had dominated the airwaves that year—*I'll Get By*, *Happy Days Are Here Again*—suddenly had the ring of bitter irony about them. Louis Armstrong's bluesy versions of *After You've Gone* and *St. James Infirmary* were more reflective of the zeitgeist once the market cascaded. On Black Thursday, October 13, the collapse was in full force as 13 million shares were sold on the New York Stock Exchange. The combined forces of the Morgan Bank and John D. Rockefeller and son could not prevent another rout on Black Tuesday, October 29, when 16 million shares were sold. Margin calls were being made to panicked investors, who did not have the money to cover their losses. By November 13, some $30 billion in market value had evaporated.

Despite the end of the age of jazz age prosperity, bejeweled society matrons floated into the new opera house in their minks on opening night. A legion of plainclothes detectives patrolled the perimeter of the opera house. Insull and fellow opera director Stanley Field beamed as they personally greeted as many patrons as they could when the doors opened for the first performance of *Aida* in the new auditorium. Insull's 25-year-old secretary John O'Keefe stood behind his boss as the throngs of Chicago's upper crusters first set foot into a building whose plans had been kept secret by Insull. When they entered the main performance space, however, many of Chicago's elite were aghast. Where were the boxes jutting out over the stage? How could their peers fully evaluate their fur coats, flowing gowns, and glimmering jewels? What kind of mockery was this, they wondered en masse. Insull's democratic design set the upper register's tongues on fire. The little horrid utilities monarch was humiliating them. He would *surely* have his comeuppance for his insolence, they muttered as they fumed about their slight.

ABDICATION AND EXILE

Insull Flees America

With the delicate lever of a voting trust controlling the stock of the two top holding companies he controlled a twelfth of the power output of America. Samuel Insull began to think he owned all that the way a man owns a roll of bills in his back pocket.

—John Dos Passos, *The Big Money*[1]

As Insull sat in his center box in the opera house on opening night, a broker tiptoed in when the lights went down for the opening scene of *Aida* and whispered that he needed to support his stocks, which were being sold off by the drove. Insull borrowed millions to peg Middle West at $220 a share. It had fallen from $350 on October 24. He had used the stock of his other companies as collateral. The investment dreams of a generation lay in ruins, although Insull was still in business and able to make purchases to protect his stocks from a free fall. His credit was good. He was still able to sell new issues of stocks and bonds. Bankers returned his calls. His picture had been on the cover of *Time* magazine, which covered the opera house opening. The stock market crash in October did not do any appreciable damage to the revenues of his operating companies. Like many of his fellow businessmen, he believed that the market had been grossly overvalued and the overall economy would be back to normal in a matter of months. Having elevated Junior to the vice chairman of most of his companies—the line of succession was now clear—the Insulls still controlled all of the $2.5 billion in holding and operating companies through two investment trusts with their $20 million stake. The 330,000 other shareholders had yet to complain.

Hoover had summoned Insull and a group of top business leaders to the White House to urge them to keep investing in their businesses, maintain employment, and declare that business conditions were "fundamentally sound." Treasury Secretary Andrew Mellon called for a cut in personal and corporate income taxes. Governors and mayors were urged to expand public works projects. The federal buildings budget was boosted by nearly $500 million. Newspapers were uncharacteristically cheery, blasting out headlines like "Wall Street May Sell Stocks, But Main Street Is Still Buying Goods."

Happy days were not here again, though. The stock market values of the previous two years were so far divorced from economic reality and intoxicated by margin-based speculation, that it was unlikely that investors would see those highs anytime soon. At the peak, on September 3, General Electric closed at $396 a share, General Motors at $181, Montgomery Ward at $466, U.S. Steel at $279, and Westinghouse at $313. Most of those prices had effectively doubled over the previous year, while earnings were growing in the low double digits. Pushing those stocks to those prices was sheer mania fueled by cheap money. By the end of 1929, those stocks would be worth less than half their all-time highs.

There was a respite in the financial carnage on November 13, 1929, when the Dow Industrials closed at 224, down from 452—a 50 percent decline from September 3. The news that the Rockefeller family was again buying stocks provided some hope, but it was short lived. There were more margin calls and every investor who had taken a plunge was on the verge of losing his entire investment—and more—in two short months. Taking the lead from Rosenwald at Sears, Insull stepped in to personally cover the margin calls of his employees. When the city of Chicago could not meet its payroll, he helped raise $100 million to pay teachers, policemen, and firefighters.

Wall Street had loved the party while the action was hot: it supplied $400 million a month in broker loans to investors (totaling $7 billion) during the summer of 1929. While mad money was flooding into the speculative craze, the Federal Reserve Bank did nothing to curb the enthusiasm, and there were few critical voices of the market's orgy. The economist John Kenneth Galbraith, who lived through the market meltdown and wrote the classic *The Great Crash,* noted:

> Each week during the autumn [of 1929] more such unfortunates were revealed in their misery. Most of them were small men who had taken a flier in the market and then become more deeply involved. Later they had more impressive companions. It was the crash, and the subsequent ruthless contraction of values, which, in the end, exposed the speculation . . . of Insull with the money of other people.[2]

Taking Hoover's mandate to his companies and his industry, Insull began to enlist Mullaney in an "everything is normal" campaign. Electricity and gas would continue to be sold, along with the securities of the holding and operating companies. Capital improvements would be increased. The public would be fully aware that the Insull companies had no intention of retrenching or shirking on their public responsibility to keep money flowing into the local and national economy. If Insull had any doubts about this plan of attack, he never voiced them to his executives nor revealed them in his memoirs. A one-page editorial in the trade journal *Electrical World* trumpeted the Insull credo in December 1929: "Samuel Insull Asserts 'Business As Usual.'" The piece (and press releases to all of the papers) outlined Insull's plans to spend $200 million on capital improvements in 1930, which was $32 million more than the previous year's total:

> To know where we stand, we have surveyed the general business conditions of the country to the best of our ability. We are convinced that the credit situation is good; that collections are practically normal; that there is no extraordinary accumulation of inventories; that the market disturbance was not caused by a shortage of money; that money, in fact, is plentiful.[3]

To put a gloss on his optimism, Insull mentioned that details of his companies' construction programs were "not announced as a mere contribution to a cheerful Christmas spirit." Rather, the money was going to be spent because "we feel we are in a continuing and a growing business." Since business conditions, in the Insull view, were normal, his companies would continue to pay dividends.

Cyrus Eaton knew there was nothing normal about Insull's defensive market buying. Insull was buying all of his stocks in an effort to prop up the prices. Eaton surmised that the bankers would be supplying him money for only so long in a prolonged decline. Insull wanted to end the game of chicken once and for all and prevent Eaton from dumping any more of his shares. Eaton informed Insull that he was willing to sell back 85,000 shares of Commonwealth Edison, 60,000 shares of People's Gas, and 13,000 shares of Public Service Company. Eaton's selling price was an outrageous $400 a share. At the time, Commonwealth Edison was selling for $328 a share, People's Gas, at $318 and Public at $329. Insull, who had been on a steamer returning from Europe at the time, replied by radio that he would tentatively accept the deal. Once again, the demon of losing control gnawed at his psyche. He was afraid that Eaton would sell to another investment syndicate, then combine their holdings with other investors to take over his companies. Whatever Eaton was asking, it was worth it to prevent that from happening.

When Insull returned to Chicago, he sat at his impossibly long conference table with Eaton, Junior, Martin, and Insull's brokers. Eaton broke the ice by saying that he was "satisfied with the management of the three operating companies and did *not* want control of the properties." Seeing an opening to negotiate, Insull lowered his buyout offer to $350 a share, which was hardly a bargain. Eaton balked, saying that he would rather combine his Insull stocks with those of Detroit Edison, International Paper, and United Light & Power than accept the lower price. Eaton again intoned the words that Insull loathed to hear: that some New York interests would eventually acquire his companies if he (Eaton) did not get his price. The meeting hit an impasse, and Eaton returned to Cleveland.

Not wanting to part with too much cash, Insull offered a new proposal to Eaton: trade for some of the stocks and pay for the purchase over a four-month period. Eaton finally accepted and walked away with $40 million in cash and nearly 89,000 shares in the new holding company, Corporation Securities. The purchase would be financed by more bank loans and bonds issued by the other holding companies. Insull was borrowing heavily from his other companies to pay off Eaton. Despite another trip to London to secure more financing, Insull was nearly to the limit of what he could borrow. By the summer of 1930, he had borrowed $110 million and pledged $440 million in Insull company securities as collateral. Insull instructed Halsey Stuart to sell more bonds to raise money for the holding companies, but the bond sales were thwarted by a lack of buyers.

By October 1930, Eaton was completely paid off. The devastating result was that all of the Insull holding companies were mired in debt and dangerously low on cash. Still believing that the market would turn around, Insull refused to suspend his capital improvement programs at the operating companies. To bolster his cash, though, he had to appeal to the banks personally, including (for the first time) a New York bank, the Central Hanover Bank & Trust Company. He raised $20 million, although it was of little help. The market kept dropping at the end of 1930 so that the securities held by Insull Utility and Corporation Securities depreciated in book value by $65 million and $45 million, respectively.

The market bounced back in early 1931 so that the two holding companies regained $86 million in their securities' values. Believing that the market rout was over, Insull boldly asked his 30,000 employees to start buying stock again. Obsessed by the rumor that nefarious New York bankers were attempting to wrest control of his Chicago-based empire, Insull set Mullaney to work to convince the public that Insull stocks were safe and should be purchased for the sake of local pride. Engineers, clerks, and secretaries once again hit the streets to peddle stocks to their families, neighbors, and friends. The rest of the country had no interest in stocks of any kind. A drought was ravaging the high plains, turning the soil to dust. Farmers had no credit and no money to pay their taxes. Corn, wheat, and other commodity prices were down so low that few could make a living on the land. Since there was no government support for them, farmers in the ravaged grain belt packed up their trucks and headed to California. Lines at the soup kitchens were getting longer. Men sold apples and pencils on the street. Their wives went to work as domestics or toiled in hot, steamy laundries. Insull's people mostly kept working providing power, gas, and transportation, but every household was cutting back. Not even Insull's companies would be immune from an entire country desperately clutching at the lint in their pockets.

Roosevelt was convinced America had lost its tolerance for the bravado of the utility industry's propaganda toreadors. Whatever Americans were paying for power in the midst of men begging for dimes in the street, it was too much. Educated by the experience of losing a battle to bring public hydroelectric power from the St. Lawrence River to New York State, Governor Roosevelt engaged in an informational crusade of his own. "We have permitted private corporations to monopolize the electrical industry and sell electricity at the highest rates they could obtain," Roosevelt said in 1930. Using the rates of the state-owned Ontario Hydroelectric power system as his model, he demonstrated to New York residents that they could be paying a lot less for power. He did it in terms they could understand: a completely electrified household in New York City using common appliances would pay $19.95; in Albany, $9.90; in New Rochelle, $25.63. In contrast, Canadians would pay only $3.32 for the same power. New York Republicans derided Roosevelt's assertions as the "waffle-iron campaign." The message, however, resounded deeply with the state's residents.

In what would be a hallmark of his extraordinary rapport with voters, Roosevelt was highly effective in stating his case on the radio. He achieved an intimacy with his audience that gave him credibility; he was connecting with people directly. They started to ask questions as to why their rates were so high when wages were so low and jobs disappearing. He took his estimate of $400 million to $700 million in power company overcharges and translated that into a daily life deprived of all the benefits of labor-saving appliances. Roosevelt supplemented his speeches and radio talks with fliers showing which appliances could be affordably used in Canada and how Americans were being shortchanged of those same appliances by the private operators.

The industry had always resisted telling the public how they justified their rates. Insull steadfastly refused to open his books until 1930. Disclosure was discouraged within the industry. Electric Bond & Share had to be taken to court in 1928 to open up its books. Martin Insull maintained in public that his business had "put its cards on the table" and often denied that utilities made tangible profits. Paul Douglas and his group of Chicago reformers knew that the Insull concerns were profitable, although they were likely shifting around the money to the various holding companies. Douglas was impressed with Roosevelt's attack on the utilities and accepted an invitation to become a consultant for his Committee to Stabilize Employment. Also opposed to the destructive Smoot-Hawley tariff, Douglas joined a group of more than 1,000 economists opposing the antitrade measure, which was blamed for deepening the Depression. As he learned more about Roosevelt and his brave struggle against polio, Douglas became an admirer and supporter. His cadre of Chicago progressives also came into the Roosevelt camp. Ickes and Lilienthal, by virtue of their knowledge of Insull's operations, would play major roles in expanding public power in the Roosevelt Administration.

Insull was emotionally, physically, and financially exhausted. His complexion was sallow and he walked with a pronounced hunch. You could see the stress in the hollow of his cheeks. Since the crash, his life had been a series of pleadings before bankers, shifting his debts among the holding companies, selling bonds, and giving speeches imbued with blind optimism. Employee activities, though, continued as if there were no Depression. The good ship *Edisonia* was to set sail on its 23rd annual dinner cruise on January 8. The electric light association's essay contest promised cash prizes totaling $1,750. Edison and Electra club officers for 1931 would be formally installed at a Palmer House dinner. The opera was hosting a "utility employees Sunday." Featured was *Camille,* an opera written by Hamilton Forrest, a former Insull office boy who had been discovered by Mary Garden. After a hiatus, the employee stock program started up again, offering attractive terms to participants, who were "limited to 50 shares." Employees were allowed to buy stock with only 10 percent down, with the remainder paid in nine monthly installments.

Insull had little to say in the January issue of the company newsletter as 1931 began. There was no mention of his frustrating and costly effort to pay off Eaton, nor his many trips before the bankers, nor of the staggering debt he took on to maintain his control. "It was a trying year," he stated in the *Edison Round*

Table, "but through the ability and fidelity of our personnel we have fulfilled our obligations to our customers, to our community and to our owners—the holders of our securities. . . . If the year has taught us anything, it is that work and thrift are the basis of comfort and security."

Gladys began the New Year by putting on a show for society. Her elegant "watch night party" closed out an otherwise ominous year for the Insulls. Hosted in the gallant new penthouse apartment in the opera building, she arranged small tables and cornucopias with hot house fruits at every table, symbolizing the hope that 1931 would be a year of plenty. She gave an odd toast that was picked up by the *Tribune* columnist "Cousin Eve." Draped in a silvery white gown, she spoke in her lovely, dramatic voice: "To the ladies, who are beautiful in spite of the fashions, and to the men, who are brilliant and scintillating in spite of their perplexities." The strains of cello, harp, and violin graced the spacious apartment with stunning views of the city, followed by various vocal renditions by opera stars such as Salvi a la Velasquez, who was adorned in "ruby velvet, comb and Sevillian veil." As the perfect hostess, Gladys graciously introduced each performer and charmed them. After one singer concluded, she dropped to one knee to present a basket of lilies, upon which the singer kissed Gladys's hand and curtsied. Cousin Eve even complimented Insull on the decoration of his office with "quaint, old English paintings, bought abroad years ago and never shown until the present."

Junior was standing in the corner with his tousled hair, short black jacket, and gray worsted trousers, wondering if this would be the year he would be given even more responsibility. He was now 31 and knew most of his father's financing mechanisms. At the table with Eaton, he knew what needed to be done. Charged with taking over the South Shore railroad under Britton Budd, he had done a remarkable job in turning the interurban around. It was as if Dad handed him a dismantled model railroad set and he had successfully reassembled it, adding a new roadbed, hourly service, and new speed records. He could boast that passenger revenue was 247 percent higher in 1930 compared to 1926. Freight revenue was up 650 percent. If he was heir apparent, he was convinced he had the proper credentials. In deference to his father, he, too, was a nominal teetotaler, devoting his life to work. Yet he was perhaps more isolated from the real world than his father. He built a "simple house" in the English country style on an island on a lake stocked with bass a few miles from his father's estate. There was only one way of accessing it other than by a boat: a narrow bridge. The house appeared as if it was surrounded by a moat. As 1931 arrived, Junior mused about what great enterprise he would be able to leave *his* son, who was in his wife's womb. Like his father, he kept a confident and often cocky face in public. In private, though, the balance sheet troubled him. Junior pondered some of the public relations moves of the previous year as well. It seemed that each step forward was matched by one backward. He and uncle Martin earned the scorn of the press when they launched a $500,000 propaganda campaign to defeat a state referendum in Maine, thus blocking those utilities from exporting cheap hydropower from the state. *Was it not legal to protect the interests of one's business?*

While breadlines snaked around the block, his father was still building and improving the Commonwealth Edison portfolio. What other company in 1930 could make that claim? Two new buildings costing $1.3 million were erected, both sleek art deco monoliths that would artfully hide transformers and heavy equipment. Despite the crash, all of the operating companies showed improved earnings in 1930 over 1929. Middle West posted a record $25 million in profit, a 43 percent increase from the previous year. Commonwealth Edison earnings were up 4 percent, Illinois Northern Utilities up 14 percent. In the midst of the chaos on Wall Street, Martin even managed the takeover of National Utilities Corporation. The Insull interests could prevail if the economy improved.

Conservative optimism was Insull's theme as he opened the doors of the annual meeting and some of the books of Insull Utility Investments and Corporation Securities in February 1931. The Insull *glasnost* was designed to show the public that their companies were thriving, had nothing to hide, and that they would prosper when the market rebounded. Both companies were presented as profitable: Insull Utility showed a profit of $10 million, while Corporation Securities posted a profit of $8 million. The main holdings of these companies, of course, were the securities of the operating companies, which were still making money in the Depression. The slight upturn in the market toward the end of 1930 meant that the portfolio of the companies was only down 6 percent. Cash dividends would continue at the rate of 1.5 percent quarterly.

The new employee stock plan was the highlight of the reports, having brought in 10,000 new stockholders for Commonwealth Edison, 5,000 for People's Gas, and 7,500 for Public Service. On the floor of the new Civic Theatre, Insull told shareholders:

> Investors have thoroughly recovered from the hysteria of the big break in the stock market and now have adopted a much saner view of conditions. . . . With the unprecedented large volumes of deposits in banks throughout the nation, it is only logical to presume that there will be ample funds to finance the extension of business and commerce this year.[4]

By August, neither the economy nor the stock market was following Insull's forecast. Banks, overleveraged from buying stocks and lending to speculators, were not lending to any but their largest clients. Employers kept cutting jobs and personal income evaporated. Hoover's policies were relying on industry to bootstrap its way out of the Depression. Ramshackle collections of shacks and tents called "Hoovervilles" were slapped together in every major city as men lost their jobs and their homes and took to the streets or the rails. While the economy slipped further into a stupor, Insull was summoned to the home of 84-year-old Thomas Edison, who had collapsed. The wizard was dying and running one last experiment to see if he could survive diabetes, a stomach disorder, and a host of other ailments. The two men chatted for about 45 minutes and Insull told reporters, "he looks feeble, but alert mentally, if not more so than I've ever known him to be." Edison quipped, "I'll live ten more years," hoping to live as long as John D. Rockefeller. Edison then went on a 20-mile auto ride. Ever attached to his lab, Edison, at the request of Harvey Firestone, spent the last years of his life trying to find a substitute for rubber. The commodity was controlled by a cartel in southeast Asia and Firestone wondered if there was a material that could be used as a substitute that could be grown in the U.S. After hundreds of experiments, Edison discovered that goldenrod, a weed that grew in every state, could be synthesized to form a type of rubber. The inventor spent untold hours in his lab in Florida over the winter trying to find the right combination for the process, which would never be commercially viable.

Edison and Insull reminisced and laughed about the time they spent together getting the Pearl Street station off the ground and the time when Edison found Insull snoozing on the streets of lower Manhattan. The two men had built an entire electrical system together starting with a single power company and ending with General Electric. The skinny and eager cockney boy, who struggled to make himself understood on that day in 1881 when Edison first met him, was now portly, powerful, and the overlord of an empire that was as frail as Edison, although he did not mention this to Edison. Insull had lost most of his accent and peered through his pince-nez glasses with a cord hanging from an earlobe. His face was flush and his hands still soft, looking more like a decaying viscount than a former London stenographer. Once the manager of thousands of pages of Edison's bills, finances, and correspondence, at 71, Insull refused to read any letter of more than 200 words. Generous to a fault, yet brusque and short with his subordinates, Insull had no patience for those who could not follow his lead. Edison remembered all of this as he peered into Insull's dark eyes, the windows to a powerful gulf of vitality. He could see Insull the organizer, financier and salesman, the master planner, and

the political operator. Edison had the insights, the ideas, and the perseverance
to get his scintillating projects in front of rich men. Insull got inside the heads
of the financiers to learn what they knew, then vaulted beyond their knowledge to make Edison's dreams tangible realities. If Edison was the seed of the
apple, then Insull was the fruit, providing sustenance for the seeds to grow as
they were scattered across the world. All of this was unsaid as they grasped
each other's hands tightly and began their new journeys.

Insull had cause to improve his outlook for his companies in early 1931. Most
of the bank loans he had taken on were short term and were being repaid on
schedule. All but $11 million of the $28 million he borrowed from Middle West
had been repaid. He had an outstanding debt of about $11 million, although he
was sure the banks would extend more financing. Since his lines of credit were
nearly tapped out in Chicago, he went back to New York, obtaining $5 million
from the Guaranty Trust, $1 million from the Irving Trust, and the balance from
his Corporation Securities and the First National Bank of Chicago. Harold Stuart suggested in June that Insull make another trip to New York to secure funds
to cover future obligations, so Insull personally called upon the Bankers Trust,
Central Hanover, Chatham-Phenix, and other banks with whom he had done
business. His use of company stock for collateral, however, held little value for
the bankers. By the middle of 1931, the market price of Insull Utility and Corporation Securities was $100 million below its liquidation value. Since that
strategy was not producing any new loans, Insull did something extraordinary:
he obtained $5 million in personal loans through Charles Mitchell of the Na-
tional City Bank of New York. His own name and fortune was now pledged as
collateral as he paid the money over to Corporation Securities to cover other
loans coming due.

The market tumbled again as he left New York for London in September.
The banks naturally wanted more stock as collateral, since the value of what he
had already pledged dramatically declined in value again. Then horrible rumors
began as word spread that Insull was backing up his loans with an empire whose
worth was eroding with every minute the market was open. The whispers became shouts that reverberated from Wall Street to LaSalle Street in Chicago: Insull was seen leaving a New York bank sobbing after being refused a loan. Insull
was being pilloried and humiliated by the House of Morgan for refusing to do
business with them over the prior four decades. London bankers had called him
to pay up. He was dangerously ill. He was dead. He was actually Jewish and the

WASP bankers were punishing him. None of it was true as he was in transit in the middle of the Atlantic.

When Insull reached London, the Bank of England went off of the gold standard, meaning that the bank would no longer make free delivery of gold in exchange for its notes. For the already precarious state of the world's stock markets and economies, this was the equivalent of catching pneumonia. Prices on the New York Stock Exchange resumed their precipitous decline as Insull watched the ticker show steady declines hour by hour. He sailed for home immediately and instructed Junior to bring together a pool of executives and business friends to raise $5 million and start buying Middle West at a meager $10 a share. As their last public pretense of the "everything is normal" policy, Insull, Martin, and Junior agreed to pay a dividend on Corporation Securities in November. The following month, the only person Insull had not asked for money was his friend Owen Young, chairman of GE. Insull asked Young to back him in a request to the New York banks for $10 million. Knowing that Young had the influence to persuade the bankers to loan the Insull companies more money, Insull agreed to tell Young and the bankers anything they wanted to know about the holding companies, as he was desperate to avoid receivership. Insull had little recourse. The value of all of the securities he had pledged as collateral was falling by the minute and there was nothing he could do about it. The banks demanded more collateral:

> Unfortunately, at this time the market price of all securities including those of the Insull group, showed a steady depreciation, and the amount of prime securities at the disposal of the Insull Utility Investments, Inc., and Corporation Securities Company of Chicago, showed steady shrinkage, owing to the constant demands of the banking creditors for additional collateral.[5]

Junior was now emerging from the trenches and facing the ire of the bankers. Insull sent him to assure all of the Chicago banks that they would have their collateral if they would agree to a "standstill agreement" freezing their repayment demands until the companies could assess what stocks could be pledged. Junior then traveled to New York with Harold Stuart to ask for the same forbearance from the Gotham bankers. Incensed that Junior, and not Insull, had been sent to parlay, Mitchell angrily sent Junior back to the train station because he had made a *personal* loan to his father and "I will not discuss it with anyone but Mr. Samuel Insull." On December 21, Insull returned to New York with Junior, renewing their mercy rounds with the banks. They wanted to show the bankers how much their securities had declined and wanted to negotiate a more lenient schedule for repayments. At this point, though, the banks were fighting with each other over what little money would be repaid by the Insulls. Irving Trust objected to Central

Hanover receiving $1.5 million. The banks reluctantly agreed to freeze the loans for six months, as Insull gained a reprieve. By the end of the year, all of the Chicago banks had essentially agreed to the same arrangement.

As 1932 dawned, the Insulls were still hoping for a revival in the market. They had no more collateral to offer and were almost completely in the thrall of the banks. In New York, the skittish financiers were demanding more information on all of the Insull companies in a continuing attempt to see if the firms were still solvent. By the end of February, Central Hanover, like most banks at the time, was pressed to obtain any cash it could, and told Insull that it was backing away from the standstill agreement and demanded immediate repayment. By now, Young was Insull's only remaining advocate with the New York bankers and assumed the role of chief negotiator. Young came to Chicago on February 27 to confer with Insull, then returned to New York, where he obtained an agreement with Central Hanover to release payment to Insull and forego loan repayment for the present. All of Insull's companies were now on the precipice.

The New York banks were watching Insull like a raptor hovering above a hunting ground and told Young that they would not approve of a dime coming out of Insull's treasuries. Now demanding that Insull's books be inspected by a qualified, independent accountant, they called upon Arthur Andersen, a chartered accountant in Chicago who had a sterling reputation at the time. The bankers now effectively controlled Insull's companies as he could not even write a check reimbursing himself for travel expenses without their approval. Andersen was given "absolute jurisdiction" to dissect any or all of Insull's books, much to Insull's chagrin. While Andersen pored over the arcane and complex accounting that Insull employed throughout the spring and early summer, Insull needed cash to keep his companies afloat. The newspapers now began diligent reporting of Insull's woes and there was little the public did not know of Insull's financial straits. *The Financial World* reported that the aggregate value of the portfolios of the two main holding companies was "$112 million, or $285 million below cost." Since 90 percent of the holding companies' holdings were pledged as collateral against $100 million in securities, how would the companies pay for the $166 million in new debt they acquired over the past year? "No equity remains for either preferred or common stocks." Unlike the past, when Insull could sell new shares or float bonds, there was no market for either. Nobody was buying securities in 1932. Everyone was selling to get their hands on hard currency.

Royal Munger, the financial columnist for the *Chicago Daily News*, echoed what little hope Insull retained. The operating companies, after all, were still profitable during the recession. Commonwealth Edison earned $10.40 a share in 1931, down from $11.51 the previous year; People's Gas earned $10.96, also down from $11.51. "The business of the operating companies is perfectly satisfactory," Insull gruffly told Munger from his office in the Commonwealth Edison building; "there is every reason to believe that 1932 will be even more satisfactory." In noting that the directors of Insull's companies all stood behind their chief, Munger sounded this vote of confidence: "The Insull holding companies have experienced a terrible loss, as every one knows. In that loss, Insull himself has shared. Their recovery, if they do recover, must be built up of the earnings of the operating companies, which, in turn can, over a period of years, by their own earnings, restore the price of the stocks held in the trust portfolio."[6]

Only $10 million stood between Insull and receivership in the second quarter of 1932. As Andersen was recommending the reorganization of Insull's companies, Insull, Martin, and Stuart headed back to New York for one last round of pleading for their financial independence. Young insisted that, at the very least, everything be done to save Middle West. So he convened a summit of all the Chicago and New York bankers involved and attempted to iron out an agreement. Young was now the only person who could resolve the crisis. Stuart and Insull were asked to remain outside the conference room as the "bankers only" meeting began on April 8. It only took the bankers an hour to decide their course of action: no more money would be lent. Most of them left without saying a word to Insull and his party. Then Young came out to talk with Insull.

"Does this mean receivership?" Insull asked dourly.

"Looks that way," Young said in a reserved tone.

Although he was shaken to his core, Insull was not disconsolate. He took the next train back to Chicago and was meeting with Chicago bankers on Saturday, April 9. They all knew him and were convinced he had some more financing ideas. Many of them were directors in his companies, bought his stock, and financed his expansion. Almost to a man, Insull had put money into each one of their pockets. They were anchored to him as to an errant family member who needed to be bailed out of jail. Despite all of the obvious conflicts of interest, they appointed *Insull* as one of the receivers of his own companies. Insull objected, perhaps mildly, but the bankers insisted because Insull had earned a solid reputation as a turnaround artist. They had seen him take all of the two-bit, struggling power plants, the gas company, the traction lines, and the interurbans and infuse them with a new vitality and profitability that was holding up even during the country's economic nightmare. What human being understood the Insull holding companies better than Insull himself? So the magnate joined a committee of three receivers. Charles McCulloch and Edward Hurley were named as the other two. On April 16, papers were filed in federal court to put Middle West, Insull Utility, and Corporation Securities into receivership with the intention of reorganizing the companies. Insull's main holding entities were bankrupt while his operating companies remained solvent.

Insull turned his attention to the management of the operating companies. Throughout May, he spent his time shoring up their finances and was ready to launch a $60 million sale of senior securities for Commonwealth Edison, People's Gas, and Public Service. Although Insull did not know it at the time, the independent directors of the companies had cabled fellow director James Simpson, who was vacationing in India, to return to Chicago. Stanley Field surprised Insull when he walked into Insull's office on June 3 to ask for his resignation from the operating companies, saying that McCulloch had also wanted him to resign. Insull blustered at first, saying he wanted to do it in a proper way, and promised he would resign the next day at the Edison offices. Ironically, even though the directors suddenly wanted Insull out of the picture, they requested that Junior stay on with the operating companies, which was some consolation to Insull.

The reason for the forced resignation was the discovery that Martin was using company funds to cover his personal stock margin accounts. He had set up dummy accounts and channeled $268,000 to cover his debts—and Insull had perhaps unknowingly signed the checks from Middle West accounts. Insull wept when he heard the revelation. On top of everything that he had been through, he was now betrayed by his own brother. McCulloch sent for Martin, who was told to resign. Martin was truculent and demanded to know the reason. "Because you have mismanaged the company in the most outrageous way," McCulloch groused. Martin silently sat in his chair stunned, knowing there was nothing more he could do. It was over. Meanwhile, on June 6, Insull signed the resignations from the 65 companies he chaired and the 85 companies for whom he had been director in suite 1700 of the Edison building. It took him nearly three hours. He asked his secretary to phone Gladys. "But do not disturb her if she is resting." Gladys called back immediately.

"Hello," he said sweetly. "How are you? Well, it's all over. I am out of a job. It was a very trying day and I will be home in a while. After dinner we will take a drive. Goodbye."

One of his teary assistants blurted out as he resumed signing, "you will come back in six months! Your stockholders will demand it."

"No," the fallen titan replied. "I shall not come back. I am through."

When Insull finished, he walked out of the conference room and reached the street, where reporters swarmed him like yellow jackets on a watermelon: "Gentleman, I have worked continuously since I was 14 years and 7 months old," Insull said, his voice cracking slightly. "I was fired from a job one time on a Saturday afternoon and had a job another job Monday morning. And I have worked hard, but I can truthfully say in the whole 58 years this has been the hardest day of all. I am out of a job. I don't know how I shall like it."

Since his debts exceeded his net worth and he had no way of immediately re-paying the banks, Insull was technically bankrupt when he left his companies. He had personally guaranteed the loans he had taken out from the New York banks, which would not have been unusual for a nineteenth-century magnate, but was unheard of for a twentieth-century one. Most of the assets that he pledged for collateral did not belong to him; they belonged largely to the share-holders of his companies. The market spiraled downward that June, leaving the owners of his companies with stock that did nothing but depreciate. All told, Insull's investors—truck drivers, power plant foremen, meter readers, bank offi-cers—lost $750 million. That would be $10.5 billion in 2005 dollars, or $500 million short of the $11 billion WorldCom accounting fraud. Had Insull com-mitted fraud? Cook County and federal prosecutors thought they had a solid case. With more than 600,000 people sitting on nearly worthless stock, surely some legerdemain was involved. Insull, and his brokers, bankers, and directors would be called to account for it.

Having gone from a cardinal of commerce to public thief in less than three years, Insull had no pretensions about getting a fair hearing in Chicago in 1932. People who had invested their life savings with him and trusted in his ability to turn around the most hopeless business situations felt more than deceived. They wanted revenge. They wanted to see Insull's head on a pike on the Michigan Avenue bridge. The public did not know that Insull had per-sonally lost more than everything he owned. Stanley Field got what he could for his friend in terms of severance, but the directors were furious at Insull and refused to grant him a $50,000 annual pension and three months' salary as severance. Field convinced Insull that he had to cut his pension and make an-other sacrifice that would allow the boards to get their pound of financial flesh. The only thing that Insull had to offer was something that was not even his right to give: Gladys's dower rights, or the share of one-third of his estate. Now his creditors could take everything of value from his wife as well. As a consolation, Gladys would be granted a $25,000 annual pension when Insull died. She reluctantly signed over her rights. Insull agreed to a $21,000 pen-sion. "I'm a damned fool," Gladys said bitterly. "But I'll do it." Now she was nearly back to where she was when she was a poor actress, only without her youth and with her career well behind her. She hated the Chicago bankers for imposing this upon her, this final humiliation. She did not care if she set foot in another Gold Coast salon. She would live in Paris, a place of elegance—and no memories.

Emotionally, mentally, and physically spent, Insull knew it was time for him and Gladys to leave Chicago. He could not manage his companies back to health if he was forced out of the boardroom. There was nothing he could do about the morbid stock market and there was little Mullaney could do to convince his shareholders that they were not robbed. Insull was not convinced that he was permanently barred from running his companies; for now, though, it was essential to leave Chicago to get a fresh perspective and let the new management team have their chance. Gladys was not envisioning a return to the Windy City anytime soon, although she was going to miss Junior and his new darling son, Sam III. Junior was staying behind to see what he could do to repair the damage. He was his father's son, not his apologist. He would soon be his sole defender as the prosecutors starting reviewing the evidence. Martin had slipped out to Canada and Insull followed on June 14, meeting with his friend P.J. McEnroe in Montreal. After traveling on to Quebec City, Gladys and Insull breakfasted at the Chateau Frontenac before boarding the *Empress of Britain* to Cherbourg. The Insulls kept their names off the passenger list, as had been their custom for years.

Chicago, for the most part, did not see Insull's departure as an overdue vacation. The headlines blared that the utilities kingpin was now on the lam—a fugitive from justice—even though he had yet to be charged with a single crime. Junior played go-between with the prosecutors, who were under tremendous pressure to produce an indictment. The Chicago papers fumed. The colonel and the Hearst editors smiled. While the Insulls found a low-key hotel in Paris, Junior was busy meeting with lawyers and company executives. By September, Insull agreed to meet Simpson in London, who was on his way back from a vacation in Scotland. Insull's successor at Commonwealth Edison, who was part of the new executive team along with George Ranney of People's Gas, was asking Insull for his advice on how to manage the electric company. The men dined and talked until midnight. The following month Junior arrived in town to brief him on his legal situation and talked about how the local politicians were making him a scapegoat. It appeared likely that Insull was going to be indicted. At that point, Insull decided to extend his stay in Europe to avoid the political witch hunt. "I don't want to put my head in the lion's mouth," he told Junior.

FDR saw Insull as more than a campaign issue. Insull symbolized everything that was repugnant about the rapacious utility barons. What is more, Insull's abuse of his monopolies and his unfettered stock sales and holding companies had contributed to the ruin of the economy. With Hoover failing miserably to reignite the economy, the governor of New York was now on center stage and about to present a frightful tragedy to the American public in which Insull was to play the role of Simon Legree. FDR was alarmed by the headlines when Insull's companies first went into receivership in April. Insull was more than a failed utilities baron, FDR surmised. This man had single-handedly set out to undermine democracy through his 6,000 power stations in 39 states. The greatest single business failure in American history was an instructive lesson in the ways that unchecked commercialism could wreck people's lives.

On Jefferson Day, April 18, 1932, FDR began his crusade against the "Insulls and the Ishmaels" of the world. Building on his theme that private utilities had been gouging customers for years, FDR proclaimed that "electric utility companies have sought, and in many cases have succeeded in obtaining permission to charge rates which will bring a fair return, not on this cash investment [in power plants], but on a definite inflation of capital." FDR found another connection between Insull and the wretched economy: one of the banks Insull got a loan from received money from the Hoover administration for a bailout. The year also marked the wholesale collapse of 389 banks. Bank holidays and withdrawal restrictions had been ordered in Iowa, Michigan, New Jersey, Indiana, Maryland, and Arkansas. The Senate Banking Committee's brilliant counsel Ferdinand Pecora started to probe some of the higher-profile failures such as Charles Dawes's Central Republic Bank in Chicago. Pecora forced Dawes to admit in testimony that 90 percent of the bank's deposits were lent to the Insull companies, in clear violation of state law, which forbid more than 10 percent of a bank's loans to a single entity.

Back in Chicago, Douglas and attorney Harry Booth formed the Illinois Utility Consumers and Investors League and aimed their protests at the Illinois Commerce Commission. They asked the commission to probe Insull's practices and to immediately reduce utility rates. Douglas and Booth were outraged that the commission had approved a $40 million bond issue by the Insull companies that would prop up the holding companies at the expense of diluting shareholders' interests in Commonwealth Edison. Booth also was challenging People's Gas, claiming the company was substituting cheaper natural gas for manufactured gas without charging lower rates. Booth and his partner Joseph Swidler, frustrated by the commission's indifference to their case, were cited for contempt of court when they went to Chicago newspapers to expose the commission's friendliness to every People's Gas rate increase. Around the same time, with Insull no longer in the picture, Booth filed suit against Public Service to reveal how it determined rates. Taking a lead from Roosevelt, Booth's group charged that the utility's rates were "exorbitant, unlawful and discriminatory." In what would be one of the arguments used in the prosecution against the Insull executives, Booth claimed that Insull was transferring funds from the profitable operating companies to keep his holding companies afloat. In a letter to Professor Robert Lovett of the University of Chicago, Booth charged:

> Our [Consumers League] report revealed that these [operating] companies suffered many millions of dollars of losses due to speculation with employees' investment funds, annuity and insurance funds and loans and advances to officers and employees, some of whom were not even connected with the operating companies. The last item alone resulted in write-offs in the surpluses of the three companies in excess of $5 million. The total losses admitted by the companies exceed $85 million.[7]

Roosevelt was on the march across the country to inform Americans that they were being fleeced by the private utilities. Like errant brats, the companies needed to be policed by the parental authority of the U.S. government, FDR argued. "You can see that this 'lusty younger child' of the U.S. needs to be kept very closely under the watchful eye of its parent—the people of the United States." FDR reasoned that Americans were getting shafted by the utilities despite the $8 billion they had invested in buying the stock of the companies. In a seminal September 21 speech in Portland, Oregon, FDR reiterated his findings that most Americans were being deprived of cheaper utility rates, citing his Canadian study as governor. He claimed that the reason Americans did not have rates as low as Canadians was that the "selfish interests in control of light and power industries have not been sufficiently farsighted to establish rates low enough for widespread public use." Casting himself as the "dangerous man" the utilities wished to vanquish, FDR moved deftly into personifying the struggle for utility regulation, casting himself as the candidate who sought to "protect the welfare of the people against selfish greed." Then he inveighed against Hoover's stance against federal regulation and the freewheeling days of the holding companies. In the emotional focal point of the speech, where Jonah emerges from the belly of the whale, FDR lashes out against Insull:

> The crash of the Insull empire has given excellent point to the truth of what I have been arguing for four long years. *That* great "Insull monstrosity," made up of a group of holding and investing companies *so long,* and exercising control over hundreds of thousands of operating companies, had distributed securities among hundreds of thousands of investors, and had taken their money to an amount running over $1.5 billion, *not millions, but billions! That* "Insull monstrosity" grew during the years of prosperity until it reached a position where it was an important factor in the lives of millions of *our* people. The

name was magic. The investing public did not realize then, as it does now *today,* that the methods used in building up of these holding companies were wholly contrary to every sound public policy. [8]

FDR tied the Insull failure to "ultimate ruin" and the "wildcatting days of the railroads." Punctuating his campaign to end the foul practices of the utilities was FDR's famous call for a "New Deal," which then was an eight-point plan to disclose corporate financing, stock ownership, regulation of holding companies, federal power supervision, and utility rate making. No fewer than five of these points became law over the next few years. Insull was now more than just a political scapegoat; his folly was the impetus for modern securities and utility regulation. Within the first 100 days of his administration, in fact, FDR was able to usher through the Truth in Securities Act of 1933, a law aimed squarely at preventing another Insull disaster.

It is unlikely that Insull heard any of FDR's speech. Nevertheless, Junior had talked his father into leaving Paris, where he might be extradited. Leaving Gladys behind in the hotel, Insull and his son took the late train to Italy, where his lawyers believed that extradition would not be processed under Mussolini's government. Only two years earlier, Insull was invited to Mussolini's Palazzo Venezie to discuss the electrification of Italy. Il Duce kept Insull waiting an irritating half hour before he showed up in his black shirt and military uniform, his chin jutting out like a giraffe. They met in a vaulted hall. The dictator's desk occupied the extreme end of the hall in the style of a Roman emperor. Impressed by his "tremendous force and power," Insull suggested that Mussolini rely more upon hydropower than coal, since the country had to import the mineral. Insull came away from the meeting "feeling that it had been my privilege to meet one of the great statesmen of Europe." This was before Mussolini had aligned himself with one of the other great statesmen of Europe, Adolf Hitler.

As Insull sought asylum in the fascist state, the Chicago papers screamed "Ask Mussolini to Catch Sam Insull." Arriving in Turin, Insull decided that it would be only a matter of time before the authorities tracked him down in Italy. On the following day, Insull booked passage to Greece, which lacked an extradition policy with the U.S. at that time. He had to fly to Salonika (Thessaloniki) through Tirana, Albania, in a three-motored plane, the first time he had ever been off the ground in an airplane. Before he left Milan, he sent a letter to Gladys, a missive that ended up being printed in the Chicago papers, which then sent reams of reporters to rifle through Gladys's trash in Paris and track down the mogul as if he had murdered the Lindbergh baby:

> My Dearest Gladys: Tonight I am feeling as if I am going on a real adventure. I am going by plane to Salonika, Greece, early tomorrow morning. . . . All these changes have been made on the best [legal] advice and Junior will tell you all the details. . . . I feel very badly about leaving you, but there is nothing else for me to do, in view of the advice I received this morning before we left Turin. . . . I am afraid that you have had an awful time with reporters, but it will all be over by Saturday night and I am hoping Junior will be with you Saturday night or Sunday morning. I am so glad he is over here. He has been a tower of strength through these terrible days. I feel very sad at heart tonight, mainly on your account, but my courage had not left me, and when these dark days are over we will have some happy times together. With best love. From your devoted husband, Sam.[9]

The flight across the Adriatic was rough as the small plane kept jerking up and down when it hit air pockets. Insull's nerves and ever-weakening heart were rattled from the flight and he was relieved to be on the ground again. Upon arriving in Salonika, he had dinner and took the late train to Athens, where he checked into the well-appointed Grande Bretagne Hotel.

While Insull lodged and dined in relative comfort, Chicago fell deeper into the throes of the Depression, and politicians were increasingly pointing to Insull's European exodus as evidence of his guilt in hoodwinking investors. The Civic Opera did relatively well in 1930, attracting larger audiences than in its Auditorium days. Yet the Depression blackened even the glittering hall of the city's wealthiest patrons. Artists agreed to a 20 percent pay cut for the 1932 season, even though ticket prices remained the same at $1 to $6 apiece. Attendance plummeted as the opera board solicited $500,000 over five years. It received only $234,000 in pledges. After staging *Martha* on January 30, 1932, the curtain came down and the opera company was forced to dissolve.

By October 10 of that year, Insull was heeding his lawyers' advice and staying put in Athens, even though the Illinois prosecutors knew he was there and the papers had located his hotel. The Hearst *Herald & Examiner* broke the revelation: "Find Insull In Athens Hotel—Fugitive Slips From Extradition Net; Dodges U.S. Arrest; Faces Deportation; Ex-Magnate Seems Well Supplied With Cash; Chicago Officer May Go Abroad For Capture."

The symbol of corporate evil, a fugitive, and fallen utilities emperor was not merely in exile, however. He would become, in the words of the *Washington Post,* "the bane of nations," as FDR did everything in his power to bring Insull back to Chicago to justice.

FACING THE MUSIC

Insull Tried for Fraud

Einhorn was among the first to be wiped out, partly because of his own mismanagement. Thousands of his dough were lost in Insull's watered and pyramided utilities . . . .

—Saul Bellow, *The Adventures of Augie March*[1]

The bright Greek sun soothed Insull as he casually strolled around the Acropolis and relaxed in the *kaffeneion*. His lawyers had told him that the Greek government had no extradition treaty with the U.S. and no intention of drafting one. The U.S. was pressuring the Greeks to deport him as an "undesirable alien," although it had yet to establish a case. Back in Chicago, his assistant John O'Keefe had been caught sending coded telegrams to him, yet refused to decode them for prosecutors, who then promptly subpoenaed him. Insull did not know a soul in the Greek capital and worried about Gladys in Paris, who had managed to receive $25,000 he had wired through the Morgan bank. Junior had gone back to Paris to be with Gladys. Contrary to newspaper reports at the time, Insull did not come into the country with $10 million. All he had were his clothes and a suitbag, attaché, and portmaneau. The first person to tell Insull the complete news of his indictment for fraud and embezzlement in Chicago was a Greek newspaperman and lawyer named Christopher Protopappas. Working for the International News Service, Protopappas explained Insull's unfolding legal situation to him and conducted an exclusive interview with the magnate. The reporter first tracked Insull down in the Athens police station, where the confused Greek police "examined" him. They could not deport him, since all of his papers were in order. Exhibiting the legendary Hellenic hospitality, the police commissioner was

extraordinarily kind, turning one of his offices into Insull's bedroom and allow-
ing him to dine at a nearby hotel during his 36-hour detention.

Insull calmly replied to Protopappas's queries: "I am innocent of wrongdo-
ing. I have lost everything I have ever owned." That was not true at that point—
he technically still had possession of his estate, pension, and other homes—but
it made for a great lead paragraph in papers around the world. Insull openly described his departure from Paris to elude the *gendarmes* and his short stay in
Italy, where Mussolini later said he did not want Insull in his country since he
represented one of the worst examples of capitalist exploitation, something that
Il Duce would end with his fascist "reforms." Though he had heard that he was
indicted, Insull had yet to receive a summons and was anxious to defend himself. Showing an uncharacteristic display of nerves, he fidgeted, repeatedly
folded a newspaper and bit his nails in front of the reporter:

> Of all of the companies controlled by me, only Middle West, Insull Utilities
> and Corporation Securities went into bankruptcy. Their liabilities were about
> $250 million while their actual losses were in the neighborhood of $100 mil-
> lion. I attribute these bankruptcies to the general world crisis. I, my wife and
> son have lost all of our property. We have nothing left except for my pension
> of $19,000 a year.[2]

The Greek police apologized to Insull after this arrest, saying that they had
acted beyond their authority. The Hellenic constables then began to quarrel
with the U.S. Embassy, which was mounting a campaign to place Insull in custody until the State Department could negotiate his extradition. The embassy
succeeded in obtaining a second arrest a month later. Insull appeared before the
country's supreme court and the justices agreed to detain him. After examination by several doctors, who determined that he was too infirm to incarcerate
because of his heart condition, the court remanded him to a hospital, where he
was again treated with deference. Insull's Greek lawyers Christos Lada and Denis
Lazaremos told Insull that it would be difficult for the U.S. to extradite him.
The Hellenic procedure was a preview for Insull's upcoming American trials.
The U.S. submitted evidence, Insull's lawyers would defend and the justices
would decide, not if Insull was guilty of crimes committed in the U.S., but if
those crimes could be proved under Greek statutes. After two months, the Greek
supreme court decided in Insull's favor. The court did not find that there was
sufficient evidence that Insull committed fraud, and he was free to stay in
Athens. Insull was released on December 27 and returned to stay in the Petit
Palais hotel. Before the end of the year, Hoover had signed a warrant for Insull's
arrest before leaving office. It must have been a bitter experience for the presi-

dent, who supported the unbridled growth of the holding companies and personally trusted businessmen like Insull.

Athens society was quite taken with Insull and welcomed him into their company. Madame Helene Coyimzoglu practically adopted Insull and became close friends with Gladys when she arrived in March 1933. The Insulls moved freely in Athenian society, attending soirees, and discussed the possibility of improving the country's primitive power system. Officials from the consular service and the Cook County state attorney's office also came to Athens, although there was nothing they could do legally to remove Insull from the country.

In an appeal, the U.S. government again argued that Insull had committed a fraud and deserved to be deported. Once again, the Greek court found no lawful ground for extradition and annulled the arrest warrant for Insull. The jurists accepted the argument that Insull was trying to save his companies with his stock transactions and borrowing, and that dire economic conditions forced his holding companies into bankruptcy. Although the appeals court mischaracterized his standing in Chicago, they did not find that he intentionally defrauded his shareholders:

> It must not be overlooked that the petition in bankruptcy [the receivership of the holding companies] was not filed for a long time after the Corporation Securities company became insolvent, and that it was not until May, 1933, that the prosecution of the accused began, who in the meantime had left the country with the good wishes of a goodly number of his fellow citizens, after having ceded to his creditors his entire real property in the United States. All these facts show that even in the United States, the acts committed by the accused were at first not considered fraudulent or as independent of the general financial crisis.[3]

FDR was working every diplomatic channel in an attempt to wrest Insull from Athens. One way was somehow to force Insull to leave Greece and arrest him in Turkey, which was on better terms with the U.S. and would approve the extradition. Outside of kidnapping Insull, that proved nettlesome since Insull had no intention of leaving Greece on his own. Although he had absolutely no influence with FDR—the one president of the twentieth century he had not met—Insull boldly forwarded a letter directly to FDR in May proclaiming his innocence and asking that his associates not be named in indictments. "If anyone is guilty of the offense charged, it is I, and not these other persons," Insull began.

Insull admitted to "mistakes of judgment" in the extraordinary letter, and predictably declared he was "innocent of any crime." Then he explained to FDR why he fled to Europe: "I declined to return to Chicago to be hounded by the late prosecutor's office of Cook County, Illinois, on charges which were then a part of a local political campaign. . . . I am willing, however, to return to prove my innocence of the charge by the Federal Government or a similar charge in connection with the Insull Utilities Investments Inc."

Roosevelt must have chuckled at Insull's moxie when he read the letter. Not only was Insull requesting a trial in a federal court, he wanted a separate trial for his associates and personal protection from the Department of Justice. Insull knew that facing a Chicago prosecutor and jury and sitting in county jail would be rough justice, indeed. There was nothing the U.S. government could do if they could not remove Insull from Greece, though, whose courts favored him at every turn.

O'Keefe was not faring as well as his boss. Under intense questioning, the young aide was revealing details of Insull's loans from the New York banks and the involvement of Owen Young. O'Keefe was now answering questions in federal court concerning the bankruptcy of the holding companies. Explaining how Insull obtained the loans with holding-company stock pledged as collateral, he detailed the last days of the Insull empire. Meanwhile, the U.S. government was successful in its efforts to arrest and extradite Martin from Canada. Asked by reporters about his stay in a Canadian jail, the aristocratic-looking Martin replied "it's too terrible to talk about."

When asked about the Insulls, Mary Garden, traveling through New York in a mink coat and two strands of pearls, was not the least bit reserved about her former supporter, enraged that the Civic Opera had been dissolved. "He has destroyed a healthy and beautiful organization," she told reporters. "I loathe destroyers. This man wiped out one of the most marvelous institutions in the world. He is a financier, not an operatic director. You put me in a chair at a director's meeting of the Insull utilities companies and see how I would make out. That's how ridiculous Insull was in opera. He knew nothing about opera."

The animus against Insull was festering in Chicago as the papers reported that Insull was living in Athens in relative comfort. Each movement of Insull was now being tracked daily: his trips to the police station, the hospital, and turkey dinners during the holidays. A contingent of newspapermen awaited Insull as he left his hotel and took his stroll. In the middle of his Athens stay, when the Greek courts decided that there was no legal reason to extradite him, Insull volunteered a news item that he hoped would generate sympathy. He had learned of a "plot" to kidnap him. With his young British lawyer Douglas Page at his side, he waved a cablegram telling him of the plan. According to the fugitive executive, "Chicago authorities have hired four Greek American detectives in Athens to kidnap and remove me to a country more favorable to their ends." The plot was derided as "absurd" by William Rittenhouse, the Cook County assistant state attorney.

Insull bided his time by making a complete study of the Greek energy situation. He advised his hosts to exploit brown coal (lignite) resources in the north of the country for the production of power. Having studied the dramatic influx of Greeks from Asia Minor, he was confident that the Balkan country could be successfully industrialized. Since the end of World War I and the fall of the Ottoman Empire, some 750,000 Greeks came back into the country. The Chicago papers reported on his master plan for the Greek economy, which included a bid to become minister of electric power. Insull did not gain the post when his principal sponsor failed to win reelection to the Greek parliament.

Chicago writers gleefully mocked Insull's respite in the birthplace of democracy. Edgar Lee Masters, whose law partner Clarence Darrow had joined Ickes's utility league to fight the remaining Insull companies, tinged his contemporary assessment of Insull with poetic vitriol:

> There was no Aristophanes to satirize him [Insull], no Demosthenes to denounce him. He was the consummation of Chicago as a megalopolis, and the whole world was in the throes of a changing era. Whether it was to be a rebarbarization of the world or a decline of civilization everywhere was a matter of deep speculation. If American civilization perishes, as the Mayan did, the steel towers which carried the wires of Insull may remain to tell the story of the epiphytes which drew sustenance from the electric plants which rested upon the land once owned by the Pottawatomies.[4]

The city that embraced Insull, however, had much better things to do than to focus on the ruminations of its former business boss. Chicago was opening another World's Fair—The Century of Progress. In the midst of the darkest days of the American economy, the exposition's unofficial theme was light in all of its glory. Building on its success with the Columbian Exposition, the 1933 fair was a dazzling display of electricity. Every art deco or modern building looked like something out of Flash Gordon, poised to hurtle into the sky at any moment. This time around, though, GE would not miss an opportunity to fully exhibit its wares. Millions of lightbulbs illuminated the fair, an orgiastic celebration of light and power in every form. As the fair was dedicated firmly to promoting commerce, nearly two dozen corporations had their own pavilions, compared with nine in the 1893 event. General Motors built a soaring monolith of a tower and transported some 20 million attendees throughout the fair in its sleek buses, which were fast supplanting—with the help of concerted well-funded political campaigns—trolley car systems in major cities.

Every building had its own electric signs, lighting design, and exhibit halls. Decorative pylons with fins seemed to be infused with light. Electric murals designed by Charles Fall that flowed upward into the sky charmed the long lines that waited to enter the "GE House of Magic." Everywhere throughout the fair, lights were opalescent and acrobatic, dramatic and practical. GE promoted every conceivable use of its appliances, power systems, and lighting. It handed out brochures telling fairgoers that modern street lighting saved cities $32 million. An "Electricity at Work" exhibit showed how a beauty shop, restaurant, bakery, dress shop, and grocery would look with the most efficient lighting scheme. GM had a working model of its assembly line. The Midway featured a skyride nearly 20 stories tall, an "Odditorium" housing a freak show and Sally Rand, the scandalous fan dancer. The attendance was so impressive—more than 40 million people walked though the gates—that FDR requested that it reopen the following year because he thought it might stimulate consumer spending. Henry Ford, who declined to participate in the first opening of the fair, probably because GM was there, built an exhibit for the 1934 version. Frank Lloyd Wright, excluded from building anything at the fair, called the exhibition's architecture a "sham."

Had he been in business in Chicago in 1933, Insull would have spent an enormous amount of money to outpromote the corporations that anchored the fair. GE and the other electrical exhibitors were capitalizing on techniques that Insull had developed 20 years earlier and, as a result, electricity was the unstoppable commodity that was taking over the modern home, even in the Depression. Mrs. Robert Bourland of Rockford, Illinois, was a living commercial for Insull's product. "In our homes today, our schedule is run by electric clocks," she said during a "Golden Jubilee of Electricity" in her town. "We clean our rugs with electric vacuum cleaners. We polish our floors with electric brushes. We turn night into day with our electric lights. I have turned day ahead several hours for my chickens with the alarm clock that switched on the lights and set the chickens scratching two hours before I awakened each morning."

The political weight on Greece to expel Insull was as heavy as a fleet of ocean liners. After the Roosevelt administration threatened to curtail trade with the Balkan country, the Greek government relented and asked Insull to leave by January 1, 1934. Insull was at the center of what was becoming an international incident. Washington did not want to inflame Greek-American relations any more than it had. Insull became a unique diplomatic and logistical problem because he could not pass through certain countries that were hostile to the U.S. Could he be sent through Europe on the Orient Express? That would not work since he would have to pass through Greek territory again. It was essential to get Insull into Turkish hands, where that government could hand him over to American authorities. Insull was effectively at the mercy of the State Department, which had managed to cancel his passport and told European countries not to issue him a visa. The defiant Greeks then issued Insull a temporary visa that expired April 5, while doctors confined Insull to bed because of his worsening heart condition and diabetes.

The Chicago papers played a game of speculation as to where Insull might land when he left Greece. One paper had him flying to Afghanistan, another to Romania. As a result of being blackballed by every government he applied to for a visa, Insull decided to slip out of the country in the middle of the night in disguise. His Greek friends had provided him with enough money to charter a 40-year-old tramp steamer, so he bade farewell to Gladys and Madame Coyimzoglu. His destination was unknown and he was relying upon the ship's captain, who spoke little English, to find him a friendly port. Several possibilities loomed and he had authority to order the captain to take him anywhere the ship could sail. Would he go to an obscure place like Jibuti (now spelled "Djibouti," in what was then French Somaliland)? Or enter the Black Sea through the Dardanelles and settle in northern Turkey? Port Said also was a possibility. He was now in the hands of his Greek friends, who worked diligently to find a place for him to dock once his ship left Piraeus. Darkening his hair and moustache and removing his glasses (one report claimed he dressed as a woman), Insull walked unnoticed by police onto the S.S. *Maiotis* on March 13, 1934.

Sailing as far as Crete, the ship turned around and headed back to Piraeus, although the only way Insull discovered the retracing was by observing the position of the sun. The captain explained in broken English that if he did not return to port, the Greek ministry of marines would arrest him and his first mate. During Insull's brief voyage, the Greek police rounded up the usual suspects, which included Gladys and Madame Coyimzoglu. The women were questioned in separate rooms about Insull's whereabouts. Gladys had attempted to secure a visa to England, which was denied. The harbor police in Piraeus nosed around the *Maiotis* and perfunctorily asked Insull where he was headed. He replied, "that's my business," then the police mysteriously let him go. The captain was told to stay in contact with the marine ministry and leave Greek waters as soon as possible.

The *Maiotis* left port and sailed into the Bosporus and anchored outside of Istanbul on March 29 to await fresh water and supplies. The Turkish harbor police detained the ship and sent guards aboard to question Insull. The captain went ashore to contact the Greek consulate and his lawyer. After several days, the guards arrested Insull and took him into court in Istanbul, where he appeared before three judges without an interpreter. In a mock trial, a document in French, signed by the American ambassador, was shown to him. As no one offered to translate it to him, the only words he could recognize were "Corporation Securities Corporation." It was likely an arrest warrant. Surprisingly, though, the court set him free since he was not guilty of any military offense nor was he a Turkish citizen. After spending a night in a seedy hotel, Insull was escorted by a police officer to another hearing in a prison. Although Insull demanded that his lawyers be present, the Turkish police continued to question him without representation. After three days in the dank jail, Insull begged his lawyer A.A. Mango to turn him over to the American ambassador. Mango advised against it, believing he had a chance to get Insull released on appeal through the Turkish high court. Insull now believed that the Turkish detention was nothing more than a kidnapping orchestrated by the American government, which was the likeliest scenario given the circumstances.

The Turkish court ruled against Insull and handed him over to the police, who put him on a Turkish steamer bound for Panderma. From there, he was taken to Smyrna, where he was escorted aboard the American Export Company's S.S. *Exilonia*. With an extradition request personally signed by FDR and Secretary of State Cordell Hull, Burton Berry, the third secretary of the American embassy in Istanbul, took custody of Insull. While Insull did not greet Berry with open arms, he was relieved to be out of the Turkish justice system, such as it was. Other than confiscating Insull's razor and posting a guard with him, Berry was cordial to Insull. The two men got to know and like each other as Insull prepared his memoirs. The voyage home was pleasant, with Insull and a handful of newspapermen chatting about events in Chicago and abroad, smoking cigars, and relaxing on deck. Insull was actually having a good time: "In the 53 years I had been crossing the Atlantic, it was the longest voyage I had ever made, both as to mileage and as to time in transit, but it really was most enjoyable, and I would be very glad to make the voyage again, but under different circumstances."

The Chicago papers were feverishly running daily stories that laid the foundation for the charges against Insull. Junior was called before G-man Melvin Purvis for questioning. Although Commonwealth Edison paid a dividend and earned a profit of $10 million in 1932, Junior was forced to resign as vice chairman of the company. He would be replaced by George Ranney, a former People's Gas and International Harvester executive. Stanley Field, another defendant in the upcoming Insull trial, also resigned as director of Commonwealth Edison and as chairman of Continental Bank.

Owen Young defended himself by claiming that his intervention with the New York bankers "delayed the Insull crash." The Utility League released a report to their friends at the Hearst papers dissecting the securities trades among the holding companies, charging that "by the end of 1931, the [holding] companies transferred $170 million . . . for speculation without stockholder or public scrutiny." The U.S. Senate banking committee was preparing its investigation into the Insull scandal. The committee would later report that there was a $44 million discrepancy between the income of the Insull holding companies and their income-tax returns. Failed Chicago banker Charles Dawes said he lent Insull $12 million and passed along the collateral to the Reconstruction Finance Corporation, the agency the Hoover administration created to bail out troubled banks. Arthur Andersen, the accountant who audited Insull's companies when he was a receiver, told the federal court how Insull almost collapsed when his audit was presented. The auditor even spared a few kind words to describe Insull: "He possessed the keenest intellect I ever knew and retained unlimited courage, business judgment and integrity."

Insull's defense team planned to transform Insull into a victim of the Depression. The idea was to get a positioning statement to Insull as he landed on American soil. Before reporters could besiege him and get the obligatory pictures of him being carried off in handcuffs, Insull would proclaim the first words of his defense. The government was careful to avoid a New York City pier, where reporters could have free rein. Their objective was to get him to Chicago as quickly and as quietly as possible and let the Chicago press feast on him. The State Department also had no intention of letting him near his lawyers, who could possibly file a writ of habeas corpus in New York or tie up the case in other legal actions. Only H.R. Bannerman of the State Department and the Coast Guard knew the exact details of Insull's transfer to authorities. A phalanx of reporters and Junior were led onto the cutter *Hudson* on May 7. Junior was not searched. At that point, John Young, the cutter's captain, was under sealed orders. As the *Hudson* drew up alongside the *Exilonia,* a sailor shouted, "Tell Insull his son is here."

Insull heard the seaman and screamed, "Where is my son, where is my Chappie?" Junior swiftly climbed a ladder on to the steamer and bolted up a flight of stairs, where his father was standing, his eyes tearing. "Why hello, Junior dear." At that moment, Junior hugged him and handed Insull a piece of paper, which was his statement.

At 6:47 a.m., Insull was transferred to the cutter from the *Exilonia* near the Ambrose Lightship off Sandy Hook, New Jersey. Facing the throng of reporters, Insull pulled out his one-page declaration and started reading:

> I am back in America to make the most important fight of my life—not only for freedom but for complete vindication. I was told that I was no longer needed. Tired from the sleepless struggle to save the investments of thousands of men and women, discouraged in my attempts to defend the investments of my friends and associates as well as everything I had, I got out. I wanted to rest. . . . Arbitrarily I had been instructed to resign the head of these companies which I had built and which I had tried to protect. No charges had been brought against me until I had been away for three months. My return at that time would have further complicated the problem of the reorganization of the companies. . . . I had heard that my greatest error was in underestimating the effects of the financial panic on American securities and particularly on the companies I was working so hard to build. I worked with all my energy to save those companies. I made mistakes, but they were honest mistakes. They were errors in judgment, but not dishonest manipulations. The whole story has not yet been told. . . . When it is told in court, my judgment may be discredited but certainly my honesty will be vindicated.[5]

After the statement, Insull was brought ashore to New Jersey at Fort Hancock and whisked onto a train at Princeton Junction, where he was sent straight to Chicago. The statement painted a picture of Insull as the doomed corporate savior, protector of other people's money, and scapegoat for a crime he had not committed. While few people outside of the inner circle of Insull associates believed that, the statement formed the bedrock of his legal defense.

In Chicago, he was clearly public enemy number one. The federal court set bail at $200,000, which was four times the bail for Capone in the same courtroom. The mobster had been tried and sentenced several years earlier for tax evasion by Judge James Wilkerson, the same judge who would preside over the Insull trial for fraud. The judge refused to reduce the bail, but permitted Insull to be examined by doctors, who placed him in St. Luke's Hospital after he was released from a prison hospital. In St. Luke's, he was given considerable attention mostly because he had raised hundreds of thousands of dollars for the institution. Following a brief rest, he was allowed to take up his residence at the Seneca Hotel at 200 East Chestnut.

Before they decamped to the Seneca, the Insulls staged a photo opportunity in the hospital, where the utilities chief was a nonpaying patient. The picture that ran across the world as Insull talked to the radio, print, and newsreel reporters, showed the old man with his son and grandson. Sam III offered a

Mother's Day rose to his gentle, white-haired grandpa while his son looked on. Three months earlier, the three-year-old boy had lost his mother to a sudden illness. The tender scene begged the question "do you want to send this kindly grandfather to prison?" and was orchestrated to generate sympathy.

Insull, dressed in an impeccable blue suit with striped shirt and gray spats, put the white rose in his lapel and began to take questions from the media after he firmly read a statement from four notecards:

> I have been fighting since boyhood. My whole life has been a struggle. When I first arrived in this country 53 years ago, all I had in the world was $200 and the promise of a job as secretary to Mr. Thomas A. Edison. Today I haven't that $200 or a job, either. . . . The Depression was too much for me. I went down with my ship. You will be convinced that although my judgment was bad, I was not dishonest.[6]

Insull was feisty with the cameramen, reminding them that he still preferred to be asked when a picture was taken. Ever conscious about his height, Insull never liked random photographs. After Junior gave a one-paragraph statement, the family left, confident that they had provided the right image and words to bolster their defense.

Insull hired one of the most-respected lawyers in Chicago in Floyd Thompson. The tall, distinguished counsel had been a newspaperman, states attorney, chief justice of the Illinois supreme court, and a Democratic party candidate for governor. He had the rare ability of being an aggressive defender who could sway juries with emotional arguments. On the prosecution side was federal district attorney Dwight Green, a quiet intellectual who ceded much of the prosecution to Leslie Salter, a sharp-tongued Oklahoma-born lawyer who was able to consistently raise the ire of the defendants. Judge James Wilkerson was perceived as stern yet fair. The government's case was neither simple nor concise. On October 4, when Green gave his opening statement, he warned the jury that it would be "slow and tedious." And he kept his word. The opening address alone was 28 pages long and detailed the complex allegations against Insull and the 16 other defendants, which included Junior, the brokers Harold and Charles Stuart, and Stanley Field, one of the directors. The trial would cover an unprecedented number of financial transactions, stock sales, accounting methods, and management decisions. The prosecution had been preparing the case for two years and was now ready to expose every errant stock trade made in the Insull companies.

"The scheme to defraud was extensive in its operation," Green stated; "thousands of persons were victimized, and many millions of dollars of worthless securities were unloaded on the public."

At its heart, the prosecution's case centered on how the Insull holding companies became "dumping grounds" for overvalued or worthless stock. Green charged that Insull and Stuart kept selling the stock to the public, even though they knew that the underlying value was less than what they had claimed. The trial would become the quintessential examination of how stocks should be valued in a time in which there was very little government regulation. The most prominent complaint was that the Insull stocks were "watered," that is, their prices were deliberately inflated and not backed by solid assets. This was the central argument against the stock of all holding companies at the time. Prior to the strong securities regulation that emerged in Roosevelt's second term, companies had a great deal of freedom on how they could state earnings, value assets, and sell their own securities.

Green contended that the Insull holding companies were able to sell stocks at grossly inflated prices even though they were technically insolvent. The top holding company, Corporation Securities, was $6 million in the red on September 15, 1931, Green claimed. Moreover, Insull only had to pay $15 a share for the stock while the public was paying $40, thus guaranteeing him and his associates a tidy profit on a company that was losing money.

The government, in trying to prove that Insull swindled the public out of $120 million, endeavored to show that numerous stock transactions benefited his group and shortchanged anyone outside of his cadre. One of the first witnesses for the prosecution was Jesse Scheinman, head of the Chicago brokerage J.D. Scheinman & Co. The broker claimed that Insull set him up in business with the sole purpose of "rigging the market through dummy accounts." Scheinman would receive orders from Insull to start buying either Insull Utility or Corporation Securities when the utilities operator thought the price was too low. While the prosecution did not dwell very long on the dummy account concept—in which a fake account would be set up for the sole purpose of propping up the market for Insull stocks through a nonexistent buyer—it introduced one of the more popular unsubstantiated rumors of that time. Defense attorney Fred Reeve expounded on the rumor: "'Isn't it true that certain financial interests were trying to *get* Insull?'"

"There was a report on LaSalle Street [Chicago's financial district] that Morgan [the New York investment banks and its affiliates] was out to kill Insull," Scheinman replied. While the newspapers highlighted "'War' With Morgan Told" in its headlines, neither Scheinman nor any other witness in the month-and-half-long trial offered any evidence that the House of Morgan was trying to depress the price of Insull stocks. While nearly every investor was dumping In- sull stocks in the last years of his holding companies, the possibility that Wall Street had a key hand in destroying Insull was probably less credible than that his leverage and Eaton buyout were far more damaging.

Green would return to his assault on price rigging later in the trial. In the most comprehensive part of his prosecution, he would bombard the jury with withering accounting details, parading seven expert witnesses who would pick apart the books of the Insull companies. R.A. Knittle, a "scientific" (forensic) ac- countant who had spent the previous two years poring over the Insull company books, presented a picture of the holding companies as little more than recepta- cles for other Insull company stocks. Knittle showed a smokestacklike graph of the securities owned by each company and explained in a monotone how the companies accounted for those securities. Green was using his expert witnesses to show that Insull's companies not only claimed fictitious values for their stocks, but also put those values down on the company's ledgers as fact.

Thompson angrily objected to the questioning of P.J. Fallon, who was an as- sistant treasurer of Insull Utility, at one point getting into a shouting match with Salter.

"By your legerdemain, you're trying to make something look *screwy,*" Salter bitingly said to Thompson. "You will admit there's something *screwy,* won't you?"

"If there is," Thompson barked, "it's because you introduced *screwy* evidence."

Over the course of several days, Salter argued how Insull's stocks were being hawked by his companies even as they kept spiraling downward. On October 19, 1929, Corporation Securities sold for $40.30 a share. A year later it was at $18.50 a share. By April 16, 1932, it was worth twelve and a half cents. The price declines were displayed in a chart Salter showed the jury.

Leaping to his feet, Salter shouted in his Oklahoma drawl, "the charts are so simple, so truthful, it hurts. We made those charts up from *their* own records."

"Speaking of *hurts,*" Thompson retorted; "I never saw anyone so hurt as when counsel with its jaw hanging down was listening to our examination of their witness."

"You didn't destroy one iota in these charts," Salter said.

"Let it pass," Thompson shot back.

There was little that Thompson could refute at this point in the trial. Salter had established that the Insull stocks were devastated along with every other industrial stock after the crash and that the intrinsic worth or "liquidation value" of those stocks also declined. It was a common trait of any popular stock from 1929 into the mid-1930s. As the eyes of the jury collectively glazed over during the volley of financial details, the prosecution had yet to prove that there was intent to defraud.

Green and Salter also lacked a key element: the emotional grief of the victims. The next wave of witnesses, Green hoped, would cement in the minds of the jury the misery that the Insull debacle inflicted on his more than 600,000 shareholders.

Green lined up 23 witnesses who personified heartbreak and turmoil. Each witness had one thing in common: they were average folks who believed in Insull and bought and held onto his stocks at the wrong time. Mary and Albert Jones were farmers from Ridott, Illinois, who mortgaged their farm to buy $16,000 in Insull stocks. Clad in undertaker black, the 70-year-old Mrs. Jones said she "accepted this stock because we relied upon the judgment of the men in the Insull company. We had explicit faith in them—that's why we are where we are today."

Mrs. Lulu Blumberg traveled from San Francisco to testify that she bought Corporation Securities because it was recommended to her through the mail as a "No. 1 investment."

George Bond, a 75-year-old car loader from Geneva, Illinois, bought Corporation Securities between 1930 and 1931 "for investment, not speculation. I still have the stock."

Thompson's cross-examination of witnesses such as teacher Olga Lovgren of Wilmette, Illinois, simply consisted of a bow and a thank you. There was no way of contesting their experience.

Salter emphasized that nearly all of the victims had been sold the stock either through the mail or through company salespeople. In many cases, the buyers were discouraged from purchasing other Insull stocks and were led into Corporation Securities, which in the early 1930s was "the best buy on the market."

The tragedies of the stock buyers darkened Insull's prospects considerably. The stocks had been peddled so aggressively that few people could resist buying them. May Stoetzel of Chicago, whose husband lost her business in the Depression, kept on buying on the way down between $27 and $15 in an attempt to "average up" her losses. Mabel McDonnell, also of Chicago, bought 25 shares of Corporation Securities because she needed a $500 down payment for some real estate in six months and was told by a salesman that she could reap that amount by holding the Insull stock. Among the 599,977 shareholders who were not represented were Studs Terkel's mother, who owned a rooming house in Chicago and lost $2,000. Most of Insull's investors were people who thought their purchases were a sure thing because they paid dividends, were associated with the Insull brand name, and represented something they could see every day—electricity, gas, and transportation. The securities were peddled by a highly competent salesforce consisting of nearly every stripe of Insull employee, and of mailings, print advertising, and radio ads. Neighbors sold to neighbors. Installation engineers sold to their customers. It was an impressive salesforce of people who already owned—and believed in—the stocks.

Insull did not react when the housewives were on the stand, but closed his eyes and put his hand on his head when the terms of the nightmarish Eaton buyout were presented by Salter. The $48 million that came out of the Insull coffers to purchase Eaton's 160,000 shares formed the foundation for the prosecution's attack on Insull's dividends. Harold Huling, the government's star accounting witness, testified that Insull had "written up" or inflated the value of his companies' assets by $23 million, which never justified the payment of dividends. Green brought out a new chart that showed how $10 charged to income of Middle West was pyramided through Insull Utility and Corporation Securities to become a $518 dividend once it reached the treasuries of those companies. Although the math was ultimately befuddling to the jury, the logic was simple: phantom profits created false dividends to lure more buyers into the stock.

Thompson challenged Huling by claiming that the three bookkeeping systems used by the holding companies were comparable to the ones employed by Huling and the other accounting experts. Arguing over accounting methods, however, proved to be a distraction and it is unlikely that the jury connected the fact that all of the holding companies were losing money with any motivation to pursue a widescale fraud. In fact, as the prosecution wound up its round of witnesses, it became more evident that Insull was doing everything he could to *save* the companies from bankruptcy. The $6 million in last-hour loans from the New York banks was revealed. More details concerning the Eaton transaction were examined. If Insull was out to fleece his investors, why would he have borrowed extensively when the price of the holding companies was falling? That was Thompson's contention. The man who could answer that question—and put a face on the company's demise—was put on the stand in his own defense.

Normally, putting the defendant in the witness chair makes defense lawyers cringe. Defendants can break down, forget details, become argumentative, and alienate the jury. Yet the only man who could properly defend Samuel Insull was Insull himself. At age 75, Insull had a stoop, a husky voice, and walked with a cane. He appeared "near physical collapse" as he took the stand on November 1 with the courtroom filled to capacity. Appearing in a perfectly pressed blue serge suit and white linen shirt, he began one of the most unorthodox testimonies of the time as Gladys listened intently and knitted in the back row of the courtroom. After Insull glared at the prosecutor's table and said "if the prosecution will excuse me, they [the other defendants] have no more to do with this case than you have," he started to recite the story that only he could tell.

Looking like a beaten, shrunken bulldog on the stand, Insull meandered into his all-but-gone cockney accent at strategic points near the beginning of his testimony. As more of a bard and infinitely less of a public enemy, Insull took the court back to his earliest days as a poor boy in London. His stunning memory recalled his "'umble" beginning on the poor side of town and going to work at age 14. From there, he joyfully recited one of the great American sagas of his generation. Working in London for a few shillings a week, he studied good literature and learned shorthand at night. He jumped from job to job, advancing each step of the way until he landed in the office of Thomas Edison's agent. Proudly looking directly through his pince-nez glasses, he spoke directly to the jury: "I happen to claim the distinction of operating the first telephone exchange for one-half hour outside of the exchanges erected within the United States."

Then he was sent to America to meet with the great Edison, working with the inventor on every detail of his life from his letters to pressing his clothes. His eyes misted up and his walrus moustache drooped when mentioning Edison's first wife, a surrogate mother and friend. He glanced over at the jury again and charmed them with a number of Edison anecdotes (which became a series of illustrations in one Chicago paper): "Once Edison proposed me for membership in an engineering society, but there was a line of the application that said 'Where was the applicant educated?' Mr. Edison put on that line 'in the College of Experience.' If I may be excused for saying so, I came under Edison's spell and it lasted as long as he lived."

Now the jury was under *Insull's* spell. No matter what the prosecution had claimed Insull had done, it would be difficult to remove the halo from one of the most genuine American success stories any of them had ever seen in person. Insull wiped the tears from his eyes and continued with how he helped Edison raise money, start General Electric, and enthusiastically took his mentor's admonition to "make it go, Sammy."

Salter saw the powerful effect Insull was having on the jury and abruptly shot up in his seat and objected. "This is all very interesting, but we should be getting to what this has to do with the fraudulent sales of Corporation Securities."

Thompson smiled and slowly moved Insull along to his first days with Chicago Edison. After a few minutes of describing how he came to Chicago to head a puny, undercapitalized company with an insulting salary of $12,000 a year, Salter rose again to object. "What bearing has all this on the issues of the case?" Thompson quickly laid out his rationale: "Perhaps counsel can't see the purpose of it, but the strongest test I know of a man's actions in the later years of his life are the character in him during the time he is building his life and his experience and it is impossible for Mr. Insull to even describe the course of his actions in the last few years of his life without giving this jury some knowledge of them during the first years of his life."

Insull explained how he obtained financing for Chicago Edison, his $250,000 loan from Marshall Field, and how he averted an early financial disaster by selling stock. He was feeling his oats and jerked up his head and explained that he had a firm idea of how securities were valued—then and now. A spectator near the press section wisecracked, "the old man is selling himself. I bet he could sell Corporation Securities stock right now."

As his testimony reached the present, Insull transformed himself from a ruined has-been into the utilities emperor of 1928. Deep into his testimony, his voice became clearer and more resolute, and he emphasized points with his right forefinger and lectured the jury with authority. Employing his crisp articulation, he became increasingly detailed as he described how his companies spread wealth to the entire Mississippi Valley and beyond. Regaining his defiance, he described his multiple takeovers of small utilities: "they said I was consolidating piles of junk." He softened his tone and looked sadly at the jury when he told them how he lost everything trying to save his companies and how he could have cashed out in Chicago to become head of the British Power Commission at the request of Prime Minister Stanley Baldwin in 1926. In a surprise turn, he offered his one mea culpa in not courting Eastern banks before the 1929 crash: "If I had some interest in New York or Philadelphia, I think the situation here in the spring of 1932, when I needed money badly, might have been very different."

Despite Salter's outbursts—he was writhing in his chair during Insull's life story—Thompson urged Insull to explain why he had continued to obtain loans for his companies in the face of the Depression. Insull recounted how he and other top businessmen met with Hoover on November 28, 1929, and were told that "the fundamental business of the country is on a sound and prosperous basis." Insull was one of the many industrial titans who believed Hoover's pronouncement, even though with regret, he said, "I was wrong, as everybody else was wrong, but that was my opinion at the time." Insull also had been influenced by the actions of John D. Rockefeller and his son in late 1929, who announced they were buying stocks and were confident in the fundamentals of the economy.

Salter did not care about Hoover and Rockefeller. He fumed that Thompson "should get down to the issue of false representation."

Thompson immediately led Insull into the Eaton affair and how Insull had met him on a transatlantic crossing, knew Eaton was buying his stock, yet did not say a word about it to the Cleveland financier. Thompson then deftly led

Insull through the financing of the holding companies, the myriad loans, and the questionable accounting. The defense attorney was reestablishing Insull's rationale to save his companies through the sales of securities to the holding companies. Having bolstered Insull's contention that he was desperately working to preserve the solvency of his companies, Thompson yielded to the anxious, yet now soft-spoken Salter for his cross-examination.

Gladys, wearing a fashionable velvet turban and a caracul coat, looked dour as her husband concluded his autobiography. She was one of the few members of the Insull contingent who retained her composure. The codefendents at this point were all crying, overwhelmed by the sheer emotional gravity of Insull's heroic effort to save himself and his companies.

Salter ignored Insull's life story and began to attack his financing practices, particularly the issuance of stock in 1930 and the declaration of dividends.

"Why did you not tell the public how much you put down in this way?" Salter asked, referring to how the company calculated its dividends and earnings.

"I presume it didn't occur to us," Insull replied.

"Isn't it the reason that if you had told them [the public] the truth you would not have been able to sell the stock?"

"No, sir," Insull said, upright and agitated. "That is not true. There was no trouble at all to sell that stock if no statement of earnings at all had been made."

During the time in question, Insull's stocks had ranged from $5 a share to $1,250. Salter wanted a precise answer on how the stocks were valued. Insull attempted to explain that his stock values represented 40 years of earnings instead of just one year.

"It is like acquiring a corner on a street at $1.25 an acre and having it go to $10,000," Insull retorted. "It might go back to the Garden of Eden, even."

Salter changed his line of questioning and asked Insull if he knew about his brother Martin's use of company funds to pay off his margin account. Insull denied knowledge of the misappropriation and Salter challenged his honesty.

"I am telling the truth," Insull insisted.

"Don't get excited," Salter shot back.

"I am *not* getting excited. You are getting me very earnest when you question my veracity, sir," Insull said in the proper English way. After a few more heated questions, Insull relaxed, crossed his legs, and clasped his hands.

Salter fired a long barrage of questions about supporting the holding company stocks, bank loans, and rumors about his health when the last loan requests were refused by the New York bankers. In the climax of the cross-examination, Salter cornered Insull on a circular that promoted Corporation Securities stock when it had little real capital behind it.

"Well, didn't you really intend and expect the public to believe from this statement that the corporation already had assets of $80 million and that they were purchasing an equity in that?"

"That was the situation gentlemen," Insull said directly to the jury, using both hands for emphasis. "Because the contracts had already been made that guaranteed to the company that it would have the necessary funds to put themselves in that situation."

"Well, then, why did you not take the public into your confidence and tell them that?"

"Show me any circular where it is done any other way," Insull answered defiantly, noting that securities laws of that era required almost no public disclosure of stock offering details.

"Is that your only answer?" Salter shouted.

"It is my answer," Insull bellowed.

Now the two men were locked in a tête-à-tête over the fine points of the Corporation Securities financing. Insull would practically scream his responses, lean forward, and shake his finger at Salter as if he were an impudent child. Insull was losing his composure and would admit a $10 million error, then retract it. Thompson would jump in to curb Salter, although it had little effect in tempering his questioning. One headline describing the brutal cross-examination read, "Insull Winces Under Heated U.S. Quiz."

Salter moved on to a new strategy of undermining Insull's claim that all of his actions were designed to protect his investors, unveiling a new chart showing that Insull drew $1.4 million in salary from 13 companies and nearly $471,00 in dividends from Insull Utility and Corporation Securities from 1929 through 1931. The strategy flopped as Insull showed that he donated more than he earned to charity and was "now dependent upon my son to pay my current expenses and to provide me with pocket money." Friends were paying for his defense.

Stopped cold on the salary argument, Salter examined Insull's exodus to Europe.

"Now what were your reasons for leaving Chicago in June, 1932?"

"I was pretty well broken down, and I was not so very young. I had been through a terrible ordeal; my career had been wrecked, and it affected my health, and I went for rest and quiet, to get away from things."

Insull's honest account of his travels from Paris to Italy to Greece did little to arouse the jury's enmity. After all, he was truly tired, elderly, and broke at the time. "I think I would have been crucified if I had come home, and self-preservation is the first law of nature."

Salter changed direction again, digging back into his sale of the holding companies before they filed for receivership. While the prosecutor made few points on describing how Insull fled the country, he knew he could anger him by impugning his integrity again.

"You invited the public to contribute $31 million," Salter said of the stock sales.

Insull blew up. "Yes. I can't get myself into the mental attitude of yourself. I was doing everything I had in my integrity, which I still have!"

"Do you not think that belief would have been shaken a little if you had told the whole truth?"

"I do not."

Salter continued to stab away at inconsistencies between Insull's stock sales and what he reported on his corporate income tax forms, the reorganization of Middle West, and the undisputed fact that the holding companies were losing money during Insull's most aggressive sales campaigns. Knowing he was fraying Insull's nerves, Salter was looking for Insull to completely lose his emotional resolve.

"Mr. Insull, the question of just what the securities which you put into these companies cost you is a rather touchy subject with you, isn't it?" Salter goaded Insull.

"No, sir," Insull said emphatically. "Not a bit of it, it's not gotten under *my* skin, and if that is your effort, you are failing signally."

On the fourth day on the stand, Insull prepared for one last confrontation with Salter before Thompson began his redirect examination. Salter kept badgering Insull about why his companies paid dividends even though they were losing money.

"Now, Mr. Insull, isn't it right that the reason you put that stock [Corporation Securities] on a dividend-paying basis, against your own judgment and the judgment of H.L. Stuart, was simply to make the stock look more attractive to the public, whom you were asking to invest in this company?"

"No," Insull stammered. "*You* stated it was against my judgment and against Mr. Stuart's judgment. A man's judgment is arrived at after discussion with his associates," Insull yelled, pounding on the railing.

Realizing that Insull was not going to make a new admission with this line of questioning, Salter retreated into questioning the employee stock sales campaign in which Insull agreed that everyone in his companies from the "elevator boys to the coal passers" were selling stock. Insull said that he did not favor the employee plan, preferring to make it optional, but was overruled by others within his companies.

In the redirect, Thompson only asked a short series of questions on whether Insull had received a salary from the holding companies. Insull had not.

Insull concluded by telling the court that he had pledged all of his and his wife's assets as collateral for his loans, including the 4,000 acres of Hawthorn Farm and a $1 million life insurance policy.

"Anyway, you signed away everything you had?" Salter asked incredulously. "Yes sir."

Insull smiled as he left the stand. After the grilling, Insull joked to reporters, "I thought they had me on the ropes for a minute."

A young lawyer (and future Chicago alderman) named Leon Despres was watching Insull as he jousted with reporters. He noted that the defendant looked small yet wiry and had the glow of confidence even though he had lost all of his corporate power and material wealth. All Insull had now was his integrity, a lance with which he fought Salter with all his might.

The next witnesses were an anticlimax to Insull's testimony and provided no support to the prosecution's case. The baronial Stanley Field highlighted his service to Chicago through the Field Museum, Chicago Zoological Society, Shedd Aquarium, and Chicago Orphan's Asylum. Cardinal Mundelein, appearing in black clerical street garb, appeared briefly as a character witness for Harold Stuart and offered that his reputation for integrity was "splendid." Eaton came on the stand and corroborated details of Insull's buyout. Harold Stuart described his $2 billion in stock and bond deals with Insull and joint efforts to try to save his companies.

Junior, the last witness, further corroborated his father's testimony, adding that after donating his salaries to charity and paying tax, he was "$137,044 in the hole as far as salaries were concerned." Salter attempted to get Junior to shed some more light on the last-ditch efforts to prop up the Insull companies with stock transactions, but Junior managed to deftly summarize his defense and that of the other defendants.

"We could not pay all of our debts, but we wanted to clean ourselves out, so we did," young Insull said succinctly.

Alongside headlines that announced "Power Output Now Highest In Nearly 4 Years" and "Edison Shows Earnings Gain," the Chicago papers carried the dramatic closing statements of Thompson and Salter. Salter assailed the defendants with the mountain of forensic evidence that was presented and sealed his accusations with an assortment of scripture quotations, which he read directly from a Bible he was holding: "Beware of false prophets, which come to you in sheep's clothing, but inwardly they are ravening wolves. Ye shall know them by their fruits. Do men gather grapes of thorns or figs of thistles?"

Adding Newton and Emerson into his statement for good measure, Salter once again claimed the Insull stocks were "cleverly manipulated" and they [Insull and his associates] "deliberately moved it up. They wanted it to rise so that could make their inflated holdings in it the cornerstone of Corporation Securities. And all of this was *before* the Depression."

Thompson began his closing statement in a somber, intimate tone, employing a highly emotional plea: "The government must show these men are guilty. We have shown they are innocent. If you jurors see two hypotheses—honesty and dishonesty—it is your obligation to acquit the men, for they have been honest. Are we to take these men away from their families, their positions in the world? I have said my last. The government is to reply. But I beg you by your verdict to remove the stain from these men. Send this old man back to his home. Send his son back to the companies he works for and back to his motherless boy."

Thompson wiped his tears away as he sat down, drank a glass of water, and looked away from the jury. His associates were crying. The defendants were crying. Insull was sobbing. After a long-winded set of instructions by Judge Wilkerson, the case went to the jury.

IN THE FULLNESS OF TIME

The Insull Legacy

Most sentimental of towns, she weeps over defaulting financiers and loads the coffins of gunmen with tons of flowers.

—Christopher Morley, *Old Loopy: A Love Letter for Chicago*[1]

Insull was confident and exultant after the trial as the jury went into deliberation. He gleefully posed for photographers in Judge Wilkerson's chambers. When one photographer complained that there was not enough light, Insull jovially said, "Shy on light? Tsk. Tsk." Another photographer asked Insull to pose with Thompson. "Look at him; I'd kiss him for you," Insull laughed. He then predicted that he would be found innocent after a two-hour deliberation. Perhaps he had been buoyed by the emotional power of Thompson's final pleading before the jury or had reacquired his mountainous self-assurance based on the defense of his integrity and telling of his personal saga. Or possibly he had been convinced that a jury of his "peers," who could empathize with his plight in the Depression, would not see any fraud in his actions when he had lost everything he owned and donated more than he earned to charity.

The jury would be swayed either by Salter's ultimate comparison of Insull to Napoleon or by Thompson's lachrymose *cri de coeur*. After 45 days, a blizzard of arcane accounting presentations, stock transactions, blistering cross-examinations, Insull's compelling autobiography, and defiance of Salter, the trial was in the hands of the jury. The exhausting record of the trial was covered in a two-million-word transcript of more than 9,500 pages. The jurors, who earned every penny of their $3-a-day pay—$162 total ($2,318.78 in

2005 dollars)—were sitting in the courthouse and sequestered for 54 days. The government covered their room and board at the commodious Great Northern Hotel, ironically Insull's residence when he first came to Chicago in 1892. Western Union and the postal telegraph wire alone sent out 1.5 million words from reporters during the trial, which cost the government an estimated $250,000.

As the world awaited the verdict, the jurors bided their time. They had decided in minutes, but decided to wait for at least two hours so as not to make it appear they reached an unduly hasty conclusion. They found Insull and all of his codefendants *not* guilty.

The corners of Insull's mouth arched up to his prominent cheekbones when the clerk read the verdicts. He hugged Junior and shook Thompson's hand vigorously with tears in his eyes. All the wives of the defendants burst into tears. Mrs. Stanley Field wiped away her tears with a white glove and exclaimed, "Isn't it wonderful? It's the only thing that could have happened." Stanley Field dabbed at his eyes, blew his nose and muttered "I'm very, very, very happy. I can't conceive of any other verdict."

The celebration continued long after the judge and jury had left the courtroom. The din was so loud outside of Judge Wilkerson's chambers that he stuck his head outside to glare at the crowd with his robe half off.

"If you don't stop this noise I'll reconvene court and have every one here arrested!" Despite his shortness with the jubilant defendants, the judge was photographed leaving the courthouse with a jaunty fedora and a sly smile.

Gladys was in her hotel suite with her French maid Nana at the Seneca when a *Tribune* reporter reached her with the news. She translated the news to her maid, whose face lit up. They embraced each other as they both wept. "Oh, I am sooo happy! We have suffered *so* much. There is justice in the world."

Reporters corralled Green and Salter as they were leaving the courtroom. Although Green had no comment, Salter, puffing on his pipe like a steam locomotive, said calmly, "we tried the case thoroughly and did the best we could." Green was able to send Capone to Alcatraz on income tax evasion, yet Insull, a man reviled by hundreds of thousands, eluded his best prosecutorial effort. Green retired from the U.S. attorney's office the following year, engaging in state politics. He became governor of Illinois in 1941 and served until 1949.

The all-male jury was happy to be returning to their families. Grocer Louis Bending from Woodstock quipped that his wife was "going to kill the fatted calf tonight. The trial was a good experience. My receipts in the grocery make me look like a piker, and I'm accustomed to tossing off millions."

Diamond dealer Roy Richardson from Evanston was "glad Insull was released. But my wife hardly knew me. I'm going to sit down and have a glass of wine." William Austin returned to his dairy farm in Woodstock, only to find that his wife, who was not expecting him home so soon, had gone to a movie.

In addition to the Insulls, the Stuarts, and Field, the others acquitted included John O'Keefe, Insull's former secretary; Edward Doyle, a director of Corporation Securities; Frank Schrader, a vice president of the brokerage house Halsey Stuart; Waldo Tobey, Insull's personal attorney; Clarence MacNeille, a secretary of Halsey Stuart; Clarence Sills, a vice president of Halsey Stuart; Fred Scheel, vice president of Utility Securities, a marketing company for Corporation Securities; Frank Evers, a secretary of Utility Securities; Robert Waite, vice president of Utility Securities; George Kemp, assistant secretary of Utility Securities; and Philip "P.J." McEnroe, vice president of Corporation Securities.

With a crowd trailing behind them, Junior whisked Insull out of the courtroom ahead of the throng, hoping to find a taxi. Bailiff Marshal Langer cleared the way for the Insulls and gave yeoman's advice as they hailed a cab: "if I were you, I'd go out and get pickled tonight, Mr. Insull." The acquitted financier looked back and smiled, "I would—but I don't drink."

Back at the Seneca, a wave of reporters streamed into the lobby. Gladys came down and tried to hug them simultaneously, and failed, because of the rotundity of her husband. She then hugged them individually and shouted, "Thank God, Thank God." Husband and wife went up to their suite as Junior headed for "The Deck," the hotel bar. Breaking his pledge for this November 25, he defied the reporters to tell him he did not deserve a few drinks. After quaffing two cocktails, he headed upstairs for a private dinner with his family.

The following day, the Insulls posed for photographers with their grandson and Scottish terrier Colin Glencannon. Insull was wearing a dark suit with a light waistcoat and spats. Gladys wore a white blouse with a red tie.

"Look at grandpa, he's all dressed up," Gladys said, glancing over at Insull. "Now Glencannon, I must smile and you must hold up your ears." The scottie yelped.

"I've been out celebrating," Insull guffawed.

Headlines across the world announced the Insull group's acquittal and sidebarred the dispatch with his remarkable rise to power. It was a front page story in London and Athens, where his Greek friends said they felt vindicated in their efforts to aid his escape from extradition.

While the Insull group had reason to rejoice, their legal troubles were far from over. The Insulls still faced charges of embezzlement and bankruptcy fraud in two other cases. Although they would also be acquitted in those trials, Insull personally owed a number of creditors millions for the loans he took out during the last months of his holding companies. Thousands of investors were not quick to forgive, either. The Insulls still needed a bodyguard. After the collapse, a bullet narrowly missed Insull as he was riding in his limo. The bullet wounded his chauffeur, who survived. After the attempted hit, Insull bought a 16-cylinder armor-plated Cadillac with one-inch-thick plate glass windows. The Insulls were getting 20 letters a day threatening shootings, stabbings, and bombings. They were postmarked from the West Coast to the Midwest.

Insull's multiple acquittals were not seen by Roosevelt as a signal to abandon his securities and utility reform legislation. The opposite occurred. Using the Insull debacle as a basis for regulatory reform, Roosevelt and his progressive allies lobbied for and eventually got passed into law the Public Utility Holding Company Act, which reined in the lion's share of abuses that Insull and his industry were accused of in the first third of the twentieth century. The holding company structure, as shown by the Insull trial, was a straw house that could not have been sustained during any economic downturn. Its complexity and reliance on consistent streams of income made it precarious, particularly when cash was tight. The Insull group was a case in point: at the top of the holding company pyramid were the Insulls and their inner circle, who controlled 69 percent of Corporation Securities and 64 percent of Insull Utilities, the two main holding companies or trusts. These companies owned 28 percent of the voting stock of Middle West Utilities, the middle holding company and all of its operating subsidiaries. Middle West owned 99 percent of National Electric Power, which owned 93 percent of National Public Service, which owned 100 percent of Seaboard Public Service, which owned all of the assets of Florida Power, Eastern Public Service, Georgia Power & Light, Virginia Public Service, Florida West Coast Ice, Tide Water Power, and dozens of other subsidiaries. This is the brief description of the Insull holdings, which cannot be legibly and comprehensively displayed on two book pages. The far-flung Insull interests were so extensive and complex that it is unlikely that FDR knew that an Insull company was supplying him power at his Warm Springs, Georgia, home.

The holding company structure allowed Insull to control company assets of $500 million in 32 states and 5,000 communities with only $27 million. It was such a profitable entity that the number of holding companies increased from 102 to 180 between 1922 and 1927, while the number of subsidiary operating companies fell from 6,355 to 4,409. The master consolidators such as Insull and the Morgan-affiliated interests held most of these companies: only eight holding companies controlled 75 percent of the investor-owned utilities in 1932.

The wide latitude the pre-New Deal securities laws gave to holding companies to trade in and rig their own stock gave them a free hand to speculate. Imbued with a faith in his own companies and management, Insull kept borrowing in 1930 and 1931 to prop up his stocks. In handwritten notes he used for the first trial, he recorded that the market value of Insull Utility climbed from $188 million at the end of 1930 to $237 million as of February, 11, 1931. The value of Corporation Securities also rose from $95 million to $133 million. Hobbled by his own hubris and misjudgment, Insull wrote, "everybody thought the troubles were over in the early months of 1931." Moreover, since stock was the basis of the holding company capitalization, he was encouraged to buy more of it at the depressed levels following the crash, loading up the portfolios of Insull Utility and Corporation Securities with even more securities he felt sure would rebound. Instead of being a manager of properties, operations, and people, Insull essentially turned into an overconfident stock trader, trying to outguess the unpredictable and rampantly bearish stock market.

Like many stockholders blinded by their own overconfidence, Insull and his companies were buying on the way down, convinced they were getting a bargain price and would profit on the rebound. This behavior was not exclusively practiced by Insull, however. Academic research by behavioral economists shows that most investors tend to be handicapped by self-confidence in investing: they generally buy at the peak of the market and do not sell when they should. Daniel Kahneman, a cowinner of the Nobel Prize in economics, found that humans seemed to be hardwired to make bad financial decisions because personal optimism overrides logic in almost all cases.

The laws at the time permitted and encouraged Insull to act in the doomed role of a steadfast trader protecting his portfolio. Being a hostage to the mercurial nature of the stock market is an impossible position to manage, though. A combination of general business conditions, market rumors, and a continued sell-off always works against buy-and-hold traders. Insull was unable to immediately deny rumors that the House of Morgan was behind the dumping of his holding company stocks, he was ill or died as he returned from England. In a market that moves second by second, information is critical. Like his peers, Insull also had no idea when the Depression would end. "I thought as everybody else did, that prosperity was around the corner," he wrote in his notes. As a result, Insull borrowed or endorsed loans for $7 million at the worst possible time for his holding companies in an effort to keep those companies solvent. While his survival instinct was overpowering, he had no idea how bad his timing was, given that moment in history.

The holding company act effectively dismembered the utility investment structures. It is unlikely they would have survived the 1930s—even without the legislation. The extensive borrowing, or leverage, to buy stock to retain control of the holding company shells magnified the disaster of the Insull conglomerate. When bankers called loans, they wanted more collateral. In a short time, Insull had pledged all of the security he had, which was in the form of holding company stock that did nothing but decline in value. By making a show of corporate confidence and refusing to cut back on capital spending for power plants and facilities, Insull exacerbated the collapse. The Eaton buyout also vacuumed cash from his corporate treasuries, leaving him with no hard currency to repay the bank loans. Dubious accounting practices inflated both the value of the securities and the underlying operating company assets. Without rigorous accounting controls, the holding company pyramids were nothing but legal shell games.

Roosevelt also succeeded in curbing the unfettered sales of securities. Targeting securities sales misdeeds, the Securities and Exchange Commission (SEC) was formed with Joseph P. Kennedy as its first chairman. The law creating the commission mandated fuller disclosures about stock offerings and sales, interested parties, and transactions fees. The deals between the Insull holding companies were brimming with conflicts, although there was no federal law preventing them from conducting business the way they did before the New Deal laws. The holding company act was upheld in its first major court challenge when Electric Bond & Share sued the nascent SEC and lost in 1938.

Public disclosure of company finances was a major problem prior to the New Deal. As evidenced in the Insull trial and documents from his companies, there was very little information that was required to be distributed to investors, particularly concerning the holding companies. The balance sheet portion of the 1915 Commonwealth Edison annual report, for example, was all of 12 lines long. The section on the company's financial state was two pages long. The last line logically should be net income, but it is "balance carried to surplus." You cannot tell precisely if the company is making a profit. Fifteen years later, the Commonwealth Edison annual report, at 10 pages (annual reports today can be hundreds of pages long), contained details on the company's stock and bond sales, although a passing mention of "the Subsidiary Corporation," whose investments are "in the interest of the company," was not clearly explained. The following year, the annual report did not mention that the Subsidiary was purchasing Commonwealth Edison's stock in the open market, the impact of the Depression on the company, the relationship of the holding companies to Commonwealth Edison nor much significant detail at all about anything in the seven-page report. Considering what had happened to the economy and the stock market, the report is laughable in its lack of detail and forward-looking statements. For the 1932 report, with James Simpson having replaced Insull's executive Ed Doyle, there are several indirect admissions of stock purchases among the holding companies and the new board's policy of "gradually eliminating investments of this class and of restricting the operations of the Company to the generation and distribution of electrical energy." Finally, in 1933, the company disclosed in a 24-page report its interests in the holding and affiliated companies, which included real estate, Federal Electric (a sign company), Lake Lawn Hotel (an employee resort), the Century of Progress, Peabody Coal, Chicago Rapid Transit, five railroads, and People's Gas. Shareholders undoubtedly had the right to know about all of the Insull cross-investments prior to 1933.

Roosevelt was better schooled in the holding company legerdemain than any other president. In his 1935 State of the Union address, he promoted his bill to curb the utility industry financing abuses, actually misreading a line about "abolition of the evil of holding companies." He meant to say "evil *features*" of holding companies and corrected himself in a subsequent press conference. Seizing upon the threat to its modus operandi, the utility industry revived its propaganda machine, even spreading a rumor that Roosevelt was insane. The campaign had little effect. Throughout the country, the idea stuck that the Insull monstrosity of holding companies had been partially responsible for the Depression. In Chicago alone, 700,000 people were out of work as 40 percent of the city's workers were on the street.

Roosevelt's case for the Public Utility Holding Company Act was bolstered considerably by the Federal Trade Commission's 84-volume *Utility Corporations* report on the industry. The mammoth study, conducted between 1928 and 1935, not only examined the Insull empire in great detail, it also showed the pervasive influence of New York investment bankers in controlling the United Corporation, which owned interests in five major holding companies from the St. Lawrence River to the Gulf of Mexico. The FTC report described the utility propaganda machine, stock ownership, and accounting practices in exhausting detail. The revelations were scandalous. In one case, the $1.2 billion Standard Gas & Electric group was found to be controlled by only $23,100 of common stock. The 151 companies examined were also found to have inflated the value of their assets by $1.4 billion. Both the FTC report and the National Power Policy Committee headed by Harold Ickes came to the same conclusion: eliminate most, if not all, holding companies.

Insull's reputation was further blackened by the FTC report. He was indirectly portrayed as a dark manipulator in an industry that undertook a massive propaganda campaign to vanquish its enemies. Roosevelt's speeches attacking "the Insulls, whose hand is against everyman" still resonated long after the Insull group disintegrated. John Flynn, writing in the *Nation,* remarked that "There will be a good deal of un-Christian satisfaction at Mr. Insull's embarrassment. The foes of the Power Gang can hardly be blamed for remembering that Insull was the sponsor of the unholy publicity drive exposed by the FTC and that he has been the most arrogant, insolent and unsocial of all of the power barons."

The holding company act, among other things, effectively broke up any combine that was not physically connected. So if a holding company owned operating companies in Atlanta and St. Louis, they would have to divest their interests unless they were linked by power lines. Insull's concept of superpower, however, fared well under the new law, as the legislation promoted the interconnection of power systems to form the modern electrical grid.

While Roosevelt targeted Insull most prominently in his campaign plank to rid the country of holding company perils, the Insull group was not the largest utility holding company of its day. The $3.4 billion Electric Bond and Share and its subordinate holding companies American Power & Light, National Power & Light, and Electric Power & Light owned 234 direct or indirect subsidiaries and was nearly twice the size of the Insull concerns. When Electric Bond lost its Supreme Court case, it took two years to dismember the company and at least 20 years to completely reorganize it. The holding company act gave the government the authority to dissolve several Electric Bond holding and subholding units. Also at issue was the concentration of corporate control and wealth. With the Insull group, the Electric Bond combine produced more than half of the power in the U.S.

As a believer in public power, Roosevelt had created the Tennessee Valley Authority in 1933. The public corporation was designed to bring electricity, recreation, and jobs to one of the poorest regions of the country. It did so by building a number of dams, hydroelectric plants, and lakes throughout the impoverished Tennessee Valley. The sister Bonneville Power Administration did the same thing for the Pacific Northwest. And the Rural Electrification Act in 1936 created a new agency that, ironically, would build upon Insull's vision of supplying power to exurban areas. Only the new agency would work directly with nonprofit farmer's cooperatives to distribute power. Having failed to build a hydropower plant in upper New York State during his term as governor because he could not get a treaty with Canada, Roosevelt saw power as an egalitarian issue: Everyone should have power at the lowest-possible cost, no matter where they lived.

Roosevelt felt that all large federal dams, such as the Muscle Shoals dam built in World War I to power a nitrate (fertilizer) plant, should be controlled by Washington and provide power through a publicly controlled distribution network. Senator George Norris was one of the progressives in the Senate who succeeded in keeping Muscle Shoals under the federal aegis. In contrast, Boulder Dam was originally supported by Hoover, who wanted the power generated from the Colorado River south of Las Vegas to be sold directly to investor-owned utilities controlled by people like Insull. In 1936, Boulder (later renamed Hoover) Dam was completed and pumped power into a 287,000-volt line that ran 266 miles, a triumph of alternating current and the superpower technology that Insull championed.

During the period of the new Roosevelt securities and public power laws, the nature of energy generation was undergoing a world-changing transformation as well. In 1934, physicist Leo Szilard described how a nuclear chain reaction would take place. Every nuclear physicist at the time knew that this discovery also translated into the creation of nuclear power and an atomic bomb with a destructive force the world had never seen. By 1938, physicists in Germany were able to start a man-made fission of uranium during the horrific rise of Hitler. Enrico Fermi and his team at the University of Chicago, only a few blocks away from Frank Lloyd Wright's electrified Robie House, were able to control the first sustained chain reaction four years later.

Despite his ongoing financial travails—he still had to sell his property to settle with creditors—Insull was energized after the trial and wanted to reenter the business world. Nikola Tesla surfaced after the trials to engage Insull in a new business proposal. Heartened that "the vicious attacks" of the trials were over, Tesla was hoping Insull would be interested in promoting a novel motor dynamo that consisted of a piston vibrating in a casing filled with gas. It was an ultraefficient generator that would be virtually unaffected by friction. Like many of Tesla's ideas, it was revolutionary and would take millions to develop and test. After his triumph with the alternating current system, Tesla had moved on to radio technology and began to experiment with a large-scale project that would transmit electricity through the earth and large steel towers. In theory, it was a compelling idea: the earth's core is primarily iron and nickel and could be used to conduct electricity under the right conditions. Under Tesla's theory, you conduct produce power in Chicago and send it to China without the use of wires. After spending all of the investment capital he had, Tesla abandoned the project and kept experimenting in myriad other areas.

Like Insull, Tesla never lost his self-confidence and his proclivity for imagining great, pragmatic electrical systems. He enthusiastically wrote Insull and outlined his "Tele-Geodynamic" invention, which had, in his estimation "incalculable importance to the world." From his description, the system sounded like a giant radio transmitter that "will be sufficient for transmitting mechanical effects over the entire globe and thus afford an unfailing means for universal communication, which is to be adopted by all countries." Not only would this device send and receive signals from any point on the planet, it would allow ships to "be steered accurately along the shortest route," and be able to "locate all underground deposits of ores, coal, oil, sulfur and other minerals in any part of the world."

"The invention would be able to lay bare the secrets of physical constitution and properties of the earth and its scientific importance can not be exaggerated," Tesla wrote Insull in 1935. Tesla not only foresaw and outlined technologies such as radar and geographic positioning systems, he had a plan for Insull's resurrection as well:

> You passed through a fierce crucible and came out as pure as gold and all fair minded people, friends or foes, should respect you more now than ever before. But your vindication was only the first part of your task, the second is to recover the great losses sustained by yourself and those who had faith in you. Two requirements are exacted to this end: One, to take care of your health, the other to introduce some new invention of wide commercial value. . . . In exploiting an invention such as my alternating system you could regain your old place of wealth and power while remaining perfectly independent.[2]

Tesla concluded the letter by asking Insull for a few thousand dollars to get his new project off the ground. While Insull agreed to meet with Tesla, it is likely he told him that he had no cash, securities, or credit and that all of his property was either in the hands of the banks or the auction houses. While he argued with Gladys on where they would settle, Insull already had a new business plan in mind. He planned to start a network of radio stations with Junior. Financing the operation of the Affiliated Broadcasting Company were two large (unnamed) companies that would contract for enough advertising to cover operating expenses. All local advertising would be sold at a profit. Insull lined up partners, tapped friends for capital, and launched the venture. Unfortunately, the advertising never materialized. It was a short-lived venture, as one of the employees was suspected of dipping into the company's treasury and the company never got off the ground in 1936.

∝∞∞

The liquidation of Insull's assets took several years as he and Junior were eager to settle every claim as best they could. He had assigned title of Hawthorn Farm to the Central Republic Trust Company as well as everything in the house and on the property. The bank gained possession of all his furniture, horses, cattle, farm equipment, autos, wagons, carriages, household supplies, paintings, tapestries, and silverware. The bank even had title to the swans in the lake and all of the window shades. His extensive book and document collection was also put on the auction block. It included a copy of the Magna Carta, the marriage contract of Louis XVI and Marie Antoinette, and first editions of Thackeray's *Vanity Fair*, Izaak Walton's *Compleat Angler*, and Captain William Bligh's *Narrative of the Mutiny on the Bounty.*

When nearly everything he owned was either auctioned off or sold, $933,000 in assets remained. Yet Insull still owed his creditors $19.3 million. As he had maintained in court, Insull was more than bankrupt after the trial; he owed the banks far more than he was worth and had no way of repaying them in his lifetime. In addition to Central Republic, he owed GE, the National City Bank of New York, and Continental Bank of Chicago. The only income he had was $21,250 from his pensions, about $20,000 in annual interest from bonds and savings accounts, and $400,653 from a trust he had set up prior to filing for bankruptcy. The radio company he established paid him a $4,000 salary before it folded.

The utility baron's charitable donations had not been exaggerated, either. He also owed $182,750 in unpaid pledges. Some of the donations were to pay for a wing on the London Temperance Hospital ($22,500), the Prince of Wales fund ($40,000), the Boy Scouts ($17,250), Queen's University of Kingston ($4,800), St. Luke's Hospital ($7,500), the Tuskegee Institute ($1,500), and the Glenwood Manual Training School ($7,500). When the estate was finally settled in 1940, the *Tribune* reported that creditors received one-thousandth of a cent on the dollar.

Junior did almost all the dealing with the creditors while Insull and Gladys went back to Europe. Gladys was vehemently opposed to staying in Chicago and she did not like London, either, so they compromised and settled in Paris. Insull came back to visit Junior in Chicago in the spring of 1938 for one last time. On the voyage back to Paris, after crossing the Atlantic more than 200 times, he was in his first shipwreck when the *Asconia* ran aground in the St. Lawrence River. When all on board were accounted for, he made his bed on a pool table on the rescue ship. Gladys had no interest in seeing all of their personal possessions auctioned off. It was a bit ghoulish. The 10-room penthouse auction in the opera building charged admission of $1 and featured Insull's four-poster bed with gold and rose bedspread, tortoise shell brushes, Sheraton dressing table, 205-piece Wedgwood dinner service, Royal Worcester tea service, and a refrigerator capable of making 224 ice cubes. Her olive oil and powdered alum were still sitting on her Sheraton dressing table at the time of the auction, waiting for her as if she was going to the opera in an hour. With the English furniture, paintings, and Oriental rugs, the lot totaled a meager $26,000 for the banks. The only possessions she kept were a $200,000 necklace of 101 matched Oriental pearls. Not one for tiaras or neckbands, the necklace was the only piece of jewelry she cared about. Since she could not afford the $3,000 insurance premium on them, she had kept them in a bank vault since 1932. Missing her family, she eventually returned to stay in Chicago with Junior, who married Margaret Byrnes in 1936. Gladys died September 23, 1953.

Mary Garden, who lived to be 90, began a second career as a voice teacher after her singing days were over. She provided instruction and inspiration to future divas such as Beverly Sills, the only other woman to head a major American opera company. Mary was paid $1,500 a student to guide her charges through the French repertoire, which was her natural forte. She taught Miss Sills *Manon* and *Thais,* speaking only in French during their sessions. Miss Sills recalled her grueling lessons with Mary:

> Although I'd already started concentrating on French opera because of my love for Lily Pons, Mary Garden *really* got me hooked. That was in spite of her teaching methods. Charming, she wasn't. Mary Garden often struck me as the meanest woman I'd ever met. She was generous when it came to showing me how she performed *Manon,* and absolutely awful about allowing me room for a single creative thought. . . . When we weren't actually working, Mary seemed to undergo a personality transplant—she became patient and friendly. . . . She gave me several fans she used on stage, and when we finished *Thais,* Mary gave me the tiara she'd worn during the years when she alone owned that opera. . . . "From now on, nobody but *you* can wear that crown."[3]

Unable to work in the utilities business, Junior served in the Navy during World War II, receiving a citation from the Secretary of the Navy for outstanding performance of duty. Worth $13.6 million in early 1929, he, too, lost all of his assets in the 1930s. He was moderately successful in the insurance business, starting his own agency in 1950. Throughout the rest of his life he was consumed with trying to pay off his father's debts and clearing the family name. In 1958, he sued three publishers for libel after they claimed that "the Insulls ended up in jail and bribed public officials." The Harvard historian

Arthur Schlesinger, Jr., had made the factual error in his *Crisis of the Old Order.* Kenneth Trombley had committed a similar error in his *Life and Times of a Happy Liberal.* The suit was dropped after a court ruled that the publishers did not do business in Illinois. After donating his family's papers to Loyola University, he assisted Forrest McDonald in the writing of the authoritative biography *Insull,* published in 1962.

As a director in most of the Insull companies, Junior still faced several lawsuits, which he finally settled in 1948. Engaged in public service, he was a trustee of the Museum of Science and Industry, the Field Museum of Natural History, and Loyola University Chicago. While acutely aware that his name still invoked anger 40 years after his father's demise, he was seen as a "modest, considerable gentleman with a keen sense of humor." He noted to *Tribune* correspondent R.C. Longworth in 1977, "I walk into some place here and say I'm Samuel Insull, Jr. They may hate my guts or think I'm a hero, but at least I don't have to draw them a map." He died in 1983 at the age of 82.

While Insull's reputation remained clouded long after he passed from the scene, his failure formed the bedrock for many of the protections enjoyed by investors today. The New Deal laws on securities regulation and holding companies— while constantly challenged and amended—serve to promote corporate transparency, and fairness, and expose conflicts of interest. Had not the rise and collapse of the Insull group aroused the indignation of FDR during the Depression, contemporary safeguards would not have been as strong or as comprehensive. An Insull contemporary, lawyer Francis X. Busch, puts the Insull-inspired legislation into context:

> . . . long before the echoes of the resounding crash of the Insull enterprises had died away, there was legislation on the statute books regulating the issuance of securities, outlawing holding companies, governing stock exchanges, and, in general, giving assurance to the shorn lambs and the lambs yet unborn that the same instruments would not be used to fleece them again. It is not an exaggeration to say that the beneficent Federal Securities and Exchange Act was reared on the ashes of the Insull empire.[4]

The public memory would not treat Insull kindly because of the widely held perception that Insull was the malevolent Croesus of his time and built his companies out of an all-consuming avarice, even though he financially ruined himself in an effort to save his companies. Consumer lawyer Donald Richberg once asked one of Insull's confidants during one of his many battles with the titan, "How can a man who has a brain think it worth while to corrupt our morals in order to light our homes?" The associate replied in a way that could have been taken as a description of Thomas Edison, George Westinghouse or Henry Ford:

> Insull doesn't ask "Why?" He doesn't speculate about the future. He isn't looking all around him to see everything that is going on. He has his eyes fixed on the job in front of him. He sees that plant which he is going to build, that will produce so many kilowatt hours. He is going to build it and get the machinery going smoothly and then go on to the next job. He knows that this job ought to be done. He sees the one way it can be done and he goes that way. He doesn't ask "Why?"[5]

After Insull died in the Paris subway on July 16, 1938, the first reports were that he was robbed as he lay in the Metro station. The French authorities then refused to release his body from the morgue at Marmottan hospital pending a coroner's report. Gladys, quietly grieving by herself in Paris, requested that his body be sent to London. Junior, who was unable to attend, was not among the 17 mourners. The Reverend John Bird read the Church of England burial service in a whitewashed chapel in Putney Vale cemetery on the edge of London, even though Insull and his family were not Anglicans. He did not mention Insull's incredible ascent from London office boy to become one of the world's wealthiest and most influential businessmen. His oak casket was lowered into a grave under a hawthorn tree, not far from where his mother and father were buried. The only account of what was said at the funeral is an observation of Harry Selfridge, a former Chicago businessman who then owned a London department store. "I attended out of admiration," he said. "He once stood for hours in a rescue boat so a woman could have a seat."

Throughout the world, newspapers carried the story of his demise, emphasizing his colossal failure in 1932. In Chicago, where bitterness over his group's stock losses still left an open wound that would fester for generations, many Chicagoans wondered if the old man had not stashed his fortune somewhere. Many were still haunted by his perhaps apocryphal answer that all of the money invested in his companies went "where the woodbine twines." Was it an ancient reference to losing it to the pawnbroker? Or was it a quotation from the perpetrators of an 1872 scam called the Credit Mobilier scheme that involved widespread corruption and greed? Or, in homage to an 1870 song, did it simply mean it went away and died, smote by the unforgiving hand of the Depression?

The woodbine or bindweed, known in North America as the honeysuckle plant, is a nonnative and unflappable bush that, once established, is extremely difficult to eradicate, no matter how severe the climate. While its flowers are sweet, it often chokes off resources from other native plants. Nevertheless, it grows prodigiously. Once Insull had found a way to plant electricity in nearly every factory, office, commercial building, and home, his garden grew unceasingly to become the indispensable tool of the electrical and information age from which the modern metropolis emerged—and continues to thrive. While Insull may have seeded and lost a terrific fortune, the forests of his creation, for better or worse, are still with us, growing daily.

EPILOGUE

Full Circle

The creation of a ubiquitous world of energy played an integral part in the new culture of consumption, turning a technological vision of the American dream into everyday reality.

—Harold Platt, *The Electric City: Energy and the Growth of the Chicago Area, 1880–1930*[1]

As I write this, the criminal aftermath of the late 1990s stock-market bubble is still being adjudicated in a number of courts throughout the world. A frenzy for stocks of all stripes consumed investors during this period, which in many ways bore striking similarities to the 1920s. Driven by titanic compensation packages anchored by stock options, executives of public corporations obsessively drove their companies to report ever higher earnings—sometimes illicitly—to nudge up their stock prices to absurd heights. Instead of electric utilities, information, telecommunication, hardware, and software technology companies were the apples of Wall Street's eyes. Corrupted by stock-option awards, these executives and their experiences recall the Insull story with one exception: none of the executives involved in the 1990s scandals made any voluntary attempt to make their companies or shareholders whole.

WorldCom chief executive Bernard Ebbers was convicted of participating in an $11 billion accounting fraud that, to date (2006), has eclipsed the Enron and Insull failures as the largest corporate bankruptcy ($107 billion) in history. His sentence was 25 years and he is appealing as of this writing. John and Timothy Rigas, formerly of Adelphia, the fifth-largest U.S. cable company, were found guilty of fraud in the collapse of that enterprise and sentenced to 15 and 20 years in prison, respectively. Other executives from Enron and Parmalat are due in court. Has history repeated itself? Were these corporate leaders so smitten with power and avarice that all of the New Deal securities laws were minor stumbling blocks as they reaped billions? It is remarkable to note that despite millions of investors losing more than $3 trillion in the bear market of 2000 to 2003, a global Depression did not follow. Although half of all Americans invest in the stock market, the vast majority of them kept their jobs and saw their home equity skyrocket in that period as cheap money flooded the market. Of course, other calamities loom in the future—that's guaranteed—yet it is important to review Insull's legacies with the lens of our own time.

The securities laws that Insull's failure ushered into existence, strengthened over the last five years by stricter accounting laws such as Sarbanes-Oxley, may have prevented unbridled corporate malfeasance in the 1990s. As Indiana University Law Professor William Henderson and Federal Appeals Judge Richard Cudahy observed in a study comparing Insull's travails with the Enron bankruptcy, "Insull's greatest legacy may be that history has *not* repeated itself." The accounting firm of Arthur Andersen, which was so instrumental in exposing financial mischief in Insull's companies in 1932, met its undoing over its complicity in the Enron failure and other accounting misdeeds. The firm also audited WorldCom and several other companies that had severe accounting irregularities. The new, post-Enron level of transparency tools would not have been possible without the foundation of the Insull-era laws. Even corporate directors may be held accountable by the courts and stockholders for their actions if they are judged to be unworthy company stewards.

Secrecy is always the bane of an open society, whether it is in the boardroom of a public company or in government. New measures are needed to shed light on the decisions and actions of executives, directors, and a government that is supposed to be policing the public interest. Insull's cloak over his activities in the 1920s and early 1930s was harmful to investors then and were an instructive prologue to the modern corporate veiling of conflicted, overcompensated executives, directors, and powerful shareholders. Yet, hardly chastened by the excesses of the Insull era, the latest generation of corporate barons managed to skirt FDR's best efforts at protecting investors. Now those very laws are under attack and revision on many fronts.

Weakened by several amendments, the Public Utility Holding Company Act is a shadow of the bulwark FDR had hoped it would be in preventing a consolidation of power in the utility industry. Since an amendment to the act was passed in 1978, there were more than 120 utilities mergers—75 occurring in

1999 and 2000 alone. Holding companies once again have returned to dominate utilities, as 54 were created since 1978 and the industry is being controlled by fewer and fewer companies. The renewed consolidation, permitted by the government as the industry deregulates, has also resulted in the loss of some 150,000 jobs. As this book goes to press, Exelon Corp., the descendent of Insull's family of companies, is preparing to merge with New Jersey Public Service Enterprise Group for $12.8 billion to create the nation's largest utility. Duke Energy, the other dominant U.S. utility, plans to acquire Cinergy, Inc. for $9.1 billion. Megainvestor Warren Buffett has offered to acquire Pacificorp, a Western utilities concern serving 3 million customers in 10 states for $5.1 billion. Buffett said he would invest from $10 to $15 billion in his utilities if the holding company act is repealed. Insull certainly would have applauded the industry's ongoing reconsolidation and deregulation. Progressive critics are much less sanguine. While these new combines will certainly produce economies of scale, it's hard to say if the renewed concentration of corporate power in the industry will be positive for utility customers and shareholders.

Deregulation—the dismembering of Insull's state regulation structure—is producing mixed results. Consumer electricity prices in the deregulated environment, particularly during Enron's existence, rose dramatically as wholesale energy traders manipulated the market. Power prices cynically manipulated by Enron traders climbed by a factor of 50 in the summer and fall of 2000, robbing the California economy of some $6 billion. As the national power system becomes more complex and in need of closer regulation, it is prone to huge breakdowns. The massive power blackout in the summer of 2003 stretched from Detroit to New York, leaving 50 million Americans without power.

An even darker side to the unrestricted expansion of the industry—fed by insatiable demands for power from the home to industry—is the environmental legacy of the electric generation industry. Coal is still the main fuel that powers generation plants throughout the world. As a plentiful and inexpensive commodity compared to oil and gas, coal is responsible for a host of environmental and public health maladies. The air pollution from the plants is estimated to contribute to the deaths of more than 60,000 people in the U.S. annually. Older coal plants that were grandfathered by environmental laws produce some 750,000 tons of smog-forming nitrogen oxides and nearly 300 million tons of carbon dioxide, the gas that contributes to global warming. As the economics of coal plants continue to favor their operation and expansion, it is predicted that coal-fired plants will double their energy production by 2015. One hopes the newer facilities be much less pollution-intensive than their progenitors.

The U.S. Department of Energy reports that 92 new coal generation plants are planned to be built (as of 2005), producing some 59,000 megawatts of power. As more power is produced, air quality often gets worse. While overall air quality has improved over the past 30 years because of stricter pollution laws, the U.S. Environmental Protection Agency says that 500 counties in 31 states are still failing its standards. While a large portion of that pollution can be attributed to transportation, coal plants emit everything from toxic mercury to asthma-aggravating particulate matter (the rate of childhood asthma is on the rise). Still unresolved is the other looming environmental problem of how to dispose of nuclear power station waste. Promoted by the energy industry as a "clean and safe" form of electrical production, nuclear power will never fully be worthy of that description until an environmentally secure way is found of storing the more than 50,000 tons of spent nuclear fuel that is dispersed across the U.S. at 120 sites. As a fitting tribute to Insull's penchant for investing in the newest, most efficient technology available, the operating company that he founded in Illinois currently runs 14 commercial nuclear plants, the most of any state. They also store nearly 8,000 tons of used fuel, which will be radioactive for tens of thousands of years. It is hoped that that new technology will be developed to make the disposal or reprocessing of nuclear waste safe and secure. With such an advance, nuclear power could become the "green" power of the future.

Ironically, breakthroughs in technology may eventually make central stations obsolete as combinations of fuel cell, solar, wind, and cogeneration plants emerge. It may well happen that small, compact power plants will ultimately provide the sole source of power for individual buildings and homes—much the way it was before Insull breathed life into the mega-power station era. It is heartening to note that GE—molded by Insull's management genius in the 1880s—is doubling its investment in environmentally progressive energy technologies.

Insull's dream of electrifying the workplace and home continues apace, however. Today more than 80 percent of American homes have microwave ovens, clothes washers, videocassette recorders, blenders, cordless phones, and electric coffeemakers. More than a third of the electricity in the home is consumed by lights and appliances, the remainder by heating and cooling. With hundreds of new electrical appliances introduced every year, it is doubtful that consumers will be cutting down on their electrical consumption anytime soon. This power lust translated to 3.9 billion mega-watt hours of electricity in the U.S. in 2003, a 25 percent increase from 1992. Overall, growth in electricity usage roughly tracks the Gross Domestic Product, which has been growing between 3 and 4 percent annually over the past decade.

It is encouraging that, along with the increased use of power, every new appliance is using progressively less energy, which follows Insull's dictum for continuous improvement in operating efficiencies. While representing only 6 percent of U.S. energy consumption, renewable energy such as wind power is becoming a leading source of clean energy. "Green" technologies will only become more feasible as more power companies install renewable energy plants and realize economies of scale—and citizens and politicians alike demand comprehensive laws that support renewable energy and conservation measures on a national and international level. It is simple: we all need to use green technologies in our homes, businesses, and government facilities if these technologies are to become economically feasible.

In placing Insull and the industry's need to act in the public interest in context, James O'Connor, the former chairman of Commonwealth Edison, who quoted Insull in his speeches more than 40 years after Insull was forced from his companies, told me that "Insull extols the satisfactions gained from working for a business which provides both public benefits and personal rewards. And to Insull, these personal rewards are measured not only by the recompense of salary but by the pleasure and excitement realized in working with an organization dedicated to helping solve 'the great problems' of the day."

Ultimately, public officials need to better police the way in which electricity is produced and marketed to balance environmental and economic impacts with the growing demand for power from all sources. To do so will require an overriding joint mission of government—*and* corporate—responsibility to resolve "problems that not purely political, or financial, or economic or technical," to quote Insull. Under this transparent dome, investor and environmental protection should be a priority. Shareholders and directors should be given even more opportunities to monitor boardroom activities and to boot irresponsible and greedy managers. Government should be given even more powerful tools to detect company fraud, and rigged markets, and to keep the earth, waters, and sky free from power-plant pollutants. Now that the entire world is virtually one great information metropolis practicing Insull's gospel of consumption, it is clear that these mandates are even more essential for the health and survival of our species.

NOTES ON REFERENCES

The well-organized collection of Samuel Insull papers at the Loyola University of Chicago archives (hereafter referred to as the Insull Archives [IA]), expertly managed by archivist Kathy Young, has been instrumental in opening up Insull's life. Donated by Insull's son, the archives represent the most extensive collection of Insullania in the world. I am also highly appreciative to Father Michael J. Garanzini, S.J., the president of Loyola, and Timothy O'Connell, Ph.D., the director of faculty administration, for granting me swift access to certain parts of the collection. Professor Harold Platt, another Loyola luminary, whose *Electric City* is a classic examination of Insull's modus operandi, was also generous with his time and insights. I have also gleaned useful insights into Insull from the two volumes of his speeches, which were self-published by Insull and given as gifts.

The original manuscript of the Insull Memoirs (IM), which were essentially written at sea as Insull was being extradited from Turkey, are archived in the Lilly Library at the University of Indiana-Bloomington. Professor William Henderson of the Indiana University School of Law and the honorable Judge Richard Cudahy provided their incisive interpretation of Insull's legacy and were generous in sharing their research and paper on the subject. The most accessible version of Insull's memoirs is *The Memoirs of Samuel Insull: An Autobiography* (Transportation Trails, 1992), edited by Larry Plachno. The Insull Memoirs became the core of my narrative and are extensively referenced and quoted with permission.

The only biography on Insull—*Insull* by Forrest McDonald (University of Chicago Press, 1962)—was a prime source as well. I thank Professor McDonald, who is retired but still answers media inquiries on Insull, for his telephone interview in ironing out some major details.

There also is a tremendous body of documentation within the Commonwealth Edison archives, maintained by Exelon Business Services. After the Insull archives and memoirs, this was next most important source of Insull material, and it is a priceless vein of information on everything electrical in the early twentieth century. The 9,000-plus boxes of this collection hold most of the modern history of electrical generation. Roberta Goering and Meg Ruddy were immensely helpful and patient in pulling boxes laden with 100-year-old dust out of warehouses (boxes that then sat next to their cubicles for months), executing my hundreds of copy requests and sending the boxes back to storage.

The Chicago Historical Society, an august institution that Insull supported financially, was a surprising repository of documents, letters, photos, and books that could be found nowhere else. Many thanks to the society's patient, professional staff. It was my friend Bill Barnhart, the esteemed columnist for the *Chicago Tribune*, who guided me to this excellent resource.

The undisputed mother lode of Edison material is archived by the Thomas A. Edison Papers at Rutgers University (hereafter the "Edison Archives [EA]). While the website (http://edison.rutgers.edu/index.htm) will only allow one to access a fraction of the five million pages of information online, the digitization of the material is ongoing.

The Libertyville-Mundelein Historical Society, a volunteer group housed in the basement of the Cook House and Museum, and the Cook Memorial Library in Libertyville, Illinois, were unexpected sources of Insull information. Both the society and library maintain Insull files that focus on his role in local development. Many thanks to Jerrold Schulkin, Dean Larson, Helen Casey, Audrey Krueger, and the fine, professional staff of these bustling but cramped institutions. The librarians at the Grayslake (Illinois) Area Memorial Library were supreme in their diligence and patience in procuring old books and articles through the great Illinois interlibrary book system.

Assorted archives at the FDR Library in Hyde Park, New York; at the Baker Library of the Harvard Business School (Henry Villard's papers) at the University of Wisconsin-Madison; and the University of Texas-Austin Alexander Architectural Archive (Nancy Sparrow helped me find drawings for the Hawthorn Farm home and estate); all provided useful details on several aspects of Insull's affairs. Helen Quirini, a former GE worker and activist, helped me plumb the GE archives in Schenectady, New York.

REFERENCES

ABBREVIATIONS

EA	Edison Archives (Thomas A. Edison Papers at Rutgers University)
CEA	Commonwealth Edison (Exelon) Archives
IM	Insull Memoirs
IA	Insull Archives (at Loyola University of Chicago)

PREFACE

In the course of my research, I have visited power plants, traced rights of way for power lines, peered into transformer substations, and saw firsthand the amazing network of power that Insull created. The power lines I surveyed were feeding a substation in Lake County, Illinois, where I live. It was not until I visited some of Insull's homes that I started to appreciate his personality, influence, and legacy.

INTRODUCTION: PARIS, JULY 16, 1938

There is some dispute in the source material as to which Paris subway entrance Insull entered on his final day. The official account is that it was the Tuileries facing the Rue du Rivoli, although I have seen references to the Place de La Concorde, which is a few blocks away. I have used the Tuileries for this imagined account of his final minutes. I was also aided in the background by www.virtualtourist.com and www.discoverparis.net. Information on heart attacks and diabetes were derived from www.prevention.com, www.virtua.org, and www.medicinenet.com. The sequence of his heart attack is largely surmised from his various maladies. I relied upon the *Chicago Tribune* of July 18, 1938—and cross-checked with other newspaper stories of that day—for the account of his death. His English penchant for punctuality for business lunches was well known, as noted in the McDonald biography and from statements of people who knew him. The summary of events of that awful year were gleaned from www.algis.com (timeline for 1938). Edison, who was an admirer of Insull long after Insull left his employment, called Insull "one of the greatest businessmen in the USA and as tireless as the tides" in a congratulatory telegram (found in the Insull archives, box 16, folder 4) sent to Insull on June 20, 1917. The reason for the telegram was that Edison was engaged in government research (for World War I) and could not leave his lab. The inventor was sending his regrets that he could not attend a party for Insull celebrating his 25 years of service with Commonwealth Edison.

1. The Ickes quotation is from *The Secret Diary of Harold Ickes*, volume 2 (Simon & Schuster), in an entry from July 23, 1938.
2. The reference to a "dangerous greatness" is from Ron Chernow's marvelous *Alexander Hamilton* (Penguin Press, 2004), page 254. Like Hamilton's, Insull's beneficial deeds have often been obscured by the man's tragic end and volatile personality.
3. While Samuel Clemens piloted steamboats long before Insull came of age, this reference is from *Life on the Mississippi* (1896 edition), www.underthesun.cc/Classics/Twain/lifeonthemississippi/lifeonthemississippi57.html.

CHAPTER 1: TIRELESS AS THE TIDES: EDISON SUMMONS INSULL

1. Michael Faraday, *Experimental Researches in Electricity,* 1831 (Encyclopedia Brittanica/Great Books of the Western World), page 265.
2. George Bernard Shaw, *The Irrational Knot: A Novel* (Constable & Co., 1880), pages vi–vii.

The Shakespeare quotation has an obscure connection to Insull's "woodbine" reference. In *A Midsummer Night's Dream*, the quotation is a poetic allusion to having a frolic in the woods and losing your inhibitions, which certainly did not describe Insull's puritanical personality. The quotation likely alludes to his abandoning conventional wisdom in his line of work. Most of the account of Insull's first year with Edison is from his memoirs and is corroborated by McDonald and Edison's many biographers. Insull was fond of re-creating his formative years with the inventor and used those quotations and anecdotes countless times in the hundreds of speeches he gave when he was in Chicago. The details did not vary over the years. Several items I pulled from speeches he gave to the Public Service Company of Northern Illinois in Chicago on December 8, 1927, and to the Middle West Educational Club on January 15, 1929 (IA, box 22, folder 3), are still consistent with the facts presented in his memoirs. I have also relied upon letters in the Insull Archives that cover the same territory. For background on nonconformists, I have relied upon an excerpt from the *Oxford Concise Dictionary on World Religions* by John Bowker, on www.spartacus.schoolnet.co.uk/REnonconformists.htm. This source also had a useful piece on temperance societies in the U.K. G.B. Shaw's association with Insull is likely confined to his short-lived profession as a telephone operator, although they may have communicated in the twentieth century. All of the Menlo Park scenes and the London telephone episode with Gladstone are from Edison assistant Francis Jehl and his *Menlo Park Reminiscences* (Edison Institute, 1937). Though Insull had few intimates during his New York years, Jehl was a sympathetic listener and, unlike many of the other Menlo Park pioneers, regarded him well after his demise. I have also matched details of the New York years from the General Electric archives in Schenectady, New York. Background on the improvements in lighting prior to the twentieth century are from Malcolm MacLaren's *Rise of the Electrical Industry During the 19th Century* (Princeton: 1943), pages 66–67. To get an overview of Edison's myriad enterprises, I have used the online version of the Edison papers at Rutgers (see above). Other background on Edison has been distilled from these excellent sources: Jill Jonnes's *Empires of Light: Edison, Tesla, Westinghouse, and the Race to Electrify the World* (Random House, 2003), L.J. Davis's Fleet Fire: Thomas Edison and the Pioneers of the Electric Revolution (Arcade Publishing, 2003), and Matthew Josephson's *Edison: A Biography* (John Wiley & Sons, 1959).

CHAPTER 2: THE PEARL IN THE OYSTER: EDISON'S POWER PLANT

1. Daniel J. Boorstin, *The Americans: The Democratic Experience* (Random House, 1973), page 536. I also employ Boorstin's account of the first day of operation of the Pearl Street station.

2. B.C. Forbes, *Men Who Are Making America* (Forbes Publishing, 1917), page 207. Insull's recollection of his working hours with Edison and his observation of the Pearl Street operation were taken from an interview with Insull by Forbes. Forbes credits Insull with bringing supreme management skills to the Edison organization. "The American people owe Mr. Insull a meed of gratitude," Forbes wrote in his one-sided and upbeat appraisal of Insull.

3. Letter from Insull to Charles Batchelor, September 28, 1882, EA. This is a long missive in which Insull breaks down nearly all of Edison's operations and what they are costing Edison and his investors. The letter is impressive in its depth and detail, considering that Insull had only started working for Edison the previous year and by this time had absorbed the financial travails of his businesses and sensed what needed to be done.

4. Ibid.

5. Ibid.

6. Letter from Insull to Edison, October 7, 1883, EA.

7. Letter from Insull to Batchelor, above.

The lightbulb volume anecdote is from the Insull Memoirs. A vivid depiction of New York in the early 1880s is provided by Jill Jonnes in *Empires of Light*. Edison's recollections of the Pearl Street station's first day are found in his many biographies. I have relied on the authoritative Josephson text for most of the details. The economist John Kay's history of electrical lighting efficiency is from his *Culture and Prosperity* (Penguin Books, 2004), pages 184–185. In addition to touring the Cook home many times, I have examined the Libertyville-Mundelein Historical Society's *Ansel B. Cook Victorian Museum: A Brief History, Visitor's Guide, and Drawings.* The series of letters from Insull were obtained from the Edison Archives at Rutgers. In Mumford's *The Brown Decades: A Study of the Arts in America 1865–1895* (Harcourt, Brace, 1931), page 247, the social critic charts post–Civil War America's "steady centralization of power and wealth." Tate's recollection of the

Brooklyn Bridge opening, as well as Edison's comment on lightning, was gleaned from his memoirs, *Edison's Open Door: The Life Story of Thomas Edison, a Great Individualist, by His Private Secretary* (Dutton, 1938). Like Jehl, Tate presents a generally favorable view of Insull, even though most of the Edison loyalists probably disliked the standoffish Englishman. The section on Tesla is derived from *Tesla: Master of Lightning* (Metro Books, 1999), by Margaret Cheney and Robert Uth. The early Tesla years with Edison and Batchelor are noted by Jehl in his *Reminiscences* (volume 3), which also provided some insights into the technical challenges of that time. The electric train episode is also recalled by Jehl. The state of the Edison companies is fully elaborated by Insull in his letter to Batchelor. In his memoirs, Insull makes a brief mention of his handling of the Edison Construction Department. Many of the Edison men thought Insull mishandled the department, although there was little Insull could do with it since it was so obviously undercapitalized. Insull did Edison a favor by suggesting that it be shut down.

CHAPTER 3: CRISIS AND CONSOLIDATION: THE MORGAN TAKEOVER

1. Lewis Mumford, *The Brown Decades* (Hartcourt, 1931).
2. Insull letter to his father, November 2, 1885, EA.
3. Insull letter to his brother Joseph, July 2, 1885, EA.
4. Josephson, *Edison,* page 293.
5. Insull letter to Tate, September 2, 1887, EA.
6. Insull letter to Tate, June 11, 1887, EA.
7. Insull letter to Tate, April 15, 1887, EA.
8. Insull letter to Edison, December 27, 1888, EA.
9. *Fleet'Fire,* page 264.
10. Ibid., page 267.
11. Insull letter to Edison, January 19, 1889, EA.
12. Insull letter to Edison, March 7, 1889, EA.
13. Ibid., July 16, 1890, EA.
14. Insull letters to Edison, October 20 and December 22, 1890, EA.
15. Edison, as quoted in *Thomas A. Edison: A Streak of Luck,* by Robert Conot (DaCapo Press, 1979), page 294.

The death of Mary Edison and Edison's subsequent courtship of Mina Miller is recounted well in Neil Baldwin's *Edison: Inventing the Century* (Hyperion, 1995), in Ronald Clark's *Edison: The Man Who Made the Future* (Rainbird, 1977), and in the Josephson biography. Background on the events in the mid- to late-1880s was provided principally by these three works. Insull's recollections of Edison's darkest days are noted in his memoirs, and the anecdote about Edison returning to telegraphy was a consistent crowd-pleaser in speeches Insull gave throughout the 1920s. The Edison board shake-up is briefly mentioned in Insull's memoirs and is fleshed out by Jehl, who also recalled Insull's role in the ousting of Eaton. It is not clear how Insull made out with his entrepreneurial scheme. The scheme is not mentioned in his memoirs and there is no mention of his brother, Joseph, and how he fared. Insull was more forthcoming with his experience in building up the Machine Works in Schenectady, which he talked about in numerous interviews over the years and in some detail in his memoirs. Like Insull, Henry Villard was one of those larger-than-life figures of his time who seems to have left little biographical material behind. His two-volume memoirs encompass most of his Civil War years but contain very little on his dealings with Edison. I have relied on *Villard: The Life and Times of an American Titan* (Doubleday, 2001), by Alexandra Villard de Borchgrave and John Cullen, and on some indexed materials at Harvard University's Baker Library, where Villard's papers are archived. I also have benefited from background material found in Helmut Schwab's copyrighted paper *Henry Villard: Journalist, Industrialist, Abolitionist,* published in Princeton in 1994 and updated in 2003. Villard's Edison General Electric structuring and Edison's "safe than sorry" quotation are from Insull's memoirs. The "Battle of the Currents" section relies on Clark's *Edison,* Jonnes's *Empires of Light,* and Andre Millard's *Edison and the Business of Innovation* (Johns Hopkins Press, 1990). The Tesla references are principally from Cheney and Uth's *Tesla.* The AC/DC war is superbly profiled in *Fleet Fire.* The most thorough recent book on the AC/DC war is Mark Essig's *Edison and the Electric Chair: A Story of Light and Death* (Walker, 2003). An accessible explanation of the technical merits of AC over DC can be found in Harold Sharlin's *The Making of the Electrical Age from the Telegraph to Automation* (Abelard-Schuman, 1963). A salient account of the 1889 blackout is in a piece entitled "New York

Unplugged, 1889," by Jill Jonnes in the *New York Times,* August 13, 2004, page A23. MacLaren's *Rise of the Electrical Industry* offers key background on the electrical industry during the last two decades of the nineteenth century and a good history on Thomson-Houston. The Morgan consolidation is best detailed by Paul Israel in *Edison: A Life of Invention* (John Wiley, 1998). The deal is sparsely mentioned by Tate and Insull (in his memoirs). Insull's assertion that he acted in the best interests of Edison is based largely on his memoirs and on Edison's biographers.

CHAPTER 4: THE WIDE-OPEN CITY: INSULL COMES TO CHICAGO

1. Theodore Dreiser, *The Titan* (World Publishing, 1914), page 60.
2. Dreiser, *Sister Carrie* (Robert Bentley, 1900), page 19.
3. Herbert Asbury, *The Gangs of Chicago: An Informal History of the Chicago Underworld* (Thunder's Mouth Press, 1940), page 204.
4. Frank Lloyd Wright, *Collected Writings,* volume 2 (Rizzoli International/Frank Lloyd Wright Foundation, 1992), page 155.
5. Ibid.
6. Louis Sullivan, *The Autobiography of an Idea* (Dover Publications, 1956), pages 308–309.
7. Henry Adams, *The Education of Henry Adams* (Houghton Mifflin, 1973), pages 342–343.

The Delmonico's dinner is documented in the Edison literature, although it is not known what Villard and the Morgan interests were making of Insull's boast. The bulk of the move from New York to Chicago is noted by Insull in his memoirs. While there are hundreds of histories on Chicago, I relied on Kenan Heise's *The Chicagoization of America 1893–1917* (Chicago Historical Bookworks, 1990) and on Harold Mayer and Richard Wade's *Chicago: Growth of a Metropolis* (University of Chicago Press, 1969) for the fine points of Chicago's ever-compelling story. For the history on early Chicago and Native Americans, I found an insightful brochure by James Patrick Dowd entitled *The Potawatomi: A Native American Legacy* (St. Charles Historical Society, 1989). The evolution and biology of the tallgrass prairie is elegantly described in "The Prairies," by Roger Anderson, published in *Outdoor Illinois* in February 1972. You can also gain a sense of the interrelation between the French and the Native Americans by walking into the rotunda of the Marquette building in Chicago, which displays several reliefs of the voyageurs, Jesuits, and local chiefs before the Potawatomi signed over Chicago to the U.S. government in the early 1830s. Insull would have gleaned a sense of local history as the Marquette building is physically connected to the (newer) Edison building. For a greater sense of how the city became a network of infrastructure extensions and ecological impacts, Alvin Boyarsky's *The Idea of a City* (MIT Press, 1996) provides an overview, as does William Cronon's *Nature's Metropolis: Chicago and the Great West* (Norton, 1991). An excellent history on temperance movements and the pervasive alcoholism of the nineteenth century can be found at www.religiousmovements.lib.virginia.edu/nrms/wctu.html. I derived the Susan B. Anthony quotation and the figures on alcohol consumption and temperance from this source. William Stead's *If Christ Came to Chicago* (Laird & Lee, 1894) is subtitled "A Plea for the Union of All Who Love in the Service of All Who Suffer." It is a fascinating combination of muckraking, evangelical outrage, and lists of bordellos that gives an unstinting picture of Chicago at the end of the nineteenth century. Like Stead 50 years before him, Asbury, in his sequel to his *Gangs of New York,* provides names and places in the development of Chicago's crime scene. The Kipling quotation is from Heise's *Chicagoization of America,* which compiles vignettes on the major shapers of Chicago history such as Jane Addams, Clarence Darrow, and the other social reformers. The Edgewater development and Wright's role in it is profiled in Miles Berger's *They Built Chicago: Entrepreneurs Who Shaped a Great City's Architecture* (Bonus Books, 1992). Wright's first impressions of Chicago are culled from his autobiography, as excerpted from *The Collected Writings of Frank Lloyd Wright,* volume 1 (Rizzoli International/Frank Lloyd Wright Foundation, 1992). The city's infrastructure and history are gloriously documented in *The Encyclopedia of Chicago* (University of Chicago Press/Newberry Library, 2004), edited by James Grossman, Ann Durkin Keating, and Janice Reiff. This monumental volume is the mother lode for all facts on the Windy City. Carl Condit's *The Rise of the Skyscraper: The Genius of Chicago Architecture from the Great Fire to Louis Sullivan* (University of Chicago Press, 1952) was my indispensable text on the evolution of modern Chicago architecture. Though Sullivan's *Autobiography of an Idea* reflects his obvious distaste for traditional buildings, it nonetheless is a classic look into the mind of one of modern architecture's great innovators. Insull's memoirs are generous in describing what his early days in Chicago were like, particularly on the financial particulars. Heise in *Chicagoization* provides the basic facts of the World's Columbian Exposition. I also consulted James Gilbert's *Perfect Cities: Chicago's Utopias of 1893* (University of Chicago Press, 1991), which compares the several utopian experiments in the Chicago area before the turn of the century. Erik Larson's *The Devil in the White City: Murder, Magic, and Madness at the Fair That Changed America* (Crown, 2003), supplies interesting details about the fair and the time, and throws in a murder mystery. Daniel Burnham, who is portrayed by historians as either a master promoter or a brilliant urban planner, was certainly a man of vision. Thomas Hines's *Burnham of Chicago: Architect and Planner* (University of Chicago Press, 1979) was my reference on this most accomplished of Chicago visionaries. The Tesla profile at the fair was gleaned from Cheney and Uth's *Tesla*. Adams's *Education* offers a brief but knowing glimpse of the significance of the fair in a classic that should be a staple in every American history course. Dvorak's visit to the fair—and the U.S.—is featured in a delightful account of his 1893 American tour by Joseph Horowitz in *Dvorak in America: In Search of the New World* (Cricket Books, 2003).

CHAPTER 5: LOVE AND WAR: INSULL MARRIES, THE EVE OF WAR

1.   Alex Kotlowitz, "A Meeting of Writers: The Champions of Underdogs," *New York Times,* January 1, 2005.
2.   Frederic Edward McKay, "Dramatic World," *Mail Evening Express,* December 8, 1898.
3.   Insull letter to Alfred Tate, January 30, 1893, EA.
4.   Gladys letter to Insull, November 14, 1898, IA (box 4, folder 7).
5.   Ibid., April 29, 1899, IA (box 5, folder 4).
6.   IM, page 96.

The chaste courtship of Gladys Wallis by Insull is seen through the hundreds of letters they sent to each other between 1897 and 1899. For some reason, though, only *her* letters from that period are stored in the Insull Archives, so there is little or no additional perspective on how Insull wooed her other than the McDonald biography, which provides most of the background on Gladys throughout this book. I also conducted a telephone interview with Professor McDonald on April 22, 2005. The two reviews of Gladys's performances were found in the Insull Archives. I am approximating the date and publication of the first review; the second has no dating or publication information on it. Insull's first years and speeches with Chicago Edison are concisely detailed in his memoirs. For additional background on Gladys and Insull's early Chicago days, I looked at Emmett Dedmon's *Fabulous Chicago* (Macmillan, 1981), a thoroughly readable Chicago history. Another enthusiastic history of Chicago is Donald Miller's *City of the Century: The Epic of Chicago and the Making of America* (Simon & Schuster, 1996). The item on the pre–World War I movie industry is from Diana Dretske's *Lake County, Illinois* (Heritage Media, 2002). The importance of Lake County's and Chicago's roles in the creation of early twentieth century popular culture has been illuminated by many visits to the Lake County Discovery Museum in Wauconda, Illinois, where Ms. Dretske is an archivist. I started my earliest research on Insull in the museum's archives there nearly a decade ago. Edward Bellamy's *Looking Backward* (Penguin, 1982) is a must-read in understanding the final years of the Gilded Age and the rise of the progressives. The roles of the early progressive leaders such as Bellamy and Henry Demarest Lloyd were explored by John Thomas's *Alternative America* (Harvard University Press, 1983). Although there is no detailed written description of the Insull-Wallis wedding, the wedding album in the Insull archives is as thick as a Manhattan phonebook and contains congratulatory letters from Edison and Villard, among other dignitaries who attended. It is unlikely that the nuptials spared any expense. For a snapshot of 1898, I relied upon David Traxel's *1898: The Birth of the American Century* (Knopf, 1998), which contains some insights on Dewey and holding companies. I also relied upon an excellent timeline and chronology in Janette Greenwood's *The Gilded Age: A History in Documents* (Oxford University Press, 2000). The narrative of the installation of the Fisk turbogenerator is from Insull's memoirs and the McDonald biography. My physical description of the Fisk station is based on a tour and information culled from the plant's archives and assistance from the station's current owner, Midwest Generation, LLC (they generously prepared a scrapbook for me on the station). The plant's history is further detailed in *A Report on the Fisk Street Station of Commonwealth Edison 1902–1909* from the Commonwealth Edison archives (the author is not given). The anecdote about the janitor is from this document. The Edison-Ford quotation is repeated in all of the Edison literature. A more contemporary account of the first large power plants is in *Chicago: The History of Its Reputation,* by Lloyd Lewis and Henry Justin Smith (Harcourt Brace, 1929). A profile of the events of 1905 is in "Even Einstein Had His Off Days," by Simon Singh in the *New York Times,* January 2, 2005. Insull outlined his business strategy and concerns about the city council in letters to Edward Brewster on January 15 and May 7, 1906. Both letters were obtained from the Chicago Historical Society. I found some interesting new research on Max Weber in "Why Work? A Hundred Years of the Protestant Ethic," by Elizabeth Kolbert, in the *New Yorker,* November 29, 2004. The Lake County experiment and life before electricity in rural areas, briefly noted in his memoirs, is described in the *Edison* magazine, volume 9, number 1 (1987). The bulk of the development of Commonwealth Edison's advertising strategy is derived from H.A. Seymour's *History of the Commonwealth Edison Company,* a typed manuscript version from 1935 that I found in the company's archives. The history of Lake County and Libertyville before 1910 is gleaned from the archives of the Libertyville-Mundelein Historical Society and www.libertyville.com/history.htm. The Wright quotation is from Donald Hoffman's *Frank Lloyd Wright's Robie House: The Illustrated Story of an Architectural Masterpiece* (Dover House, 1984). Gladys's role in Junior's illness and revival (as well as her quotation) are from the McDonald biography.

CHAPTER 6: A NEW KIND OF POWER: INSULL BUILDS HIS IMAGE

1. Louis Brandeis, *Other People's Money and How Bankers Use It* (Stokes, 1914), pages 22–23.
2. Mary Garden, with Louis Biancolli, *Mary Garden's Story* (Simon & Schuster, 1951), pages 62–63.
3. Ibid., pages 212–213.
4. Brandeis, pages 80–81.
5. Ibid., pages 156–157.
6. Bernard Sunny, *Samuel Insull: A Many-Sided Man,* (Franklin Institute, 1926), an address given at the Franklin Institute honoring Insull and the unveiling of his portrait.
7. Harold Ickes, *The Autobiography of a Curmudgeon* (Reynal & Hitchcock, 1950), page 190.
8. Letter from Samuel Insull, Jr., to Insull, March 16, 1919 (courtesy of Barbara Mahoney).

Brandeis's *Other People's Money* is an essential classic that should be required reading for anyone who wants to understand the age of corporate trusts before World War II. In the course of my research, Mary Garden was a figure whose personality loomed as large as Insull's during the early part of the century, but she has been mostly lost in the fog of history. Fortunately, there is a fairly recent biography that does her justice: Michael T.R.B. Turnbull's *Mary Garden* (Timber Press, 1997). Mary's autobiography, *Mary Garden's Story,* with Louis Biancolli (Simon & Schuster, 1951), contains generous dollops of Mary's outsized personality yet nothing terribly revealing about her inner life or her relationship with Insull. These two texts were my principal sources on this fascinating woman. I was able to piece together some more background on her recording and performance history from Internet sources such as www.cantabile-subito.de/Sopranos/Garden_Mary/hauptteil_garden_mary.html (from which I pulled the first quotation), National Public Radio's "At the Opera" website, www.npr.org/programs/attheopera/archives/000408.ato.html; the "Brainy Encyclopedia," www.brainyencyclopedia.com; and the Minnesota Public Radio website, *www.news-minnesota.publicradio.org/features/2005/01/31_morelockb_pelleas-melisande/.* Oddly enough, Insull gives scant mention to her in his memoirs, which is strange considering the powerful influence they must have had on each other. All of the quotations on Mary's performances are from Turnbull's book. All of the facts on the first decades of Commonwealth Edison are from its voluminous archives (some 9,000 boxes), now managed by Exelon Business Services. Pam Strobel's recollections of her grandmother's tenure with the company are from a telephone interview on January 31, 2005. Another prime resource on Commonwealth Edison was John Hogan's *A Spirit Capable* (Mobium Press, 1986), a history of the company. I also interviewed John on December 8, 2004, and exchanged several emails. The tragic story (a continuing tale of woe) of the Cubs' last World Series and the rise of Babe Ruth is from www.chicagosports.com from October 12, 2004. Mayer and Wade's *Chicago: Growth of a Metropolis* illustrates how extensive the interurban system was and how it connected Chicago with a three-state urbanscape. Also helpful was Bruce Moffat's *The "L": Development of Chicago's Rapid Transit System 1888–1932* (Bulletin 131 of the Central Electric Railfan's Association, 1995). Specific rail lines and defunct interurbans such as the North Shore continue to have lively fan clubs. One such club—www.northshoreline.com—was extremely generous in helping me acquire materials (see "Special Thanks" below). My description of the Insull palazzo is based on several visits in 2004 and 2005 and on studying the original drawings obtained from the University of Texas. I was not able to find any of Marshall's notes on the Insull home. Most of my approximation of its Palladian equivalent was aided by Bruce Boucher's *Andrea Palladio: The Architect in His Time* (Abbeville Press, 1998). I also was unable to find Jens Jensen's masterful original landscape plan for the grounds, although I believe Marshall's drawings may have incorporated his ideas. John

Byrne, the director of the Cuneo, was particularly helpful since his father had worked on the property, so he provided some guidance on what the home may have looked like in earlier years.

CHAPTER 7: ALL THAT JAZZ: THE 1920S BOOM YEARS

1. Nelson Algren, *Chicago: City on the Make* (University of Chicago Press, 1951), page 54. Algren also makes a passing reference to Insull in this prose-poem that sums up Algren's love-hate relationship with the city that shaped his novels.
2. Commonwealth Edison ad in its company publication *Electric City*, volume 11, CEA.
3. Henry Demarest Lloyd, as quoted in Gwendolyn Wright's *Building the Dream* (Random House, 1981), page170.
4. Ibid., page 156.
5. Commonwealth Edison ad, 1925, CEA.
6. Phineas T. Barnum, *The Life of Phineas T. Barnum, Written by Himself* (University of Illinois Press, 2000), pages 394–396.
7. Insull, "My Business Is Your Business," speech before the Peoria, Illinois, Chamber of Commerce, March 11, 1921.
8. John Gruber and J.J. Sedelmaier, "SIC Transit," *Print Magazine*, May-June, 1998.
9. Insull, excerpted and edited by Bernard Mullaney, in *Principles of Utility Management* (booklet), February 15, 1924, IA (box 22, folder 7).

The Commonwealth Edison archives provide an invaluable fount of information on how electricity was sold in the first third of the twentieth century. Most of my findings on this subject were obtained from this source, including the many quotations from ads and promotions. An essential text in understanding this period and how electricity and domestication intertwined is Gwendolyn Wright's *Building the Dream*, from which several facts used in this chapter are gleaned. Commonwealth Edison documented its entire advertising strategy, peppered with figures on how much electricity they were selling, in a booklet submitted for the Charles Coffin award of 1926, which was given to the company for its prowess in selling power and appliances. Most of the facts on power usage and electrical product advertising in the Chicago area were culled from this source. The anecdote about Gladys and the bookkeeper is from McDonald's biography. John Hogan's *A Spirit Capable* also filled in many of the gaps of the company's history during the 1920s. Heise's *The Chicagoization of America* provided a brief history of the African-American community after World War I. Studs Terkel, who has documented (through his incredible interviews in print, TV, and radio) more American history than perhaps any other author, generously offered his recollections of the 1920s in a phone interview. Mary Garden's opening night on Chicago radio was briefly noted in her autobiography. I found a more extensive history of early Chicago radio on the website www.richsamuels.com/nbcmm/kyw.html. I referenced Richard Norton Smith's *The Colonel: The Life and Legend of Robert R. McCormick* (Houghton Mifflin, 1997), which is a balanced biography of a Chicago giant who was as controversial as Insull. The Insull anecdotes are from this book. Also worthwhile was Joseph Epstein's piece, "The Colonel and the Lady" in *Commentary*, August 1997. Insull's English visits are prominently mentioned in his memoirs. While Barnum's autobiography is less than reliable, I benefited from *P.T. Barnum: America's Greatest Showman*, by Philip B. Kunhardt, Philip B. Kunhardt, Jr., Philip B. Kunhardt III, and Peter W. Kunhardt (Borzoi-Knopf, 1995). Insull's repeated boasts about how many customers and investors his companies had were staples in hundreds of speeches given between 1910 and 1929. I have summarized most of his main points, including his aversion to federal regulation and takeover of his industry, from his two volumes of published speeches. The section on the interurbans was considerably aided by facts and illustrations of Ronald Cohen and Stephen McShane's *Moonlight in Duneland: The Illustrated Story of the Chicago South Shore and South Bend Railroad* (Quarry Books, 1998) and www.northshoreline.com. Another useful guide to the interurban network was George Hilton and John Due's *The Electric Interurban in America* (Stanford University Press, 1964). To understand how Chicago's infrastructure was developing, I also relied upon Ann Durking Keating's *Invisible Networks: Exploring the History of Local Utilities and Public Works* (Krieger Publishing, 1994), which contains several useful facts and insights on electrical connections, interurbans, and the Chicago sanitary system. Insull detailed how property values rose along his electric rail lines in a speech he gave before the Chicago Real Estate Board on December 14, 1924 (thanks to the City of Chicago's Harold Washington Library/Chicago Municipal Reference Library). For additional background facts on the 1920s, I consulted David Kyvig's *Daily Life in the United States*,

1920–1940: How Americans Lived through the "Roaring Twenties" and the Great Depression (Ivan Dee, 2002); Perry Duis's *Challenging Chicago: Coping with Everyday Life 1837–1920* (University of Illinois Press, 1998); General Electric's *Light* magazine from May 1923; and "Samuel Insull: His Son Remembers the Tycoon," *Libertyville Independent-Register,* February 5, 1976.

CHAPTER 8: MANAGING THE SPECTACLE: MID-1920S SCANDALS

1.   Charles R. Walgreen, founder of the drugstore chain, 1932, as quoted in *Quotable Chicago,* edited by Richard Lindberg (Wild Onion Books, 1996), page 56.

2.   Arthur Meeker, Jr., *Chicago Herald & Examiner,* June 2, 1925, as quoted in McDonald's *Insull,* pages 234–235.

3.   Pauline Kael, *Raising Kane* (Bantam Books, 1971), page 12.

4.   Ben Hecht, *Gaily, Gaily: The Memoirs of a Cub Reporter in Chicago* (Elek Books, 1964), pages 151–152.

5.   Morris Werner, *Julius Rosenwald: The Life of a Practical Humanitarian* (Harper & Brothers, 1939), page 299.

6.   Hogan, *A Spirit Capable,* page 148.

7.   Herbert Hoover, "State versus Federal Regulation in the Transformation of the Power Industry to Central Generation and Interconnection of Systems," address before NELA, 48th convention, June 17, 1925, from *NELA Proceedings,* volume 82.

8.   Insull, "Why Do So Many Bright Young Men Enter the Public-Utility Business?"—an address to the students of the University of Illinois/Champaign-Urbana, Illinois, May 7, 1925.

9.   J.E. Davidson, NELA President, address before the 49th NELA convention, May 18, 1926, from *NELA Proceedings,* volume 3.

10. *Chicago Tribune* editorial, as quoted in Ronald Davis's *Opera in Chicago* (Appleton Century, 1966), page 160.

11. Insull, address at reception for the International Eucharistic Congress, Chicago Coliseum, June 19, 1926, from the archives of the Archdiocese of Chicago.

12. Clarence Darrow, *Attorney for the Damned,* edited by Arthur Weinberg (Simon & Schuster, 1957), pages 200–201.

13. Lawrence Bergreen, *Capone: The Man and the Era* (Simon & Schuster, 1994), page 226.

The Smith episode is covered in fairly healthy detail in the McDonald biography and is dealt with almost apologetically in four paragraphs of Insull's memoirs. Hogan's *A Spirit Capable* also puts the scandal in perspective. Surprisingly, I found a relatively good account of the affair in Morris Werner's *Julius Rosenwald.* The Progressive movement in the mid- to late 1920s is profiled in David Thelen's *Robert M. La Follette* (Little, Brown, 1976). Martin Insull's broadsides against public utility ownership were on display in his speeches before the National Electric Light Association. I used his statements from a NELA speech from June 17, 1923. Gladys's reentry into the theater world was noted by every Chicago paper. My account is drawn largely from the McDonald biography. The Insull-Mankiewicz-Welles-*Citizen Kane* connection was deftly handled by Pauline Kael in her book on one of the greatest movies ever produced. Also helpful was Frank Brady's *Citizen Welles: A Biography of Orson Welles* (Scribners, 1989) and Barbara Leaming's *Orson Welles* (Viking Penguin, 1985). Ben Hecht's early memoirs give you a feel for his *Front Page* days. The partial filmography of his long, illustrious career was from www.imdb.com/name/nm0372942/. The Napoleon quotation is from McDonald. Mary Garden is coy about her romances in her autobiography, and her recent biography sheds little light on her love life. The *Tribune* editorial and an account of her management of the opera before Insull took over is in Ronald Davis's *Opera in Chicago* (Appleton Century, 1966). The quotes are from the Garden biography. Cardinal Mundelein is profiled in Edward Kantowicz's *Corporation Sole: Cardinal Mundelein and Chicago Catholicism* (University of Notre Dame Press, 1983). I also used background material—letters from Insull to Mundelein—from the archives of the Catholic Archdiocese of Chicago. Insull's hosting of the cardinals in his home was recalled by Insull, Jr. in a talk he gave before the Libertyville-Mundelein Historical Society, October 23, 1972. The figures on the North Shore Line are from www.northshoreline.com. My description of the Mundelein Seminary is based on numerous visits (it is about three miles down the road from my home). Additional facts were obtained at www.usml.edu. For an overview of the music of the 1920s, I relied upon Alec Wilder's *American Popular Songs: The Great Innovators 1900–1950* (Oxford University Press, 1972). The Lewis anecdote is from Carl Sandburg's *The Sandburg Range* (Harcourt, 1957), pages 123–124. A balanced biography on Lewis is Richard Lingeman's *Sinclair Lewis: Rebel from Main Street* (Random House, 2002). I found local newspaper accounts on the Rondout robbery in the archives of the Libertyville-Mundelein Historical Society and in Katherine Hamilton-Smith's article in the *Daily Herald,* June 20, 2004.

CHAPTER 9: ATTACK FROM ALL SIDES

1. Edgar Lee Masters, *The Tale of Chicago* (G.P. Putnam, 1935), pages 305–306.
2. IM, page 188.
3. Harold Platt, "Samuel Insull and the Electric City" as excerpted from a chapter in *A Wild Kind of Boldness: A Chicago History Reader,* edited by Rosemary Adams(Chicago Historical Society, 1998), page 218.
4. Insull, address at the opening of the Model Farm of the Public Service Company of Northern Illinois, August 11, 1928 (from the Chicago Historical Society archives).
5. David Nye, *Electrifying America: Social Meanings of a New Technology* (MIT Press, 1990), page 277.

Edgar Lee Master's depiction of the Eaton episode contained a freshness that the other accounts lacked. He would have seen Insull's grip on his companies unravel firsthand. Most of the financial particulars are derived from the memoirs and from Insull's trial notes in the Insull archives. For a comprehensive history of the 1920s, I relied upon Nathan Miller's *New World Coming: The 1920s and the Making of Modern America* (Scribner, 2003), which details the rise of holding companies and Insull's role in creating them. NELA's propaganda campaign in the late 1920s is noted in David Nye's *Electrifying America: Social Meanings of a New Technology* (MIT Press, 1990), which was instrumental in explaining how electricity came to dominate consumer culture in the twentieth century. I found a copy of the *American Mercury* from January 1929 and was more interested in the advertising than the articles. Insull appears to not have touted his stocks, and is defensive about that subject in his memoirs. The section on the model farm and Libertyville was aided by several materials (including personal recorded recollections of area residents) from the Libertyville-Mundelein Historical Society. Insull and his associates also gave speeches before the local chamber of commerce and businessmen's groups, which were also in this collection. I also have visited Junior's former house on Scilly Island. Background on the Public Service building in Libertyville was provided by an unpublished paper (June 1983) by Kelly Patrick Rafferty of the University of Illinois Graduate School of Architecture. The Westchester/Zelosky section was aided by the Westchester area historical society and their richly detailed website www.franzosenbuschheritagesociety.org, which contains an Insull profile. Nye explains the social impact of electrification in *Electrifying America,* the prime resource for this section. Additional facts on the emerging consumer culture were gleaned from Kyvig's *Daily Life.* The progressive's attack on Insull's traction proposal was best described in T. H. Watkins's *Righteous Pilgrim: The Life and Times of Harold Ickes* (Henry Holt, 1990). For a classic account of the market runup and crash, I consulted John Kenneth Galbraith's *The Great Crash 1929* (Houghton Mifflin, 1979). While Insull's opening night at the new opera house is mentioned in all of the Insull texts, extensive background on the building and Electric Club were provided by the current owner of the building, Equity Office Properties and the management of the club. The Lyric Opera also has a history of its building on its website www.lyricopera.org/about/house.asp. I have also been in the opera house several times (where there was an Insull room), toured what would have been his penthouse (now office space), toured the Tower Club, and walked around the building more times than I can remember. A summary of the songs and books of 1929 was found on *guweb2.gonzaga.edu/faculty/campbell/enl311/1920m.html.*

CHAPTER 10: ABDICATION AND EXILE: INSULL FLEES AMERICA

1. John Dos Passos, *The Big Money* from *The USA Trilogy* (Literary Classics, 1996), page 1212. Insull is one subject in a series of rollicking vignettes that includes Edison, Ford, and Hearst in this newsreel-inspired classic.
2. Galbraith, *The Great Crash,* page 135.
3. Insull, *Electrical World,* December 14, 1929, page 1165.
4. "Courage to Be Big Need of 1931—Insull," *Chicago Herald-Examiner,* February 17,·1931.
5. IM, page 203.
6. Royal Munger, "Insull Losses Leave Earning Power Secure: Directors Have Confidence in Utility Leader: Control Assured," *Chicago Daily News,* March 7, 1932.
7. Letter from Harry Booth to Robert Lovett, January 20, 1932 (Chicago Historical Society).

8.   Franklin D. Roosevelt, address at the Municipal Auditorium, Portland, Oregon, September 21, 1932, from the FDR Library; the emphases are FDR's own.
9.   Insull letter to Gladys, Milan, Italy, Oct. 6, 1932, IA (box 19, folder 10).

Galbraith's *The Great Crash* is fundamental in understanding the stock market blowup and I have used his 50th anniversary edition for background. The Commonwealth Edison publications, in contrast, are brimming with Insull's optimism. The Eaton account is from Insull's memoirs, his notes, and the McDonald biography. Key information on that time was provided by Paul Douglas's memoirs, *In the Fullness of Time* (Harcourt Brace, 1971); Roger Biles's *Crusading Liberal: Paul H. Douglas of Illinois* (Northern University Press, 2002); a profile of Insull, Jr., entitled "Samuel II" in the September 1931 issue of *Fortune;* Marian Ramsay's *Pyramids of Power: The Story of Roosevelt, Insull, and the Utility Wars* (Bobbs-Merrill, 1937); Frederick Lewis Allen's *Since Yesterday* (Harper & Row, 1986); Frank Freidel's *Franklin D. Roosevelt* (Little, Brown, 1973); and Kenneth Davis's *FDR: The New York Years 1928–1933* (Random House, 1985). Gladys's dinner party was featured in the "Cousin Eve" society column in the *Chicago Tribune* of January 11, 1931. The Edison visit and financial accounts of Insull's companies were from Chicago newspaper reports. The memoirs record his bank negotiations in fairly good detail. The aftermath of Insull's resignations is recounted in the McDonald biography and in the memoirs. I found an item on the opera's postcrash financial condition at www.niulig.niu.edu/rbsc/2coos.html. Essential contemporary accounts were found in Royal Munger's booklet, *The Rise and Fall of Samuel Insull* (no publication date discovered, but believed to be a mid-1930s compilation of his *Chicago Daily News* pieces), and John T. Flynn's series in *Colliers* magazine from December 1932, "Up and Down with Sam Insull."

CHAPTER 11: FACING THE MUSIC: INSULL TRIED FOR FRAUD

1.   Saul Bellow, *The Adventures of Augie March* (Viking Press, 1953), page 106. What a pleasant surprise to find an Insull reference in one of the greatest novels of the twentieth century. In memoriam.
2.   Christopher Protopappas, "'Innocent' Says Samuel in Exclusive Talk," *Chicago American,* October 10, 1932.
3.   "Decision of the Greek Court of Appeals on the application of the U.S.A. for the extradition of Samuel Insull, Sr., 1933," *American Journal of International Law,* 1934, page 362.
4.   Masters, *The Tale of Chicago,* page 327.
5.   Insull statement, Fort Hancock, New Jersey, May 7, 1934, IA (box 66, folder 18).
6.   "Insull to Appear in Court on Wednesday," *Chicago American,* May 14, 1934.

Insull's flight and Mary Garden's comments were thoroughly covered in all the Chicago newspapers in 1932. General Electric's *Light* magazine from fall 1933 gave an overview of the Century of Progress. The trial was covered by all the Chicago papers, which also reprinted the trial transcripts. All of the quotations before, during, and after the trial are from these sources, particularly the *Chicago Tribune, Herald-Examiner,* and *American.* The Insull letter to FDR is from the Insull Archives (box 11, folder 1).

CHAPTER 12: IN THE FULLNESS OF TIME: THE INSULL LEGACY

1.   Christopher Morley, *Old Loopy: A Love Letter for Chicago* (Argus Book Shop, 1935).
2.   Letter to Insull from Tesla, March 18, 1935, IA (box 8, folder 2).
3.   Beverly Sills, *Beverly: An Autobiography* (Bantam Books, 1987), pages 54–55.
4.   Francis X. Busch, *Guilty or Not Guilty?* (Bobbs-Merrill, 1952), page 127.
5.   Ramsay, *Pyramids of Power,* page 114.

The posttrial scenes and quotations were from Chicago newspapers. I also went into the Commonwealth Edison archives to pull annual reports and noticed how sparse they were prior to 1932. For an in-depth look at the power of the holding companies, I relied upon Ramsay's *Pyramids of Power;* www.ucan.org/law_policy/energydocs/history.htm; Leonard Hyman's *America's Electric Utilities: Past, Present, and Future* (Public Utilities Reports, 2000); Joel Seligman's *The Transformation of Wall Street* (Houghton-Mifflin, 1982); Thomas Parke Hughes's *Networks of Power* (Johns Hopkins University Press, 1983); and Conrad Black's *Franklin D. Roosevelt: Champion of Freedom* (Public Affairs, 2003). Insull's death and funeral accounts are from Chicago newspapers. I derived my woodbine references from www.wildyorkshire.co.uk/naturediary/docs/2003/6/246. html. Nearly all of the details on Insull's estate are from the Insull Archives.

EPILOGUE: FULL CIRCLE

1. Harold Platt, *The Electric City: Energy and the Growth of the Chicago Area 1880–1930* (University of Chicago Press, 1991, page 289.

Of all of the resources I used in trying to place the Insull story in a modern context, the most instructive was "From Insull to Enron: Corporate Re-regulation after the Rise and Fall of Two Energy Icons," by the Honorable Richard Cudahy and Professor William Henderson, in the *Energy Law Journal*, volume 26, number 1, 2005. Judge Cudahy and Professor Henderson were exceedingly generous with their time and resources. Key facts on energy consumption, environmental ills, deregulation, and the Enron era come from the Federal Energy Regulatory Commission, www.washingtonpost.com, Bloomberg News, the *Chicago Tribune*, the *Wall Street Journal* (May 25, 2005, page A1), www.publiccitizen.org/print_article.cfm?ID=4180, the *Financial Times*, www.nytimes.com, *Inside Exelon*, the Edison Electric Institute, the Consumer Federation of America, the U.S. Department of Energy/Energy Information Agency and Sharon Beder's *Power Play: The Fight to Control the World's Electricity* (New Press, 2003). I am also grateful to James O'Connor for a personal interview (and subsequent correspondence) on December 13, 2004.

SPECIAL THANKS

J.J. Sedelmaier of J.J. Sedelmaier Productions, Inc. (www.jjsedelmaier.com) provided a generous array of Insull images and was incredibly generous with his time and resources. John Maxson was unstinting in his generosity and helpfulness in providing me access to former Commonwealth Edison principals and others. George Travers provided some anecdotal material on Insull as well as a lively impersonation of the gentleman. John Hogan, whose *A Spirit Capable* is a finely detailed corporate history of Commonwealth Edison, and James O'Connor, the venerable former chairman of the company, also provided unique insights. Also thanks to Exeloners Pam Strobel, Jennifer Medley, and Kellie Szabo.

The GE archives in Schenectady also provided some materials on the early history of the company. Thanks to Mary Ocasek of the University of St. Mary of the Lake/Mundelein Seminary and Julie Satzig of the Archdiocese of Chicago archives. I appreciated the help of John Cuneo, Jr., whose father purchased the Insull estate in 1937; John Byrne, the director of operations at the Cuneo Museum and Gardens; and Jim Minarcik, who gives a great Insull-referenced tour. Thanks to Kate Newton, the manager of the Tower Club, and Julie Nowak of Equity Office for spending time with me and showing me around "Insull's throne." Danny Newman of the Lyric and my friend Dennis Fertig also provided some background on Insull's connection to *Citizen Kane.* Lucy Alvarez of U.S. Equities allowed me to inspect the old Edison boardroom and Insull's offices, along with Estela Beltran of the Chicago Board of Education. Susan Olivarria, John Kennedy, Dan Dammer, and Bob Balla of Midwest Generation, LLC, gave generously of their time so that I could tour and study the Fisk Street station.

Helpful background material was found in the Art Institute of Chicago's Ryerson and Burnham Libraries, which had extensive collections on the history of Chicago architecture.

Many other people provided aid in my research including, Steve Barg, Tim Girmsheid, J.B. Delacour, Joan Gottschall, Laura Heiden, Tom Herrerra, John Hotz, Christine Hides, Barbara Mahoney, Jill Crandall, Jackie Harris, George McFetridge, Sarah Skerik, John Carroll, George Ranney, Thomas Geoghegan, and Leon Despres. And thanks to my patient neighbors at Prairie Crossing, who have listened to me crow about this book for more than a year.

It is also my ongoing privilege to work with the many great editors and reporters at Bloomberg News, particularly Matt Winkler, Bill Ahearn and Jim Greiff.

None of this would have been possible without the fierce dedication of my agent, Robert Shepard, who labored through countless rejections and revisions of the book *proposal,* only to have editors say repeated times, "we don't want to publish another Edison book." He has been a friend and staunch supporter of this book and is one of those rare, brave souls who champions his clients *and* beliefs. Airie Stuart, my editor at Palgrave Macmillan, also deserves my thanks for publishing this saga. Thanks also to Melissa Nosal for her support at Palgrave.

And no author can survive without a great deal of divine intervention, in this case from my angels Kathleen Rose, Sarah Virginia, and Julia Theresa.

INSULLANIA SITES:
PLACES OF INTEREST

Many of the places most associated with Insull are still very accessible. I have visited all of them in the course of my research and found that Insull is not forgotten within the structures that he built. The crown jewel of Insull's former country estate is the Cuneo Museum and Gardens in Vernon Hills, Illinois, which is lovingly preserved by the Cuneo family. Insull would have been pleased to know that his pink palazzo in the middle of what he called Hawthorn Farm is surrounded by an energy-intensive megadevelopment and shopping mall. The home itself is a step into the life of a 1920s mogul. Although virtually none of the Insull possessions are retained in the house, you can feel Insull's presence everywhere. The grounds of the estate, which also was the location for the Julia Roberts film *My Best Friend's Wedding,* are exquisitely landscaped, although Jens Jensen's original landscape design was altered decades ago. The 75-acre estate is also home to a conservatory full of exotic plants and a herd of rare white fallow deer.

The most famous working building remaining from Insull's legacy is the 20 North Wacker building, known locally as the Opera building. Home to the Lyric Opera of Chicago, its commodious stage has been graced by everyone from Maria Callas to Luciano Pavarotti. There is no question that the building not only is home to one of the world's premier opera companies, it also is teaming with Insull references. Owned and managed by Equity Office Properties, it is also still the home to the Tower Club, a private club and restaurant that Insull established as the Electric Club for his business associates and cronies. Insull's legendary penthouse, however, is no longer there, having been refurbished into office space years ago.

While there is only one Insull interurban electric rail line still running—the South Shore line, running from northwest Indiana to Chicago's Randolph Street station—you can still get a feel for what the interurban era was like through http://www.northshoreline.com. For those who want to see a vintage Insull-era interurban stop on the North Shore line, find your way to the Dempster Street terminus of the CTA's Skokie Swift line, which is accessible by CTA's red line from the city (transfer at Howard Street). Restoration of the terminal designed by Arthur Gerber shows the attention to aesthetic details that Insull had in bolstering electric interurbans (except for the Starbucks, of course).

For those deeply interested in how power is generated, it is worth a trip to see the Fisk Generating station of Midwest Generation, LLC. While none of the original generators are there—one is at the GE complex in Schenectady, New York—you can get a feel for what an awesome process power production is, even in this age.

For an example of an Insull-commissioned northern European tudor hybrid, stop by the Harris Bank building on Milwaukee and Church Streets in downtown Libertyville, Illinois. The building, designed by Hermann von Holst, served as one of Insull's headquarters in Lake county, housing both his utility companies and bank.

A decidedly non-Insull site that is well worth the time is the Edison Ford Estates complex in downtown Ft. Myers, Florida. While there is no evidence that Insull was here, you can peer into Edison's lab and adjacent museum, which holds a surprising number of Edison inventions and gives an excellent timeline-oriented overview of the inventor's life and work. The two winter homes that Edison and Ford stayed in are well preserved. For a much better picture of Edison's early years, it is worth a visit to Ford's Greenfield Village near Detroit, where Ford preserved a good slice of Edison's Menlo Park lab.

INDEX

ABOUT THE AUTHOR

John F. Wasik is the author of ten books and a columnist for Bloomberg News. His articles have appeared in the *New York Times,* the *Financial Times,* the *International Herald Tribune,* and magazines, and are posted at www.bloomberg.com. He is the winner of 18 awards for his columns and investigative journalism, and his pieces are circulated to 400 newspapers on five continents and have been translated into Spanish, Italian, German, and Japanese. He is a graduate of the University of Illinois-Chicago, where he obtained his bachelor's and master's degrees. He resides in Lake County, Illinois, with his wife and two daughters. His website is www.johnwasik.com.